IMPROVING ON NO CHILD LEFT BEHIND

IMPROVING ON NO CHILD LEFT BEHIND

Getting Education Reform Back on Track

Edited by

Richard D. Kahlenberg

A CENTURY FOUNDATION BOOK

2008 • THE CENTURY FOUNDATION PRESS • NEW YORK

The Century Foundation sponsors and supervises timely analyses of economic policy, foreign affairs, and domestic political issues. Not-for-profit and nonpartisan, it was founded in 1919 and endowed by Edward A. Filene.

LIBRARY OF CONGRESS CATALOGING-IN-PUBLICATION DATA

Improving on No Child Left Behind : getting education reform back on track / edited by Richard D. Kahlenberg.
  p. cm.
"A Century Foundation Book."
Includes bibliographical references and index.
ISBN 978-0-87078-512-2 (alk. paper)
1. United States. No Child Left Behind Act of 2001. 2. Education--Standards--United States. 3. Educational accountability--United States. 4. Educational change--United States. I. Kahlenberg, Richard D.
LB2806.22.1477 2008
379.1'580973--dc22
                    2008029649

Cover Design by Claude Goodwin, photo by Doug Schneider

FOREWORD

In 2008, Americans are finding it difficult to maintain their optimism about how their economy works. There is a new recognition of the underlying risks of the global marketplace. The troubles of Wall Street and Main Street suggest a shared destiny. But, in fact, in recent decades the experience of those in the bottom and middle of the economic ladder has been quite distinct from the unprecedented success and affluence of those at the top. Americans with average incomes have found themselves under pressure in good times and bad. Just as importantly, sustaining the dream and expectation of upward mobility has been challenged by overwhelming evidence of increasing inequality. Wages for most workers have stagnated, while those at the top have enjoyed vast increases in income and wealth.

These trends ought to trouble all of us. Capitalism and democracy, after all, owe a large measure of their dynamism and success to the fact that, while they do not prevent substantial inequality, they do offer extensive opportunity for upward mobility. Americans still cling to the notion that it is their birthright to live in a nation where there is ample opportunity for movement up the economic ladder for all citizens. Any evidence that this part of the American Dream is at risk or in decline is likely to be disquieting.

A key component of past mobility has been the scope and success of the American public education system. Thus, data suggesting that American education, in some cases, is having the effect of reinforcing

v

existing inequalities is real cause for alarm. One piece of evidence pointing to this disturbing trend is a recent study that found that the reading gap between the average student in high-poverty and low-poverty schools—measured in terms of relative standing on a percentile scale—starts at twenty-seven points in first grade and grows to forty-three points by eighth grade. Such findings call into question the whole notion of an educational dynamic of opportunity and highlight the necessity to reform our weakest public schools.

Public education plays a key role in the life of the nation. By the time American students reach secondary school, over 90 percent of them are in public schools, managed by 14,561 different school districts. Encouraging, let alone enforcing, some degree of commonality among these diverse jurisdictions and the state governments that oversee them is difficult, and some would argue, not all that desirable. Nonetheless, there has been growing interest in an enlarged federal role in elementary and secondary education.

In recent years, much of the national attention on issues of school reform has focused on the enactment of and subsequent effects of the No Child Left Behind Act (NCLB). Today, the reauthorization or reform of this legislation is the central federal issue in elementary and secondary education. While federal funding made up only 9 percent of the $521 billion spent in 2006, the extra federal dollars provided at the margin are likely to loom large in the worlds of state governments and local school boards, both of which are perennially strapped for cash. In fiscal year 2008, NCLB added $24.6 billion to total spending. Fully funded at the authorized level, another $14.8 billion would have been available to school districts.

So, it is with this important next round of policymaking in mind that The Century Foundation commissioned this volume examining the evidence, the issues, and the alternatives for a renewed or replaced NCLB law in 2009. Richard Kahlenberg, senior fellow at The Century Foundation and editor of this volume, assembled a distinguished group of experts to offer their reporting and judgment on the experience with NCLB so far, and the present state of the debate about its future. As Kahlenberg puts it, "the basic thrust of NCLB [is] more funding in exchange for more accountability." While that idea was the essence of NCLB's approach, the devil had been in the details of implementation.

The Century Foundation has produced a number of recent and forthcoming publications that bear on the fundamental issue of equal opportunity in education. The list includes Kahlenberg's *All Together Now: Creating Middle-Class Schools through Public School Choice* (2001); Joan Lombardi's *Time to Care: Redesigning Child Care to Promote Education, Support Families, and Build Communities* (2002); and Jeffrey R. Henig's *Spin Cycle: How Research Is Used in Policy Debates—The Case of Charter Schools* (2008). In addition, we have also published a series of collected essays on education, most notably, *A Notion at Risk: Preserving Public Education as an Engine for Social Mobility* (2000), edited by Kahlenberg; *Raising Standards or Raising Barriers? Inequality and High-Stakes Testing in Public Education* (2001), edited by Gary Orfield and Mindy L. Kornhaber; *Public School Choice vs. Private School Vouchers* (2003), edited by Kahlenberg; and *America's Untapped Resource: Low-Income Students in Higher Education* (2004), also edited by Kahlenberg. Finally, The Century Foundation sponsored a task force, chaired by former Connecticut Governor Lowell Weicker, Jr., which issued a report, *Divided We Fail: Coming Together through Public School Choice* (2002). In the future, we plan to publish edited volumes on inequality in higher education and the use of legacy preferences by universities and colleges.

We hope that this volume helps inform the decisions that Congress and the next president will make about how to shape the federal role in elementary and secondary education. On behalf of the Trustees of The Century Foundation, I thank Richard Kahlenberg and his fellow contributors for their work on this important topic.

RICHARD C. LEONE, *President*
THE CENTURY FOUNDATION
September 2008

CONTENTS

1.

INTRODUCTION

Richard D. Kahlenberg

The new president and Congress will have an opportunity to revise the Elementary and Secondary Education Act (ESEA), which was due to be renewed in 2007 but was the subject of fierce disagreement. Whether the legislation continues to be called the No Child Left Behind Act (NCLB) or is renamed, the basic thrust of NCLB—more funding in exchange for more accountability—is likely to remain. NCLB was passed in 2001 with broad bipartisan support, but in the years since its enactment it has come under sharp attack from many quarters. The controversial legislation, which requires states receiving federal funding to test students in reading and math in grades 3 through 8 and to hold schools accountable for making adequate yearly progress in raising student achievement, is now widely acknowledged to need a major overhaul.

The sound idea of standards-based education reform—that states should establish clear content standards that define what students should know and be able to do at each grade level; that students should take rigorous and sophisticated tests to see whether they mastered the material; and that students, teachers, and school administrators should be held accountable for results—is now threatened by major flaws in the way that NCLB embodies such reform. NCLB is being criticized not only by those on the far Left and far Right who never liked standards-based reform in the first place, but also by moderates who find several elements of NCLB untenable. In particular, critics rightly object to three central features of the act: the underfunding of NCLB; the flawed implementation of the standards, testing, and accountability provisions; and major difficulties with the provisions that are designed to allow students to transfer out of failing public schools.

This volume lays out the original ideas behind standards-based reform as outlined by proponents in the 1980s and 1990s and suggests ways to get the reform back on track. Chapter 2, by William Duncombe and John Yinger of Syracuse University and Anna Lukemeyer of the University of Nevada at Las Vegas, examines the flawed funding mechanism of NCLB, which broke the broad bargain envisioned by early reformers: more generous funding in return for higher standards and greater accountability. In order to uphold the bargain originally set out, the authors suggest that NCLB funding should be substantially increased in order to reduce the shortfall between authorization and appropriation and, ideally, to fund the ambitious goal of moving many more children to high levels of academic proficiency.

Chapter 3, by Lauren Resnick, Mary Kay Stein, and Sarah Coon of the University of Pittsburgh, outlines the flawed system of standards, testing, and accountability contained in NCLB, including the unrealistic requirement of 100 percent student proficiency, the varying state-by-state standards, and the way in which teachers, but not students, are held accountable. In order to fix these problems, clear content standards should be set, ideally by a national entity, to guide testing and accountability. Rather than setting an arbitrary single performance standard for all students, measures should be set to move all students to greater heights of learning. And students should be held accountable as well as adults.

Chapter 4, written by Amy Stuart Wells of Teachers College, Columbia University, and Jennifer Jellison Holme of the University of Texas at Austin, discusses the broken promise of the student-transfers provision: because transfers normally are limited to schools within a district, many students in failing districts are given no real option of choosing a better public school. This limitation undermines the potential of NCLB to reduce concentrations of poverty, a promising strategy for increasing student achievement. To remedy this, genuine opportunity should be provided for low-income students in failing schools to transfer to better performing public schools. Lines between urban and suburban districts should be made more malleable, allowing low-income urban students to attend good suburban schools and drawing more affluent suburban students into urban magnet schools. To make this happen, middle-class schools must be provided with financial incentives to educate low-income students, and the disincentives must be removed by making reasonable accommodations on NCLB's strict accountability requirements for transfer students. No one has figured out how to make high-poverty schools work well on a system-wide basis, and so NCLB's transfer provisions should be harnessed to reduce economic school segregation.

The stakes are high, for NCLB's flawed implementation of standards-based reform affirms the fears of reform opponents: that if NCLB is not fixed, it actually will strengthen the case for private-school vouchers and undercut the viability of public education. If overhauled, however, NCLB could recapture the early hopes for standards-based reform and promote both equity and excellence in K–12 schooling. Rather than junking the standards movement, or leaving NCLB as it is, the thesis of this book is that we must go back to the origins and resurrect the early promise of the reform.

The Original Idea of Standards-based Reform

Standards-based reform, as envisioned by leading educators such as Albert Shanker, Marshall "Mike" Smith, Diane Ravitch, Lauren Resnick, and Chester Finn, as well as governors and business leaders from outside education, would provide a sound way of promoting higher educational achievement and greater equality of educational opportunity. These educators believed that there was a big hole at the center of American education: a lack of agreement on what skills and knowledge students should master. Teachers had textbooks but no real guidance on what to prioritize, so they were essentially asked to create their own curricula. Teachers ended up choosing very different topics to pursue, based on personal interests, which created confusion and incoherence.[1]

There was also little outside pressure for anyone in the system to work very hard. Shanker noted that when he was a teacher and gave an assignment or quiz, all the students' hands would go up, and they would ask, "Does it count?"[2] For the small number of students applying to selective colleges, doing well academically mattered a great deal, but not so for the vast majority of students going on to nonselective colleges or going straight into the workforce, where employers rarely looked at grades achieved.

In an influential paper, Smith and his coauthor, Jennifer O'Day, suggested an alternative to this chaos: standards-based reform. They outlined a systemic reform in which all horses—standards, curriculum, textbooks, tests, teacher training, and teacher development— pulled the cart in the same direction. States would establish clear content standards, which would direct the curriculum, teacher training, and assessments.[3] Looking abroad at what successful competitors did, some, like Shanker, argued for national standards to provide even greater coherence.[4] Those systems made life predictable for both teachers and students. Everyone knew in advance what was expected of them, and the systems turned teachers and students from adversaries into allies. "It's like the Olympics," Shanker said. "There's an external standard that students need to meet, and the teacher is there to help the student make it."[5]

Likewise, standards-based reform also envisioned consequences for students, teachers, and principals whose students failed their assessments. Other countries had systems of accountability in place, and standards-based-reform advocates saw this feature as critical. The key insight was that achievement is fueled by effort, as well as innate ability, and new ways were needed to create greater efforts by both students and teachers.

Early advocates of standards-based reform recognized that they were asking schools to do what had never been done before—educate all students to high levels. In the past, under a manufacturing economy, it was acceptable to hold a small group of students to high standards and let the majority slip by. But in the new, knowledge-based economy, educators needed to genuinely educate far more students, and advocates realized that in order to reach new performance standards, more funding would be required. The essential bargain, then, was more funding for greater accountability.

A final piece of the larger standards-based-reform scheme was providing a mechanism so that children stuck in failing schools had the opportunity to transfer to better-performing public schools. This provision was a part of the accountability structure, to the extent that poor-performing schools would be "punished" by losing students, with the ultimate threat of being closed down. Providing the ability to transfer was also an acknowledgment that standards-based reform was a long-term strategy and that, even as schools slowly improved, families whose children were trapped in bad schools deserved a form of immediate relief.

Although the No Child Left Behind Act was an outgrowth of the standards-based reform movement, it departs in significant ways from the movement's early ideals. Furthermore, there are technical problems with NCLB that need fixing. As outlined below, there are significant shortfalls in funding; major flaws in the standards, testing, and accountability scheme; and serious limitations in the student transfer provisions.

Not surprisingly, most researchers have found that NCLB has failed to live up to its goal of substantially increasing academic achievement and closing the achievement gap between racial, ethnic, and income groups. While there have been some achievement gains since the beginning of the standards-based reform movement, most of those gains occurred prior to the enactment of NCLB.[6] A widely cited June 2007 study by the Center on Education Policy found gains in state test scores under NCLB, but a July 2007 study by Bruce Fuller at the University of California at Berkeley and others found that on the more reliable National Assessment of Educational Progress, in twelve states studied, test-score gains actually slowed with the enactment of NCLB.[7]

As a result of the significant departures from the model, and the mixed academic results, NCLB is under enormous attack, and some are heralding its demise.[8] NCLB urgently needs mending, not ending. Rather than abandoning standards-based reform, we should endeavor to improve on NCLB. The sections that follow outline the shortcomings of NCLB and make suggestions for fixing these problems.

FLAWS IN NCLB'S FUNDING

NCLB's grand bargain—greater federal funding in exchange for stricter accountability for results—has broken down in two respects. The first problem is the obvious mismatch between authorization and appropriation. The legislation authorized substantial increases in federal funding of K–12 education, but actual appropriations have fallen many billions of dollars below the authorized levels.

In FY 2002, Congress authorized $26.4 billion but appropriated only $22.2 billion, a $4.2 billion shortfall. Over time, and in general, the shortfall grew progressively worse: from $5.4 billion in FY 2003 to $7.6 billion in FY 2004, $9.8 billion in FY 2005, $13.4 billion in

FY 2006, $15.8 billion in FY 2007, and $14.8 billion in FY 2008. Between FY 2002 and FY 2008, the accumulated gap between authorization and appropriations was $70.9 billion. Taking into account the FY 2009 Bush administration budget request, the total gap rises to $85.7 billion.[9]

In fact, the shortfall goes even deeper than that in a second respect, according to Duncombe, Lukemeyer, and Yinger's new study of how much it would cost actually to reach some of the goals of No Child Left Behind. The authors find that federal funding would have to multiply many times over to help districts succeed in meeting even the intermediate goals of NCLB (short of the act's ultimate goal of 100 percent student proficiency). In their chapter, the authors note that there are three basic ways to raise levels of academic proficiency: increase federal funding (to reduce class size, increase teacher pay, enhance the use of technology, and so on), increase state and local education funding (to accomplish some of these same goals), and increase efficiency—get more bang for the buck—through the adoption of best education reform practices.

While some commentators have argued that "money doesn't matter" in education, Duncombe, Lukemeyer, and Yinger's research is based on a careful review of the difference that resources can make in raising student achievement based on past efforts. Using "cost function" analysis, the authors look at historical data on the relationship between spending and performance to estimate the amount of funding required to produce a given level of performance.

In seeking to estimate the costs of reaching the goals of NCLB, the authors note that the per-pupil cost would vary from state to state, depending on the level of standards adopted (higher standards are more expensive to meet), the local cost of living (teacher salaries must be higher in more expensive areas), and the makeup of the student population (students from low-income backgrounds and students for whom English is not the first language are generally more expensive to educate). Duncombe, Lukemeyer, and Yinger then look at four representative states, two of which (California and New York) tilt urban and two of which (Missouri and Kansas) tilt rural. Of these states, California and Missouri had low rates of student proficiency when NCLB began in 2002 (because of high standards and general levels of student performance), and New York and Kansas had high rates of student proficiency (because of low standards and general levels of student performance).

The authors do not even estimate the extraordinary cost of trying to reach NCLB's ultimate goal of 100 percent student proficiency, which they flatly reject as "unattainable."[10] Rather, they estimate the cost of an intermediate goal of getting 90 percent of students to proficiency. Even assuming that states increase funding by 15 percent and that districts become 15 percent more efficient at spending resources (ambitious goals), the authors conclude that federal Title I aid would have to be increased by 18 percent in Kansas, 129 percent in New York, 547 percent in California, and 1,077 percent in Missouri.[11] Because NCLB's stated goal is to have children reach high performance standards—of the type adopted by California and Missouri—current federal funding increases clearly fail to come anywhere near meeting the necessary investment.

The federal government needs to meet its end of the bargain: more resources in exchange for higher standards and more accountability. The reauthorization of No Child Left Behind should reflect the real costs of trying to increase achievement significantly and close the achievement gap. These costs, as Duncombe, Lukemeyer, and Yinger note, are substantial. In addition, in years to come, appropriations should be much closer to the level authorized than has been true during the Bush administration.

FLAWS IN NCLB'S SYSTEM OF STANDARDS, TESTING, AND ACCOUNTABILITY

NCLB's three-part system of standards, testing, and accountability is deeply flawed and needs revision, as Resnick, Stein, and Coon note in their chapter.

Most fundamentally, NCLB has failed to spur states to develop clear content standards, the linchpin necessary to inform teacher development, the curriculum, assessments, and the ultimate system for accountability. Content standards, which are supposed to drive the rest of the system, are often ill defined, so teachers have to intuit the standards from previous tests. In many places, Resnick, Stein, and Coon note, we have seen "a virtual hijacking of standards and education by narrow tests."[12] The existence of fifty different state standards also introduces chaos and confusion. As Shanker asked,

"Should children in Alabama learn a different kind of math or science from children in New York?"[13]

NCLB not only fails to encourage states to set rich and consistent content standards, it also allows them to set wildly different performance standards for what constitutes "proficiency." According to a 2007 study by Northwest Evaluation Associates and the Thomas B. Fordham Institute, passing scores vary from the sixth to the seventy-seventh percentile.[14] Worse, by requiring 100 percent proficiency, NCLB actually provides a perverse incentive for states to lower performance standards of proficiency in order to avoid having districts be sanctioned.[15]

As the standards are poorly constructed, so too are the tests. In part, perhaps, because of the large number of tests required (tests in math and reading for grades 3 to 8 as well as one grade in high school), states have adopted inexpensive, low-quality tests that rely on students answering multiple-choice questions by filling in bubbles. The low quality of the assessment is critical because under any system in which teachers are judged based on test scores, they will inevitably "teach to the test." As Albert Shanker noted, "Teaching to the test is something positive when you have really good tests."[16] But when the tests are poor quality, teaching to the test devolves into rote memorization and mastery of test-taking techniques rather than rich learning.

The assessments not only tend to be of low quality, but their timing also tends to make them fairly unhelpful in diagnosing problems of individual students. Tests generally are given at the end of the year, and results do not come back until after the students have moved on to another grade. The timing and nature of the tests robs them of their diagnostic function, as former Education Testing Service researcher Paul Barton notes, and reduces their value to teachers and students alike.[17]

The third prong of the standards-based system of reform—accountability—is equally problematic under NCLB. Weaknesses in the standards and weaknesses in the assessments naturally create fairness problems in the accountability system, but there are several other issues as well.

For one thing, NCLB requires states to set a single cut point for proficiency and mandates that 100 percent of students meet the performance standard in math and reading by 2014. Most serious educators believe this goal to be a fantasy because it denies the reality of human variability. No society throughout history has ever achieved 100 percent proficiency in education. To suggest that all students, including those who are severely disabled, will reach a meaningful standard of proficiency is a nice political slogan, but it is absurd to punish schools, principals, and teachers—and ultimately students and their families—for failing to reach an impossible goal. Moreover, a single performance standard that is impossibly high for certain special education students to meet may at the same time be too low for the vast majority of students who will not be challenged sufficiently.[18] The problem, therefore, is not that the performance standard is set too high or too low—it is that a single standard will be both. Finally, a single performance standard necessarily will lead to an emphasis on helping children who are on the cusp of being proficient. As Resnick, Stein, and Coon point out in their chapter, teachers will "concentrate on students who are *almost* proficient, ignoring most of the others who are judged to be well above the proficiency mark, and those who are far below it.[19]

For another, NCLB does not separate out the effects of family and the effects of school on student achievement, thereby holding teachers in high-poverty schools responsible for factors outside their control. Research going back four decades has found that the socioeconomic status of the family is the most important predictor of student achievement, yet NCLB requires all schools to reach the same exact standard, irrespective of the number of low-income students being educated. Ironically, defenders of charter schools have underlined the importance of family influence by complaining that it is unfair to hold charter schools to the same performance standard as public schools because charter schools tend to educate more low-income students. But NCLB says that public schools with large numbers of poor students will be graded on the same scale as those in which students enjoy numerous advantages.

In addition, NCLB holds teachers and principals accountable, but not students. NCLB contains no sanctions for students who fail to achieve proficiency on standardized tests. Some states have adopted, on their own, incentives for students to work hard (to be promoted to the next grade or to receive a graduation diploma), but NCLB itself does not contain such sanctions. Most European nations have a system of incentives and outcomes for their students, Shanker noted, recognizing that academic performance represents a combination of good teaching and hard work by students. "Imagine saying we should shut down a hospital and fire its staff," Shanker wrote, "because not all its patients became healthy—but never demanding that the patients also look out for themselves by eating properly, exercising, and laying off cigarettes, alcohol, and drugs."[20]

Likewise, NCLB lacks what Paul Barton calls a "rule of reason," lumping all those schools that barely miss making adequate yearly progress (AYP) with a single subgroup of students together with schools that fail by a wide margin with all groups. NCLB's provision requiring that schools make AYP with all subgroups of students—disaggregated by race, income, special education status, and so on—is generally thought to be a good provision because it does not allow schools to hide the failure of various subgroups of students behind generally good average achievement scores. But the law does not distinguish between a school that fails to make adequate progress with one group and a school that is generally failing with all of its students; either way, the school is publicly branded as a failure.[21]

Finally, unlike the original vision for standards-based reform, NCLB contains only "sticks" and no "carrots." As Resnick, Stein, and Coon point out, a reliance on sticks alone (coupled with the goal of 100 percent proficiency) can lead to disillusionment and cynicism among teachers.[22] We may, they say, be losing some of our best teachers because of the heavy punitive sanctions applied under a system that many view as unfair.

What is to be done? Return to the original vision of standards-based reform. Establish clear and well-defined standards, set at the national level if possible, or the state level if necessary. (As a political compromise, a small number of state consortia could adopt agreed-upon standards.) Produce high-quality tests that are linked to these standards. (Federal money may be required for both to occur.) Abolish the ludicrous goal of 100 percent proficiency to a single standard, and instead set multiple standards with the goal of moving all segments of the distribution up at least one notch. (The National Assessment of Educational Progress uses such a system, identifying advanced, proficient, and basic.) Use well-constructed, value-added models of achievement that better measure what children are learning in school, as opposed to what they have learned at home, before kindergarten, or during summers. Ideally, similar assessments should be given at the beginning and end of a school year, so that we know what actual third graders learned in third grade, not how well one year's cohort of third graders does compared to the previous year's cohort.[23] Apply accountability requirements to students, as well as teachers. Adopt a graduated scale of compliance that recognizes the different degrees of school failure. Finally, use carrots as well as sticks as incentives for students and teachers.

FLAWS IN NCLB'S
STUDENT-TRANSFER PROVISIONS

NCLB provides that when Title I (high poverty) schools fail to make AYP for two years in a row, the school district must allow students to transfer to better-performing public schools within the district. The provision is meant to accomplish three goals: to serve as a sanction and form of accountability for low-performing schools, hopefully pressuring them to improve; to provide immediate relief for students stuck in failing schools; and (in the minds of some progressive reformers) to provide an opportunity for low-income students to escape high-poverty schools, thereby reducing concentrations of school poverty.[24]

In practice, however, the student transfer provisions have been one of the most disappointing features of NCLB. Various studies and surveys have found that about 1 percent of students eligible to transfer actually do so.[25] Some argue that the minute number of transfers suggests that parents simply like neighborhood schools and do not want to get out of failing schools, or that districts are not providing enough information to parents about transfer options, and there is probably some truth to both of those.[26] But there is another likely cause: many parents may not even apply to have their children transfer because there are so few good options within many urban school districts. Lacking the chance to send their children to demonstrably better schools in the suburbs, many urban parents may fail to see much comparative advantage to transferring from a failing segregated school to an almost-failing segregated school.[27] In some school districts, such as Providence, Rhode Island, there have been literally no non-failing schools to transfer into at particular grade levels.[28] It is not surprising, then, that the U.S. Department of Education found that in a survey of nine urban districts, participation in Title I school choice was about 0.5 percent, even lower than the national average of 1 percent.[29] While NCLB encourages urban and suburban districts to set up "cooperative agreements" to allow student transfers, virtually none of the country's suburban districts has voluntarily agreed to do this.[30]

It is little wonder why suburban middle-class schools do not welcome low-income transfer students: all the incentives align against their doing so. As the University of Virginia's James Ryan notes, a receiving school that takes in low-income students faces a double risk. Because low-income students, on average, score lower than middle-class children, an influx of low-income transfer students initially is likely to depress aggregate school scores, increasing the chances that the receiving school will itself fail to make AYP. The other risk stems from a laudable feature of the legislation: the requirement that schools do a good job of raising proficiency in general, but also of raising the scores of groups of students, disaggregated by race and income. Homogenous schools with few poor or minority students are exempt from this requirement, because a critical mass of students is required to make disaggregation valid statistically. But an influx of poor and/or minority students might push a school over the threshold number, triggering disaggregation, thus increasing the number of targets the school has to hit to make AYP and thereby increasing the risk of failing. This proves, says Ryan, "an incentive to minimize the number of African-American or poor students in a school or district."[31]

These disincentives to cross-district transfers are problematic not only because they undercut the accountability rationale of NCLB and fail to provide immediate relief to students trapped in failing schools, but also more importantly because they undermine NCLB's potential to break down economic segregation in our schools.

A wide body of research has found that concentrations of poverty create enormous difficulties for schools. On average, low-income fourth-grade American students given a chance to attend more affluent schools scored almost two years ahead of low-income students stuck in high-poverty schools on the National Assessment of Educational Progress (NAEP) in math. Indeed, low-income students in middle-class schools performed better, on average, than middle-class students attending high-poverty schools.[32] Likewise, data from the 2006 Programme for International Student Assessment (PISA) for fifteen-year-olds in science showed a "clear advantage in attending a school whose students are, on average, from more advantaged socio-economic backgrounds." The report continued, "Regardless of their own socio-economic background, students attending schools in which the average socio-economic background is high tend to perform better than when they are enrolled in a school with a below-average socio-economic intake."[33] Middle-class schools provide not only more financial resources on average, but also a more positive peer environment, better teachers, and more actively involved parents.[34]

More than forty school districts across the country now use socio-economic status of student families as a factor in student assignment.[35] In Wake County (Raleigh), North Carolina, for example, the school board in 2000 adopted a policy goal that no school should have more than 40 percent of students eligible for free and reduced-price lunch or more than 25 percent performing below grade level. The program has been successful: low-income and minority students are performing better than comparable students in other large North Carolina districts, and middle-class students are excelling as well.[36]

The Wake County socioeconomic school integration plan works well in part because the school district encompasses both the city of Raleigh and its surrounding suburbs. In much of the country, however, urban and suburban areas are cut into separate school districts, so it is imperative that creative efforts be made to provide meaningful choice extending across school-district lines.

As the chapter by Holme and Wells notes, there are eight highly successful interdistrict programs that consciously seek to promote increased racial and economic school integration. These programs—in Boston, St. Louis, Hartford, Milwaukee, Rochester, Indianapolis, Minneapolis, and East Palo Alto—have led to greater opportunities for the low-income and minority students who have transferred, and they have broad societal benefits.[37]

Holme and Wells, in what appears to be the most comprehensive review of interdistrict programs to date, find that after an initial adjustment period, students generally see large test-score achievement gains in suburban schools. In St. Louis, transfer students not only scored higher, they also were twice as likely to go on to two-year or four-year colleges than graduates of the schools they left behind.[38] Over the longer term, students in these programs benefit from the widely established fact that white employers prefer African-American graduates of predominantly white suburban schools over similar graduates of racially segregated inner-city schools.[39] In all the jurisdictions reviewed, there are substantial waiting lists to participate in transfer programs. In St. Louis, for example, 3,662 black students applied for 1,163 available suburban seats in the 2007–8 school year.

In Milwaukee, 2000 students applied for transfers to suburban schools, where there were only 370 slots available in 2006–7. Meanwhile, Boston's urban-suburban transfer program, known as METCO, has a waiting list of 13,000.[40]

The authors cite several key provisions of these successful programs, which could serve as models for transfers under NCLB. The programs do not allow receiving districts to reject students for academic reasons; they provide centers for information and outreach to transferring students; they provide free transportation to students; and they provide incentives for suburban districts to participate.[41]

Holme and Wells note that outreach programs have been important in St. Louis, Boston, Indianapolis, Milwaukee, and Minneapolis in helping ease the transition of students from city to suburban schools.[42] In each of the eight districts, states provide all or a very large portion of the costs of transportation, which can run more than $2,000 a year per pupil.[43] And one of the key reasons for the political success of these programs is the financial incentives provided to middle-class receiving districts. According to Holme and Wells, programs in St. Louis, Milwaukee, and Indianapolis have provided receiving districts the equivalent of their average per-pupil expenditure for resident students, while in Rochester, the suburban districts receive the city's per-pupil funding, which is close to or greater than the amount spent per pupil in the suburbs. East Palo Alto, Minneapolis, Hartford, and Boston have less-generous programs.[44] While there was strong political resistance to many of these programs initially, over time suburban legislators have often come to support continuation of the programs, Holme and Wells report. And new suburban districts have asked to be added to programs in Boston, Minneapolis, and Rochester.[45] The authors attribute the political success of the programs not only to the financial incentives provided, but also to salutary effects that the programs themselves have on the racial attitudes of students and parents in the suburbs over time.[46]

NCLB could use these interdistrict programs as a model. Under the U.S. Supreme Court's June 2007 decision striking down racial integration plans in Louisville and Seattle, interdistrict programs may not be able to use race as a primary factor, but it still remains perfectly legal to give priority to low-income students of all races, as NCLB currently does for intra-district public school choice. As is true of NCLB's intra-district transfer policy, free transportation should be provided to children in failing schools for interdistrict travel.

Former North Carolina senator John Edwards has proposed a promising two-way interdistrict public school choice program to encourage socioeconomic school integration. He called for $100 million in federal bonuses to middle-class schools enrolling low-income students and an additional $100 million to expand funding of magnet schools dedicated to economic integration that draw students from suburbs to low-income areas.[47] The money could be used on a small scale to test both the amount of financial incentive required to entice middle-class suburban schools to open their doors to low-income children, and the amount required to create attractive magnet schools that will draw middle-class suburban students into urban schools. Experience suggests that given the right program, magnet schools can attract middle-class suburban students to schools located in some of the toughest urban neighborhoods. In Hartford, for example, a Montessori magnet school, located near boarded-up buildings, has a long waiting list of white middle-class suburban children because the program offered at the end of the bus ride is excellent.[48] Nationally, an estimated 150,000 students are on waiting lists for magnet schools. Some 1.2 million students attend an estimated 2,400 magnet schools across the country.[49] Holme and Wells also suggest that for suburban districts lacking classroom space, the federal government should provide capital funds to increase capacity for low-income transfer students.[50]

In addition, NCLB should be amended to eliminate existing disincentives to accepting low-income students. Senator Joe Lieberman has proposed legislation under which receiving suburban districts would receive a one-year AYP "safe harbor" for transfer students. These students' progress would be monitored for five years, after which time they would be merged into the accountability provisions for the school as a whole.[51]

CONCLUSION

Improving No Child Left Behind will require addressing the three key problems outlined above: the underfunding of NCLB; the problems with the standards, testing, and accountability provisions; and the need to provide a meaningful right for students to transfer to better-performing public schools, including ones outside their own districts.

Failure to fix these problems could undermine the entire standards-based reform movement, and, indeed, our entire system of American public education. As currently structured, NCLB is in many ways a setup for privatization. By taking standards-based reform off course—failing to provide adequate resources, failing to establish a coherent and sophisticated set of standards and assessments, and failing to provide children stuck in underperforming schools with appropriate remedies—NCLB could fuel the argument for moving toward a system of privatized education in the United States.

The decision by Congress and the Bush administration to underfund NCLB helps make it more likely that public schools will fail to meet new standards, undercutting the case for public education generally. In addition, because the accountability provisions in the law are written in a way that overidentifies failure, and because the law allows states to skip over the hard work of establishing well thought-out standards and sophisticated assessments, it sets up teachers, students, and public schools for failure. Finally, because the transfer provisions in the law do not require that urban students be allowed to transfer to suburban schools, the resulting lack of supply of good receiving schools has been used as an argument by conservatives that private-school vouchers are necessary to meet the demand.[52]

On the other hand, if standards-based reform is put back on track, it would drown out the wrongheaded calls for privatization.[53] As Resnick has observed, the standards movement is in its adolescence, but we should not "give up on our unruly teen."[54] When Congress reauthorizes the Elementary and Secondary Education Act, it should:

◆   Raise the level of funding to meet the enormous task at hand: raising student proficiency and closing achievement gaps between groups. Careful research suggests that this will require increasing federal funding dramatically (from modest increases for states with more affluent students and low standards to ten times current levels for high-needs states with rigorous performance standards).

◆   Modify the standards, accountability, and testing provisions of NCLB by requiring states (or a national body) to set clear and well-defined content standards of what students should know and be able to do; produce high-quality tests; set multiple performance standards to encourage students at all levels to improve;

measure what students are actually learning in school, not outside of it; provide similar assessments at the beginning and ends of the school year to better capture student gains and provide better diagnostic aid to teachers; hold students accountable as well as teachers; employ a graduated scale of compliance with performance standards; and use carrots as well as sanctions, for teachers as well as students.

◆ Alter the transfer provisions in NCLB to encourage socioeconomic integration by providing incentives for middle-class schools in suburban areas to accept transfer of low-income students across district lines; increase magnet-school funding to encourage suburban middle-class families to send their children to schools in urban settings; eliminate the disincentive of middle-class schools to accept low-income students by providing a safe harbor on accountability for such students; provide free transportation for NCLB transfers, including across school-district lines; and fund information centers to educate low-income families about their rights to seek a better education for their children.

A well-constructed bill—one that fully funds the ambitious goals of NCLB; provides coherent national standards, tied to high-quality assessments and reasonable stakes for students and teachers alike; and provides a genuine transfer option for low-income students to attend high-quality middle-class suburban schools—would not pave the way for private-school vouchers. Quite the opposite, it would strengthen our public education system immeasurably.

2.

Dollars without Sense
The Mismatch between the No Child
Left Behind Act Accountability System
and Title I Funding

William D. Duncombe, Anna Lukemeyer, and John Yinger

1. Introduction

The No Child Left Behind Act (NCLB) is designed to boost student performance, especially that of low-income students and those from traditionally disadvantaged groups, through an accountability system and additional funding. This chapter describes the accountability and funding mechanisms in NCLB and explores their fairness and effectiveness, using data from California, Kansas, Missouri, and New York.

NCLB did not invent educational accountability, of course. In fact, by 2001 almost every state had some form of an accountability system. Over forty states had school report cards, over half had school performance ratings, and many provided assistance or sanctions for low-performing schools.[1] Nevertheless, NCLB represented a major change in the accountability environment because it introduced extensive federal government involvement in setting performance objectives, in implementation timing, and in imposing sanctions for inadequate performance.[2]

19

   Key to understanding the role of NCLB are the concepts of educational costs, efficiency, and accountability. This chapter begins with a detailed look at these concepts and the key accountability provisions of NCLB (section 2). We then turn to an analysis of the role of NCLB in California, Kansas, Missouri, and New York. These states provide sharp contrasts in the share of students passing state tests, in the degree of centralization in their education finance system, and in their level of urbanization. We estimate the cost of achieving the intermediate targets associated with NCLB in each of these states (section 3) and determine the extent to which the funds associated with NCLB cover these costs (section 4). In section 5 we use our cost estimates to calculate the changes in federal aid, state aid, or school-district efficiency that would be required for each state to reach its NCLB performance targets. Section 6 asks who should be held accountable and, in particular, explores the roles of schools, school districts, states, and the federal government in the NCLB accountability system. The role of the federal government is the subject of several court cases, which are discussed in this section. The final section explores the policy implications of our results, including recommendations for modifying the funding and accountability provisions of NCLB.

   The key results from our analysis indicate that NCLB leaves a funding gap between the spending required to meet NCLB standards and the additional federal Title I aid associated with NCLB; this gap is much larger in states where student proficiency rates were relatively low at the inception of NCLB (California and Missouri) than in states where they were relatively high (Kansas and New York). This funding gap is much larger in school districts with high concentrations of disadvantaged students than in other districts. Even assuming that NCLB was accompanied by a 15 percent increase in both state aid and school-district efficiency, federal Title I aid will have to more than double in urbanized states with relatively high student proficiency rates, such as New York, and increase five to ten times in states with low proficiency rates (Missouri and California) to meet a 90 percent proficiency target. Assuming that such increases in state and federal aid and efficiency are unrealistic, NCLB in its present form is both unfair, because it penalizes states and districts serving large populations of disadvantaged students, and ineffective, because it provides strong incentives for states to lower their standards.

2. EDUCATIONAL COSTS, EFFICIENCY, AND ACCOUNTABILITY

An accountability system provides an organization or set of organizations with incentives to meet specified objectives in a cost-effective manner. Accountability systems are used, for example, by businesses to affect the behavior of their branch offices, by state governments to influence their local governments, or by the federal government to influence the governments that receive its funds. NCLB creates an accountability system through which the federal government attempts to influence the behavior of schools, school districts, and state governments.

This section provides a guide to educational accountability systems. More specifically, we explore the concepts of educational costs and efficiency and show how these concepts can be used both to help design a school accountability system and to evaluate NCLB.

EDUCATIONAL COSTS

Educational cost is the amount of money that a district must spend per pupil to obtain a given output, defined as a given level of student performance. This type of cost is analogous to cost in private production, which is a central tool in economics. A cost equation explains cost as a function of output level and input prices. The relevant outputs in the case of education are graduation rates and measures of student performance on state tests. The key input price is teacher salary.

As shown by previous studies, application of this tool to education requires three principal extensions.[3] First, any estimation of a cost equation must recognize the difference between costs and spending, which, as discussed below, is school-district efficiency. Second, educational cost depends not only on input prices, but also on student characteristics, such as the poverty rate and the share of students with limited English proficiency. Third, estimation of an education cost equation must recognize that both measures of student performance and teachers' salaries are influenced by school-district decisions and are therefore, to use the statistical term, endogenous. Studies that do not account for this endogeneity yield biased results.

SCHOOL-DISTRICT EFFICIENCY

The first extension is critical for interpreting the analysis in this chapter. A cost equation indicates how much a school district would have to spend to achieve a given student performance level if it used the best available technology—that is, the best available teaching methods and management practices. We cannot, however, observe costs in this sense; instead, we observe actual spending, which may not reflect the best available technology. In other words, spending may exceed costs because some districts deviate from the best available technology, which is the same thing as being inefficient. To isolate the impact of the student performance level, input prices, and student characteristics on costs, therefore, one must somehow control for school-district efficiency.

A production activity is defined to be efficient if it uses the fewest resources possible to produce a particular output (or outputs) given current technology. A production activity that uses more than the minimum possible resources to produce a given output is called inefficient. Three features of efficiency are central to understanding school-district spending and for designing a sensible school accountability program.

First, a school district is not inefficient if it spends more than other districts with the same output for reasons outside its control. The most obvious example of this point involves teacher wages. School districts located in high-wage areas must pay more than other districts to attract teachers of any given quality. In addition, some school districts must pay more than other districts to deal with certain characteristics of their students, such as poverty or a lack of English proficiency. Methods to account for factors outside a district's control have been developed by scholars and are described below.[4]

The second key feature of efficiency is that it cannot be defined in the abstract but instead can only be defined relative to the output or outputs selected by the analyst. In the case of a firm with a single output (or multiple outputs produced with totally separate inputs), the notion of efficiency is straightforward. Inefficient firms are those that do not use the best available technology for producing the output. Examples of inefficiency include using a machine based on an outmoded technology, paying employees more than the market wage, or sending executives on expensive junkets. Given the nature of these types of activity, an "inefficient" firm is often said to be "wasteful."

When a firm produces multiple outputs with some sharing of inputs, however, the concept of "inefficiency" applies to the firm's production of each output, not to the firm as a whole, and "inefficiency" and "waste" may no longer be equivalent. Consider farms that grow corn and beans in the same fields, a practice used by Native Americans to give the beans a place to climb. One farm might be slow, and hence inefficient, in growing corn because it takes great care not to trample the beans. This type of efficiency has nothing to do with waste; instead, it has to do with the farm's trade-off across the two outputs. Of course, the farm may also be wasteful in the sense that it pays overly generous salaries or uses outmoded techniques.

Multiple outputs and input sharing are inherent characteristics of public education; the same teachers and classrooms, supported by the same administrative services, provide many different outputs. These outputs include student performance on standardized tests in English, math, social studies, and science. They also include high-school completion rates and student performance in art, music, athletics, and citizenship, which are more difficult to measure. In this setting, an analyst can ask if a school district is inefficient in producing English and math performance (perhaps over several grades), but one must recognize that this type of inefficiency reflects both spending to promote other outputs and the use of outmoded techniques or other forms of waste. For example, a school district that is efficient in delivering student performance in mathematics might not be efficient in delivering student performance in English or art. Indeed, spending on art is likely to be a source of inefficiency in the production of mathematics in the sense that it involves spending with little impact on mathematics performance. No existing study has been able to separate these two types of inefficiency.

The concept of efficiency is widely misunderstood in both the academic literature and policy debates. School districts are said to be "wasteful" if they spend more per pupil than other districts (after accounting for labor market conditions and other factors outside their control) with the same student performance in English and mathematics. In fact, districts that spend more than other districts with the same English and math performance may simply be providing relatively high levels of student performance along other dimensions, such as graduation rates or science achievement. Of course, these districts may also be using outmoded techniques or being wasteful in some other way, but spending numbers alone cannot determine whether this is true.

SCHOOL ACCOUNTABILITY SYSTEMS

A school accountability system is a state-level system intended to give school districts incentives to be efficient, both in the sense of minimizing waste and in the sense of boosting certain specified performance targets. Accountability is, of course, an issue in any type of activity, and many principles for accountability systems have been developed in the literature on performance management. Many scholars have applied some or all of these principles to educational accountability programs.[5]

According to these scholars, anyone designing an educational accountability system must address three key issues. First, they must decide who is to be held accountable. Second, they must decide what the people being held accountable should be held accountable for. The selected objectives must, of course, be measurable. Moreover, it obviously makes no sense to hold people accountable for something over which they have no control (or to hold them fully accountable for something over which they have only partial control). As a result, this step involves identifying performance measures over which the people being held accountable have control and then expressing targets for these measures. Third, they must decide on the consequences of success or failure in meeting the specified targets. This step determines the strength of the incentives in the accountability program. Larger rewards or more severe penalties lead to stronger incentives to meet the specified performance targets.

One approach to an educational accountability system is to hold students accountable for their performance in certain classes or on certain tests. Sanctions in this type of system can be severe; students may not be allowed to graduate if they do not pass a specified list of courses or tests. A more modest sanction is that students who fail to pass all the specified courses or tests receive a different type of high school degree. A system that holds students accountable provides them with incentives to perform well, but it may be unfair; students in underfunded or poorly managed schools face more obstacles in avoiding sanctions than do other students. Moreover, this type of system may boost the drop-out rate in these low-performing schools.

A more common type of accountability system focuses on holding teachers and/or school administrators accountable for student performance, usually measured by student test scores, graduation rates, or changes in test scores.[6] Systems developed to comply with NCLB fall into this category. Consequences for failing to meet standards in these systems might be as mild as bad publicity, but they might also involve financial penalties, reassignment of students, or even state takeover.[7] Several scholars have found evidence that accountability programs can have a positive impact on student performance.[8] There is no consensus, however, on the features that an accountability system must have in order to produce this impact or on the magnitude of this impact when it occurs.

ACCOUNTABILITY AND FUNDING

A key issue for these accountability systems, and for this chapter, is how to account for factors outside the control of school-district personnel, such as a high-wage environment or concentrated poverty. Failure to account for these factors may lead to an accountability system that is unfair, in the sense that it punishes or rewards school districts based on circumstances that are not of their own making, or ineffective, in the sense that it expects school districts to overcome circumstances over which they have no control. Imagine a national business that required its branches to pay the same salaries for each position regardless of the local cost of living and then used the same accountability standard for each branch. This program would be unfair, because it would be easier for the branch offices to attract high-quality employees in the low-cost locations than in the high-cost locations. It would also be ineffective because branch offices cannot influence the cost of living. If the accountability system were "high stakes" in the sense that it imposed significant rewards or punishments, then high-quality personnel in high-wage places would have a strong incentive to leave. Implementing this accountability system, therefore, could actually result in a reduction of staff quality in high-wage locations. Providing all school districts with the same funding per pupil and expecting them all to meet the same accountability standards would be equally flawed.

One way to avoid these problems is to combine an account-ability system with a funding system that fully compensates districts for the added costs associated with external cost factors. Requiring all branch offices to pay the same *real* salary—that is, a salary reflecting the purchasing power in each region—would eliminate the unfairness in the above program and would make this program more effective by allowing branch offices to focus on factors that they can control, such as recruitment and training. Similarly, a school funding system that adequately accounts for the added costs of a high-wage location or a concentration of disadvantaged students would place all school districts on a level playing field; in this case, it would be fair and effective to hold all districts to the same accountability standards. Without full compensation for external cost factors, however, a school accountability system that imposes the same standards on all districts is neither fair nor effective.

Although the first school accountability programs implemented in most states ignored factors outside the control of school personnel, many states were modifying their systems to address this issue before NCLB was passed.[9] Some states, including South Carolina, set standards for a district relative to other districts with approximately the same poverty rate.[10] Moreover, one city school district, Dallas, set up an accountability system that used statistical analysis to try to account for some of the factors outside the control of school officials.[11] The accountability provisions of NCLB, which, as we will see, contain no such adjustment, have derailed most state attempts to address this issue.

A related development is that some states have moved to accountability systems that measure progress based not on levels of, but on changes in, student performance. Some scholars argue that this is a step in the right direction because it eliminates the imposition of sanctions on a district that has a low initial performance caused by factors outside its control.[12] Other scholars are not so sure that this approach is an improvement because high-cost districts must spend more than other districts to improve their performance,[13] because this approach punishes districts that are already efficient, and hence have little room for improvement,[14] and because changes in test scores in a given grade are a noisy measure of performance change.[15] All of these issues come up in NCLB, which, as we will see, sets intermediate performance targets based on "adequate yearly progress" (AYP).

THE NO CHILD LEFT BEHIND ACT

NCLB imposed a new accountability system on schools in every state. More specifically, NCLB required states to implement math and reading exams in grades 3–8 and in at least one grade in high school by 2005–6, and science exams once in elementary, middle, and high school by 2007–8. In addition, districts are required to report participation rates on the exams and graduation rates from high school. Moreover, NCLB requires districts to collect and report assessment information by racial, socioeconomic, and special-needs groups.

NCLB sets as its target that *all* students reach proficiency on these measures by 2013–14. States are provided a fair amount of discretion in selecting exams, defining the level of performance that is "proficient," and setting intervening performance targets for the years leading up to 2013–14. More specifically, NCLB requires states to make adequate yearly progress (AYP) until 2014. Rules for determining AYP have evolved over the last five years, and states are now allowed several paths to establishing AYP.[16] Schools can be classified as making AYP if the growth in student performance is at least 10 percent more than last year ("safe harbor"), if performance falls within a "confidence interval" of the target, or some combination of these two.[17] The combination of safe harbor provisions and confidence intervals increases the complexity of determining AYP[18] and can significantly reduce the performance improvement required of a school below the performance targets. In certain situations, a school below the performance standards can still make AYP without any improvement in performance.[19] Recently, the U.S. Department of Education has approved several states as pilot sites to test the use of "growth models" as an additional component of assessing AYP.[20] Growth models represent attempts to develop student-level value-added measures for schools.

The penalty component of NCLB uses high stakes and punitive consequences for schools receiving Title I funding and not making AYP:

> After two consecutive years of failure, schools must develop a plan for improvement and are supposed to receive "technical" assistance. Students in those schools are also allowed to choose another public school, including a charter school, within the same district. After three years, students who have not already departed for greener pastures must be provided with tutoring services from an outside provider, public or private. Those schools that fail to

make AYP for four consecutive years must take one of several measures, including replacing school staff or instituting a new curriculum, and those that fail for five years in a row must essentially surrender control to the state government, which can reopen the school as a charter school, turn over management to a private company, or take over the school itself.[21]

The strong sanctions in NCLB will undoubtedly lead to some responses that are consistent with the objectives of the legislation, such as a greater focus on math and reading,[22] which corresponds to increased efficiency through cutting back on activities that do not support NCLB's specified objectives; and the use of more effective teaching and management techniques, which corresponds to increased efficiency through cutting waste. NCLB, however, also violates two of the most basic principles developed for an effective accountability system: it does not fully specify objectives, but instead lets the objectives be influenced by the people being held accountable,[23] and it does not adequately consider factors that the people being held accountable cannot control.

NCLB requires states to make AYP and, eventually, to have 100 percent passing rates, but it does not specify the tests to which these standards must be applied and allows a lot of flexibility in defining AYP. The federal law also allows each state to set its own definitions of "proficiency." Moreover, neither the funding nor the sanctions in NCLB are connected with the stringency of a state's standards, which vary widely.[24] As a result, states have incentives to set low proficiency levels and to postpone required proficiency improvements as long as possible.[25]

Consider the cases of the four states we focus on in this chapter—California, Kansas, Missouri, and New York. As shown in Table 2.1, the share of students passing the state tests in math and reading in 2003 was much lower in Missouri and California than in Kansas and New York.[26] This variation in passing rates reflects variation in the underlying quality of education as well as variation in the stringency of the state exams. In 2003, for example, Kansas and New York set their proficiency target at a much higher level (49 percent and 60 percent) than did Missouri and California (25 percent and 13 percent).[27] All the states have average performance above their targets up to 2005, but Missouri and California obviously must experience a much greater annual improvement to reach the NCLB requirement of 100 percent proficiency by 2014. Kansas and

Table 2.1 Proficiency Targets and Percent of Students Reaching Proficiency

Year	Kansas		Missouri		California		New York	
	NCLB Target	Actual Performance	NCLB Target	Actual Performance	NCLB Target	Actual Performance	NCLB Target	Actual Performance
2002	44.9	58.3	13.4	25.2	13.3	—	—	76.5
2003	44.9	63.2	14.4	25.0	13.3	37.7	60.1	76.6
2004	51.8	67.6	15.4	26.2	13.3	38.8	60.1	79.0
2005	58.6	70.5	22.1	27.4	24.2	43.5	64.1	81.5
2006	58.6	73.4	30.7	—	24.2	46.4	68.2	—
2007	68.4	—	39.4	—	24.2	47.0	72.0	—
2008	72.9	—	48.0	—	35.0	—	76.1	—
2009	77.5	—	56.7	—	45.8	—	80.2	—
2010	82.0	—	65.4	—	56.7	—	84.0	—
2011	86.5	—	74.0	—	67.5	—	88.1	—
2012	91.0	—	82.7	—	78.3	—	91.9	—
2013	95.5	—	91.3	—	89.2	—	96.0	—

Note: See text for sources of information on NCLB targets. Actual performance information for California is from the California Department of Education, *Accountability Progress Report*, for various years. For New York performance information is from the New York State Education Department, *New York: The State of Learning*, for various years. See text for sources of information on NCLB Targets. Actual performance information in Kansas is from Kansas State Board of Education, *Education in Kansas: Accountability Report*, for various years. In Missouri, performance information is from Missouri Department of Elementary and Secondary Education (2007).

New York set their targets for 2008 at 73 percent and 76 percent, compared to targets of 48 percent and 35 percent in Missouri and California, respectively.

It should come as no surprise, therefore, that in January 2004 the Missouri State Board of Education approved new cutoffs for the state tests that "should result in more students scoring at the 'proficient' and 'advanced' levels." According to the board's press release, this policy change was deemed to be "critical because federal law (No Child Left Behind) requires all children to be proficient in reading and math by 2014."[28] The percentage of proficient students jumped from 27.5 percent in 2005 with the old cutoffs to 43.3 percent in 2006 with the new cutoffs.[29]

More formal evidence on the variation in state standards under NCLB and the incentives to reduce state standards comes from several recent studies. The differences in the difficulties of reaching proficiency on state exams in math and English have been highlighted in a recent publication from NCES (2007), which compares state proficiency standards to those on the national NAEP exam for reading and math in fourth and eighth grades.[30] In states for which data are available, the NAEP equivalent proficiency scores vary widely, and almost all states have established proficiency levels below the standard set for the NAEP.[31] In an analysis of fourth-grade math and reading tests in twelve states since NCLB was passed, proficiency on state tests improved more than did proficiency on the national NAEP tests—a sign that standards on state tests may be dropping.[32]

These problems with the intermediate standards in NCLB will turn into a crisis if the requirement of 100 percent proficiency is imposed in 2014. Even if a state lowers its standards considerably, many of its schools are likely to fall short of this requirement without unprecedented increases in education funding and/or school-district efficiency. Thus, severe sanctions in many schools would be almost inevitable, wreaking havoc in every state's education system, including states that have done the most to improve student performance. Unattainable objectives cannot form the basis of a reasonable accountability system.

Instead of looking at 100 percent proficiency, therefore, this chapter examines the cost of achieving intermediate performance targets in several states and determines whether the funding that accompanies NCLB is sufficient to cover these costs. Our analysis focuses on the intermediate performance targets set for each year, which are defined in terms of expected proficiency rates rather than the requirements to make AYP. Specifically, we base our comparisons on three proficiency levels—70 percent, 80 percent, and 90 percent—which provide a range of possible targets for NCLB. This focus reflects two key features of NCLB: first, the requirements to make AYP, which vary significantly across states and even across schools, are difficult to duplicate. Second, the AYP standards just postpone the ultimate requirement of reaching 100 percent proficiency by 2014. In order to make significant movement toward this standard, schools need to make steady improvements in their proficiency rates.

Another key objective of NCLB is "improving the academic achievement of the disadvantaged." This is a laudable objective, but the mechanisms for implementing it do not adequately recognize the added costs of educating disadvantaged students. The standards for adequate yearly progress are not adjusted in any way to account for these higher costs. Moreover, NCLB places more short-run requirements on schools with disadvantaged students than on other schools. To be specific, NCLB requires adequate yearly progress not only for each school but also for a variety of student groups within a school, including students from poor families and students from various racial and ethnic groups. Thus, schools with many disadvantaged students generally face harsher sanctions than other schools,[33] which can potentially lead to a number of perverse incentives.[34] We do not consider performance of subgroups for our analysis, which implies that our estimates are likely to understate the costs of complying with NCLB.

This is not the whole story, however, because NCLB did focus federal education dollars more tightly on schools with high poverty rates.[35] In principle, this change might offset the fact that NCLB performance standards are not adjusted for student disadvantage. As discussed above, one way to make certain that schools are not held accountable for factors outside their control is to set the same standard for all schools and to give each school the resources that it needs to meet this standard, after considering, among other things, the level of disadvantage among its students. We investigate this issue in detail later in this chapter. To be specific, we calculate the extent to which the funding components of NCLB—Title I aid programs—are sufficient to compensate districts for cost factors outside their control.

3. COSTING OUT NCLB

Several approaches for estimating the cost of reaching a given student performance standard have been developed,[36] and studies of this topic have been carried out in at least thirty states.[37] We use the so-called cost-function method to estimate the spending required to meet NCLB standards. In this section, we review previous studies of this topic, discuss data and measures used in the cost function, present cost-function results, and estimate the cost of meeting NCLB standards in California, Kansas, Missouri, and New York.

PREVIOUS STUDIES OF THE COST TO MEET NCLB STANDARDS

The cost estimates in this chapter draw on previous research by Driscoll and Fleeter; Imazeki and Reschovsky; and Duncombe, Lukemeyer, and Yinger.[38] These studies estimate the school-district spending that is needed to comply with the NCLB standards and compare this spending with the funding available through Title I of NCLB and other sources.

This chapter expands on these studies by using more recent data and by conducting comparable analyses in four different states with different characteristics. As discussed above, we focus on states that differ significantly in the share of students passing state tests, their level of urbanization, and the centralization of their finance system. Kansas and New York selected tests and set proficiency cutoffs that, when combined with their education systems, resulted in relatively high proficiency levels before implementation of NCLB, whereas California and Missouri set much more stringent standards relative to the performance of their students, resulting in low student proficiency rates. In each of these pairs, one state is highly urbanized and the other is largely rural. Moreover, California and Kansas have highly centralized education finance systems, whereas the systems in New York and Missouri are relatively decentralized.

The calculations in this chapter do not consider the costs of a testing system or the costs of enforcing required change in the school finance system. Scholars have examined these costs, which are small relative to the costs that we address.[39]

Data Sources and Measures

A school-district cost function relates five factors to spending per pupil: student performance; the price of school resources, such as teacher salaries; the district's enrollment; student characteristics that affect educational performance, such as poverty; and factors that affect school-district efficiency. The cost-function estimates in this chapter are based on data for three pre-NCLB years (1999–2000 through 2001–2) for school districts in Kansas, Missouri, and New York plus either two years (Kansas and California) or three years (Missouri and New York) after the passage of NCLB. The cost model for California was estimated with only two years of data (2004 and 2005) because changes in the financial data did not permit the inclusion of information for earlier years. The state education departments in each state supplied most of the data. This section is organized by major categories of variables, and summary statistics are reported in Table 2.2. A more detailed discussion of data and measures is provided in Appendix 2.A (see page 81).

The dependent variable for our cost functions is district-operating expenditures per pupil, generally excluding special education.[40] Capital spending was excluded because capital budgeting decisions are long-term in nature, and it is difficult to capture these decisions with only a few years of data. Special education spending was excluded because NCLB is focused primarily on non–special education students and because it is not possible to obtain comparable data on special education students across states.

We measure student performance as a simple average of proficiency rates on math and English language arts exams at three levels of education—elementary school, middle school, and high school. While accountability provisions also include participation rates on exams, graduation rates, and proficiency rates on other exams, reading and math exams form the core of the NCLB accountability system.[41]

Teacher salary is the most important resource price affecting school-district spending. In addition, teachers' salaries are highly correlated with salaries of other certified staff, so that teachers' salaries serve as a proxy for all staff salaries. To develop a comparable salary measure across districts, data on individual teachers is used to predict what teachers' salaries would be in each district if teachers had average experience and education.[42]

The number of students in a district is the main factor affecting economies of scale in school districts. The measure of students used in

Table 2.2 Descriptive Statistics for Variables Used in Cost Models

Variables	Kansas (2004)		Missouri (2005)		California (2005)		New York (2005)	
	Mean	Standard Deviation	Mean	Standard Deviation	Mean	Standard Deviation	Mean	Standard Deviation
Per-Pupil spending	$6,991	$1,311	$6,112	$1,513	$7,118	$2,166	$12,843	$3,776
Performance measure	71.8	7.9	25.6	7.2	46.6	15.5	86.6	6.0
Cost variables:								
Teacher salaries	$39,427	$2,950	$27,460	$3,290	$35,521	$3,383	$54,922	$8,895
Percent free lunch students	26.7	11.3	—	—	—	—	30.9	19.7
Percent subsidized lunch students	—	—	46.1	16.0	48.0	26.1	—	—
Percent special education students	—	—	16.7	4.9	18.5	18.5	2.7	1.6
Percent limited English students	—	—	—	—	1.4	1.0	—	—
Enrollment	1,486	3,834	1,671	3,568	6,809	26,475	4,218	40,243
Enrollment categories:								
Under 100 students	0.013	0.115	0.050	0.219	—	—	—	—
100 to 150 students	0.040	0.197	0.047	0.211	—	—	—	—
150 to 250 students	0.110	0.314	0.132	0.339	—	—	—	—

Under 250 students	—	—	—	—	0.119	0.324	0.027	0.161
250 to 500 students	0.301	0.459	0.203	0.403	0.154	0.361	0.079	0.269
500 to 1,000 students	0.254	0.436	0.238	0.427	0.112	0.316	0.166	0.373
1,000 to 1,500 students	0.087	0.282	0.093	0.291	0.067	0.250	0.191	0.394
1,500 to 2,500 students	0.087	0.282	0.089	0.285	0.103	0.304	0.196	0.397
2,500 to 5,000 students	0.060	0.238	0.085	0.280	0.142	0.349	0.211	0.408
5,000 to 15,000 students	0.030	0.171	0.041	0.198	0.183	0.387	0.120	0.325
Over 15,000 students	0.017	0.128	0.021	0.145	0.121	0.326	0.010	0.101
Sample Size	299		516		925		674	

Note: Entries are simple district averages. Descriptive statistics for all variables used in the cost models are provided in tables 2.B.1–2.B.4. Teacher salaries are estimated for a teacher with average experience in Kansas, based on teachers with five years or fewer of experience in Missouri and New York, and set to the minimum salary on the district salary scale in California.

the study is enrollment, either measured at one point in time (California and Kansas) or averaged over the year (Missouri and New York). Because the relationship between per-pupil spending and enrollment is often nonlinear, we use several enrollment classes in order to allow flexibility in measuring this relationship.

Cost functions usually include student-need measures for child poverty, limited English proficiency (LEP), and special education. The poverty measures used most often in state aid formulas are the percentage of students receiving a free lunch (Kansas and New York) or a free or subsidized lunch (California and Missouri). While the reliability of these measures has been challenged, especially for secondary students, they generally track closely with the child poverty rate produced by the Census Bureau.[43]

In contrast to subsidized-lunch data, data on the number of LEP students are not defined consistently across states or even across school districts within some states. Based on the available data, we initially included a measure of the share of LEP students in the cost model for all states. The coefficient on this variable, however, was statistically significant only in California. Thus, the LEP variable was dropped in the models for other states.

Because the share of special education students can affect spending on non–special education programs, we included a measure of the share of special education students in the cost model even though special education spending is excluded. Measures of special education students can be problematic because of the potential for overclassifying special education students, especially those with learning disabilities, in order to increase state aid.[44] We included the share of students with moderate to severe disabilities when these data were available (California and New York) and the share of students with any special need when they were not (Missouri). The coefficient on the special education variable for districts in Kansas was not statistically significant and we dropped it from the cost model.

As discussed above, some school districts may have higher spending than others relative to their level of student achievement not because of higher costs, but because of inefficient use of resources or spending on subject areas—such as art, music, and athletics—with a limited impact on test-score performance in math and reading. Because efficiency cannot be measured, we control for efficiency by including variables in the cost model that have a conceptual link to efficiency and that have been found to be significant in previous cost/efficiency studies. These variables include fiscal capacity and factors affecting voter involvement in monitoring local government. Research on New York indicates that taxpayers in districts with high property wealth, income, and state aid may have less incentive to put pressure on district officials to be efficient or may be more apt to spend money on non-tested subjects.[45] In addition, voters might have more incentive and capacity to monitor operations in school districts with relatively more college-educated adults, more elderly residents, a larger share of households that own their own homes, or where the typical voter pays a larger share of school taxes (as measured by median housing price divided by property value per pupil).

COST-FUNCTION ESTIMATES

We estimate cost functions for school districts in the four states using standard multiple-regression techniques. We also take several steps to avoid potential problems with regression estimates. The regression methodology and results are discussed in Appendix 2.B. The cost-function results generally fit expected relationships, and most of the cost variables are significantly different from zero at conventional levels. We find that higher student performance, teacher salaries, and student poverty are associated with higher spending levels, all else equal. Consistent with previous research, we find that per-pupil spending drops significantly as the enrollment size of the district increases, particularly up to enrollment levels of 1,500 students.[46] The economies-of-size effects are the weakest in New York, probably because of a relatively small number of districts with under 500 students. The results of the cost models can be used to construct several cost measures, most notably cost indices and pupil weights.

COST INDICES. One measure of relative cost differences within a state is a cost index. A cost index measures how much more a particular district must spend, based on factors outside of its control, to reach any given student performance level compared to a district with average characteristics. For example, a cost index of 120 indicates that a district must spend 20 percent more than the average district to reach any given performance target due to cost factors outside the district's control. Cost indices can be calculated for individual cost factors as well:

Table 2.3 Cost Indices by Census School-district Type

Census District Type	California	New York	Kansas	Missouri
Overall cost index:				
Large central cities	111.2	149.8	105.3	112.4
Medium cities	97.6	116.3	87.9	91.1
Urban fringe of large cities	93.2	99.2	86.2	94.2
Urban fringe of medium cities	106.7	93.6	92.2	82.7
Large town	—	106.1	97.2	84.9
Small town	96.6	104.3	94.3	89.5
Rural metro	109.5	106.5	107.2	94.0
Rural non-metro	109.3	98.0	95.3	107.8
Student need cost index:				
Large central cities	112.2	148.4	118.9	112.7
Medium cities	104.1	123.7	96.3	94.7
Urban fringe of large cities	96.8	91.4	96.0	93.2
Urban fringe of medium cities	108.2	97.7	96.6	95.2
Large town	—	113.5	107.7	92.6
Small town	97.2	110.6	102.8	100.9
Rural metro	98.6	109.4	101.0	93.2
Rural non-metro	103.7	98.7	96.1	103.5

Teacher salary cost index:

Large central cities	102.7	100.6	102.8	129.5
Medium cities	102.8	96.7	105.7	127.7
Urban fringe of large cities	102.8	110.6	103.3	123.9
Urban fringe of medium cities	100.5	96.8	101.0	106.6
Large town	—	95.6	101.9	113.7
Small town	97.9	94.6	100.8	105.8
Rural metro	95.5	95.1	98.6	104.7
Rural non-metro	98.1	98.8	101.5	92.8

Enrollment cost index:

Large central cities	88.8	100.5	86.2	77.6
Medium cities	91.4	97.2	86.6	75.9
Urban fringe of large cities	92.3	98.4	86.5	81.2
Urban fringe of medium cities	97.2	99.1	94.4	82.5
Large town	—	98.0	88.6	81.3
Small town	100.4	99.7	91.1	83.6
Rural metro	115.3	102.4	107.5	98.1
Rural non-metro	110.7	100.8	97.6	113.8

Note: Indices are relative to the state average, which is set at 100. Values below 100 indicate below average costs, while values above 100 indicate above average costs. All entries are based on a simple district average of cost indices for districts in each category. The student need cost index includes a measure of student poverty in all states, a measure of and special education in all states but Kansas, and a measure of limited English proficient students in California.

teacher salaries, student needs, and enrollment size. Table 2.3 presents average cost indices by census district type.[47]

In all four states, large cities and some rural districts tend to have relatively high costs. The cost index for large cities is particularly high in New York, because this classification includes only high-poverty large cities, and the cost model for New York does not indicate significant economies of size. Large cities have higher costs principally because of higher student needs (and higher salary costs in Missouri). Rural districts have higher costs due to small scale (enrollment cost index) and, in some rural districts, higher student needs. Suburban districts on the fringe of large cities generally have below-average costs due to lower student needs and larger size even though they tend to have higher salary costs than average.

PUPIL WEIGHTS FOR POVERTY. Most states adjust for disadvantaged students either through categorical aid programs or by providing extra weights for high-need students in the basic operating aid program.[48] Pupil weights measure how much more expensive are students with a certain characteristic (e.g., living in poverty) compared to students without these characteristics. For example, a poverty weight of 0.5 indicates that the cost of bringing a student up to any performance level is 50 percent higher for a child living in poverty than for a nonpoor child.

Cost-function results can be used to estimate pupil weights for students living in poverty based on the share of students receiving free lunch (Kansas and New York) or receiving subsidized or free lunch (California and Missouri).[49] Table 2.4 reports the estimated pupil weights for poverty for all four states by census district type. Pupil poverty weights average 0.89 and 0.65 in New York and California and 0.59 and 0.62 in Kansas and Missouri. In these states, in other words, the cost of bringing a child up to performance standards is between 60 percent and 90 percent higher for a poor child than for a nonpoor child. The fact that poverty weights are higher in California and New York than in Kansas and Missouri may reflect the higher concentration of urban poverty in these states.[50]

ESTIMATING THE COST TO MEET NCLB STANDARDS

The cost-function results can be used to estimate the amount that each school district must spend to reach a given performance standard,

Table 2.4 Poverty Weights by Census School–District Type

Census District Type	California (2005)	New York (2005)	Kansas (2004)	Missouri (2005)
State average	0.65	0.89	0.59	0.62
Census district type:				
Large central cities	0.67	1.00	0.64	0.68
Medium cities	0.65	0.91	0.56	0.61
Urban fringe of large cities	0.63	0.80	0.57	0.60
Urban fringe of medium cities	0.66	0.80	0.57	0.61
Large town	—	0.89	0.61	0.61
Small town	0.65	0.87	0.60	0.63
Rural metro	0.65	0.86	0.59	0.59
Rural non-metro	0.65	0.80	0.56	0.64

Note: Entries are pupil-weighted average of poverty weights for districts in each census district type. Weights for Missouri and California are based on K–12 students receiving free and subsidized lunch. For Kansas the weight is based on K–12 students receiving free lunch, and for New York the weight is based on K–6 students receiving free lunch.

holding its efficiency constant at its current level. Because NCLB targets are based on absolute student performance, defined as the share of students reaching proficiency, we estimate costs using three different student proficiency rates in math and reading—70 percent, 80 percent, and 90 percent. Because 100 percent proficiency is unrealistic, we selected proficiency rates that might be viewed as low, moderate, or high long-term targets for NCLB. For states such as New York and Kansas, where a relatively high share of students already are classified as proficient (81 percent and 73 percent, respectively), reaching these targets will be easier than in states such as Missouri and California, which have relatively few students reaching proficiency (28 percent and 44 percent respectively).[51] In developing these estimates we are using the present levels of efficiency in each district. Later in the chapter we present evidence on the efficiency increases that are needed to reach these proficiency standards.

Table 2.5 reports estimates of the spending increase required to meet these three performance levels compared to actual spending per pupil in 2005 (2004 in Kansas).[52] In New York and Kansas, most districts already met the 70 percent proficiency standard in 2005, so no additional spending is required. The one exception is large cities, which would require significant spending increases in Kansas. With a 90 percent proficiency rate target, most districts in both states will require a substantial increase in spending, with average required spending increases of 20 percent in New York and 16 percent in Kansas. In both states, the greatest increases are in large central cities. Sizable increases would also have to occur in other cities and towns and in some rural school districts.

In Missouri and California, significant increases in average spending would be required even to meet the 70 percent proficiency target. While the large central cities would require the largest spending increases (48 percent in California and 76 percent in Missouri), almost all districts would need to increase spending by more than 30 percent. To reach a 90 percent proficiency target, the estimated spending increase would be 50 percent in Missouri and 58 percent in California. Without improvements in efficiency, required spending increases in the large cities in both states would exceed 70 percent on average and most districts are estimated to require increases of over 40 percent.

Table 2.5 Per-Pupil Spending Increases Required to Support a Particular Proficiency Rate by Census School–District Types (in 2005 Dollars)

	Actual Expenditures Per Pupil	Percent Increase in Predicted Spending to Reach Proficiency Rates of:		
		70%	80%	90%
Kansas:				
Total State	$6,118	5.3	10.0	15.7
Census district type:				
Large central cities	$6,112	14.4	21.8	28.8
Medium cities	$6,079	2.2	3.6	7.6
Urban fringe of large cities	$5,535	2.3	5.0	9.4
Urban fringe of medium cities	$5,615	0.6	4.3	10.2
Large town	$6,456	5.8	12.0	18.4
Small town	$6,105	5.4	10.8	16.7
Rural metro	$7,029	3.3	8.4	14.1
Rural non-metro	$5,901	1.8	5.8	11.6

Continued on next page

Table 2.5 Continued

	Actual Expenditures Per Pupil	Percent Increase in Predicted Spending to Reach Proficiency Rates of:		
		70%	80%	90%
Missouri:				
Total State	$6,248	38.2	44.3	49.9
Census district type:				
Large central cities	$8,742	76.0	83.8	91.0
Medium cities	$5,873	35.7	41.7	47.3
Urban fringe of large cities	$6,813	28.3	34.0	39.2
Urban fringe of medium cities	$4,720	31.6	37.5	42.8
Large town	$5,399	36.6	42.6	48.2
Small town	$5,446	40.3	46.5	52.2
Rural metro	$5,328	33.8	39.8	45.2
Rural non-metro	$5,653	40.9	47.2	52.9
California:				
Total state	$6,500	37.7	48.2	58.2
Census district type:				
Large central cities	$7,069	47.8	59.4	70.4

	Spending			
Medium cities	$6,418	37.6	47.8	57.7
Urban fringe of large cities	$6,195	29.5	39.2	48.6
Urban fringe of medium cities	$6,428	42.3	53.3	63.9
Large town	—	—	—	—
Small town	$6,627	27.1	36.8	46.3
Rural metro	$7,280	33.6	43.7	53.7
Rural non-metro	$6,548	43.5	54.6	65.1
New York:				
Census district type:				
Total State	$12,746	0.4	7.8	20.1
Census district type:				
Large central cities	$12,766	0.6	16.5	37.3
Medium cities	$12,212	0.0	6.6	20.9
Urban fringe of large cities	$14,520	0.4	1.7	5.3
Urban fringe of medium cities	$11,025	0.0	0.6	6.2
Large town	$9,946	0.0	0.3	14.2
Small town	$11,313	0.3	3.0	14.4
Rural metro	$11,608	0.2	1.8	12.4
Rural non-metro	$11,742	0.1	0.8	7.4

Note: Entries are pupil-weighted average of per-pupil spending for districts in each census district type. Spending is not directly comparable across states, because of differences in spending definitions and financial accounting systems. If the required increase in spending is negative, it is set to zero.

4. TITLE I FUNDING AND NCLB PERFORMANCE TARGETS

Title I has been the principal federal compensatory aid program for four decades. In this section, we discuss the changes in Title I funding that were passed as part of NCLB, examine the impact of these changes on different types of districts, and estimate the extent to which this funding covers the added spending needed to meet NCLB performance targets.

CHANGES IN TITLE I FUNDING

Whether Title I funds are adequate depends on the base for comparison. Appropriations for Title I have been between 65 and 75 percent of the original authorization, which has prompted some to claim a funding gap.[53] On the other hand, Title I funding increased significantly after 2001, which has been used as evidence that NCLB is not underfunded.[54]

Using information on Title I allocations (Part A) in 2001 and 2006 for most school districts in the country, we examine changes in Title I funding after passage of NCLB (Table 2.6, pages 48–49). Title I aid in nominal dollars increased almost 50 percent between 2001 and 2006; only 56 percent of the school districts, however, experienced an increase in Title I aid.[55] Aid increased more slowly in Kansas and Missouri than in New York and California, which may reflect in part more generous funding of urban states than rural states.[56] When aid is adjusted for inflation, the increase falls to 30 percent on average and 18 percent in Kansas and Missouri. An alternative change measure that focuses on the compensatory objectives of Title I aid is change in the amount of inflation-adjusted Title I aid per child in poverty.[57] Aid per child in poverty increased by only 4.2 percent nationally and has actually gone down in some rural states, such as Kansas and Missouri. When we take into account differences in geographic costs across districts, spending per child in poverty actually decreased on average; the decreases were over 20 percent in Kansas and Missouri.[58]

While average spending increases are quite low or nonexistent when inflation, poverty, and geographic costs are taken into account, the targeting of Title I aid to high-poverty districts appears to have improved. We examined changes in Title I aid for districts in several poverty classes. Low-poverty districts (poverty rate below 5 percent) experienced a significant aid decline, even in nominal terms. For other poverty classes, Title I aid increases are higher in districts with the highest poverty rates. For example, in districts with child poverty over 25 percent, cost-adjusted Title I aid per child in poverty increased by over 10 percent on average; aid increased by over 25 percent in districts with the highest concentrations of poverty (over 50 percent poverty rate). Overall, therefore, the story on growth in Title I aid is mixed; once appropriately adjusted, average aid increases were relatively small, but aid grew significantly in districts with the highest concentrations of poverty.

DISTRIBUTION AND EQUITY OF TITLE I AID

Title I, Part A, is composed of four different aid formulas: Basic Aid, Concentration Aid, Targeted Aid, and Education Finance Incentive Grants (EFIG).[59] Prior to NCLB only Basic Grants and Concentration Grants were funded. Because details of the aid formulas for these aid programs have been presented in other sources,[60] we simply summarize key components of the aid formula and examine how they affect aid distribution and equity.

Eligibility for all programs is based on either the child poverty rate or the number of children in poverty in a school. The Basic Grant has the widest distribution (over 90 percent of districts receive aid) because its poverty cutoffs are low (2 percent or 10 students). The cutoffs for the Targeted Grant and EFIG are higher (5 percent or 10 children) and over 80 percent of districts received this aid. The Concentration Grant has the highest cutoff (15 percent or 6,500 students in poverty), which results in the lowest share of districts receiving funds (under 60 percent). Aid is calculated for all programs except EFIG by multiplying the number of "formula children" (mainly children in poverty) by an expenditure factor, which is calculated based on average per-pupil expenditure in a state.[61] Targeted Aid weights the poverty enrollment count by a factor linked to the level of poverty concentration in a district.[62] The EFIG formula is different than the other formulas, because it is calculated in two stages and several other factors are considered. In the first stage the grant to a state is based on relative population, tax effort, and spending equity.[63] Allocation of

Table 2.6 Change in Title I Aid Between 2001 and 2006

	Share of Districts with Real Title I Aid Increase (2001–2006)	Percent Change in Per–Pupil Title I Aid (2001–2006)		Percent Change in Inflation–adjusted Title I Aid Per Child in Poverty (2001–2006)	
		Nominal Dollars	Real Dollars	Not Cost Adjusted	Cost Adjusted
U.S Average	56.1	$81.4	$58.2	$51.6	–$79.7
(% change)	—	47.7	30.0	4.2	–6.8
California	50.7	$84.6	$58.9	$165.9	$26.1
(% change)	—	44.8	27.5	15.1	2.7
Kansas	45.0	$44.0	$26.6	–$172.0	–$316.4
(% change)	—	34.5	18.4	–12.4	–21.1
Missouri	53.1	$53.1	$32.4	–$180.6	–$295.7
(% change)	—	35.0	18.8	–14.7	–23.0
New York	38.4	$138.1	$99.8	$26.6	–$149.1
(% change)	—	49.0	31.2	1.7	–11.2
Poverty Classes:					
Under 5%	28.1	–$6.5	–$11.8	–$780.0	–$782.1
(% change)	—	–16.5	–26.5	–49.3	–55.1
5% to 15%	50.9	$36.9	$23.3	$54.8	–$79.1
(% change)	—	37.0	20.6	4.7	–7.1

15% to 25%	66.4	$90.0	$62.4	$195.7	$55.2
(% change)	—	44.4	27.1	16.7	4.7
25% to 50%	84.3	$224.5	$174.7	$327.2	$137.8
(% change)	—	61.3	42.0	25.1	11.5
Over 50%	100.0	$440.7	$350.6	$453.3	$289.3
(% change)	—	66.5	46.5	40.8	26.2

Note: Entries are pupil-weighted averages except for the share of districts with Title I aid increases, which are simple district averages. Title I aid for 2001 is deflated using the CPI for urban consumers (base is 2006 dollars). Cost adjustment is with a comparable wage index produced for NCES. Title I aid (Part A) in 2001 and 2006 is based on data from the U.S. Department of Education.

the state grant to districts within a state is based on the district's share of Title I funding under the other aid programs.[64]

While child poverty rates are a key part of all the Title I aid formulas, these formulas have been criticized on several grounds.[65] First, the use of per-pupil state expenditure in the allocation of aid is a poor attempt to correct for geographic cost differences across states; this practice generally results in higher-income states receiving more aid. A more appropriate approach would be to adjust aid levels by a geographic cost index for each district. Second, the use of absolute counts of students living in poverty in determining eligibility (and in determining pupil weights used in Targeted Aid) assures that larger districts are more apt to get funding than smaller districts with the same child poverty rate. This is, at best, an ad hoc attempt to weight urban poverty more heavily. Third, the measures of tax effort and spending equity used in the EFIG formula are inexact and the adjustments are too small to have much influence on state policy. Minimum-aid and hold-harmless provisions limit the extent of redistribution. Liu has shown that these provisions result in striking differences across states and districts in the level of funding per child in poverty.[66]

Under NCLB the relative importance of these aid programs changed; all increases in aid over 2001 levels are distributed through either Targeted Grants or EFIG. In 2006, these two programs each accounted for 18 percent of total Title I funding; the share of Basic Aid and Concentration Aid dropped from 84 percent and 16 percent, respectively, in 2001 to 54 percent and 11 percent in 2006.

To examine the importance of the various factors in the aid formula on the actual distribution of Title I funding, we regressed per-pupil Title I aid in 2001 and 2006 on these formula factors, such as those measuring the cost of providing education.[67] Table 2.7 (pages 52–53) reports standardized coefficients, because they measure the relative importance of a particular factor in the regression model. This table reveals that the regression model for 2006 Title I aid explains a higher share of the aid distribution (32 percent) than the model for 2001 (12 percent). The generally low explanatory power of these factors may be due in part to hold-harmless provisions and to limitations on the variability of some factors.[68]

As expected, poverty is the most important factor affecting aid distribution in both years. For total Title I aid in 2006, there is a nonlinear relationship between aid and poverty, which indicates that the level of per-pupil aid increases with the concentration of poverty in a district. This nonlinear relationship did not exist for Title I aid in 2001. Among other cost factors, both district enrollment and the comparable-wage index are related to aid distribution, but they are not as important as poverty.[69]

The second most important determinant of aid distribution is the size of the state as represented by total state enrollment. We find that aid declines with the size of the state up to an enrollment of about three million students, at which point it starts to increase again. To some extent, the decline in aid over most enrollment ranges probably reflects minimum Title I aid provisions. Another important factor affecting the aid distribution is average per-pupil spending in a state, which is used directly in calculating the aid level. Higher average spending results in greater Title I aid. For EFIG, the measures of tax effort and spending equity also appear to influence the aid distribution.

The compensatory nature of the Title I aid program implies that cost-adjusted aid should be distributed in direct proportion to the share of students living in poverty in a school district. To examine how closely the distribution of Title I aid matches this equity objective and whether equity has improved since the passage of NCLB, we calculated correlations between Title I aid and child poverty rates in 2001 and 2006 (Table 2.8, page 55). Table 2.8 reveals that the equity of the NCLB aid distribution improved between 2001 and 2006. In almost all cases, correlations between aid and poverty have become more strongly positive. For the nation as a whole in 2006, the correlation between unadjusted Title I aid per pupil and the child poverty rate is moderate (0.55), which is consistent with the earlier finding that poverty, while important, is not the only determinant of the Title I aid distribution. This correlation is larger in three of the states that we examined for this study, particularly Kansas. Correlations for districts within a poverty class are smaller but still positive, except in the highest-poverty districts. For these districts, Title I aid distribution is negatively related to the child poverty rate. Table 2.8 also shows that the correlation between cost-adjusted Title I aid per child in poverty and the child poverty rate has gone from being negative in every case in 2001 to being positive in 2006 in every case except the highest-poverty districts. This finding is consistent with the use under NCLB of Targeted Grants to distribute aid increases. Targeted grants are designed to direct more funds to districts with a higher concentration of poverty.

Table 2.7 Factors Affecting the Distribution of Title I Funds Per Pupil by Grant Type (Standardized Coefficients)

Variable	Total Title I (Part A) (2001)	2006				
		Total Title I (Part A)	Basic Grant	Concentration Grant	Targeted Grant	Education Finance Incentive Grant
Cost Factors:						
Child poverty rate (percent)	0.39*	0.29*	0.43*	0.26*	0.06	0.02
Child poverty rate squared	-0.03	0.32*	0.21	0.07	0.50*	0.54
District enrollment	-0.02*	0.03*	-0.01	-0.02*	0.07*	0.09
District enrollment squared	0.02*	-0.01*	0.01*	0.02*	-0.04*	-0.05*
Comparable wage index	-0.05*	-0.05*	-0.02*	-0.03*	-0.03*	-0.08*
Other Aid Distribution Factors:						
Average per-Pupil spending in state	0.12*	0.11*	0.18*	0.08*	0.16*	0.03*
State enrollment (thousands)	-0.20*	-0.34*	-0.20*	-0.25*	-0.43*	-0.54*
State enrollment squared	0.20*	0.31*	0.17*	0.27*	0.37*	0.44*

State per-pupil spending as percent of per-capita income		0.04*			0.12*
Coefficient of variation for spending		0.06*			0.07*
Adjusted R-square	0.13	0.33	0.36	0.11	0.29	0.32
Sample size	13,658		13,679			

Note: Dependent variable is per-Pupil Title I aid.
*Statistically significant from zero at 5% level.

The use of Targeted Grants and EFIG also appears to have reduced variation across districts in the level of Title I aid per child in poverty. The coefficient of variation, which measures average percent variation in aid across districts, dropped significantly between 2001 and 2006. Despite this improvement, however, there remains significant variation across districts in the level of cost-adjusted Title I aid per child in poverty.

In addition, the distribution of Title I funds within school districts often gives short shrift to the poorest schools.[70] While requirements in Title I aid formulas are supposed to assure that state and local funds are equalized before Title I funds are distributed, the reality is that district budgeting "systematically disadvantages schools with the greatest education needs."[71] Districts are able to satisfy comparability requirements and still distribute funds unequally, largely because of what is commonly called the comparability loophole. Teacher salaries are one of the major sources of intra-district inequity,[72] but districts can ignore teacher experience in calculating a school's salary costs. Eliminating the comparability loophole should be a high priority in the reauthorization of NCLB.

TITLE I FUNDING AND STUDENT PERFORMANCE TARGETS

Building on our analysis of education costs and NCLB, we now examine the extent to which NCLB provides the funds needed for states to meet various student performance targets. Our focus, like the focus of the studies on which we build,[73] is on the cost of reaching proficiency. Testing and administrative costs associated with NCLB are relatively small compared to these costs and are not considered here.

We make two types of comparisons. First, we compare the increase in Title I funds associated with NCLB to the increase in school-district spending that is needed to reach NCLB standards. Second, given the "compensatory" focus on NCLB, we compare this increase in Title I funds to the increase in spending associated with raising the performance of low-income children from their current levels up to a state's proficiency standards.

Our results are presented Table 2.9. We assume no increase in real dollars in Title I funding after 2006, based on the relatively small increases in Title I funding in 2007 and 2008 and in the president's 2009 budget.[74] Spending estimates are based on student proficiency

Table 2.8 Evaluation of Changes in Equity of the Distribution of
Title I Aid Between 2001 and 2006

	Correlation of Per–Pupil Title I Aid and Child Poverty Rate		Correlation of Cost-adjusted Title I Aid Per Pupil and Child Poverty Rate		Coefficient of Variation in Cost–adjusted Title I Aid Per Child in Poverty	
	2001	2006	2001	2006	2001	2006
U.S Average	0.36	0.55	-0.15	0.23	0.66	0.37
California	0.31	0.57	-0.07	0.27	0.57	0.30
Kansas	0.57	0.87	-0.25	0.39	0.59	0.34
Missouri	0.65	0.66	-0.25	0.52	0.44	0.33
New York	0.40	0.40	-0.06	0.55	0.47	0.28
Poverty Classes:						
Under 5%	0.11	0.17	-0.25	0.12	1.21	0.97
5% to 15%	0.15	0.37	-0.04	0.08	0.60	0.35
15% to 25%	0.06	0.21	-0.08	0.05	0.39	0.21
25% to 50%	0.15	0.31	-0.09	0.08	0.27	0.18
Over 50%	-0.19	-0.12	-0.27	-0.16	0.26	0.17

Note: Correlations are calculated at the district level. Cost adjustment is with a comparable wage index produced for NCES. Title I aid for 2001 is deflated using the CPI for urban consumers (base is 2006 dollars). Title I aid in 2001 and 2006 is based on data from the U.S. Department of Education. The coefficient of variation is calculated using the pupil-weighted standard deviation in cost-adjusted Title I aid per child in poverty divided by the pupil-weighted average. It can be interpreted as the average percent variation in cost-adjusted Title I aid per child in poverty.

levels in math and reading exams of 70 percent, 80 percent, and 90 percent.

Table 2.9 (pages 58–61) reveals that in New York and Kansas, which had high proficiency rates before NCLB, increases in Title I aid cover a much higher share of spending increases needed to meet NCLB targets than they did in California and Missouri, which had low proficiency rates. In New York State as a whole, Title I aid increases cover 95 percent of required spending increases for a 70 percent proficiency rate; this share drops to 41 percent with 80 percent proficiency and to 17 percent with 90 percent proficiency. In Kansas, Title I aid increases cover 50 percent of spending increases for a 70 percent proficiency rate, but this share drops to 28 percent and 7 percent with 80 percent and 90 percent proficiency rates, respectively. The results are quite different for Missouri, where Title I increases cover only 3 percent of increased spending for a 70 percent proficiency rate and only 2 percent for 90 percent proficiency. Title I aid increases cover a higher share of spending increases in California than in Missouri, but the percentage of coverage is still quite low (4 percent with 90 percent proficiency to 9 percent with 70 percent proficiency). When Title I aid increases are compared to the spending increases for children in poverty (second panel of Table 2.9), the coverage ratios are somewhat higher but of similar magnitude.

5. Alternative Paths to the NCLB Performance Targets

The calculations in the previous section indicate that Title I aid does not currently provide school districts with enough money to reach the NCLB performance target of 100 percent proficiency, and it provides insufficient funds to reach much lower proficiency targets for states in which a relatively low share of students meet current proficiency standards. This section begins by showing the increases in federal aid that would be required for various proficiency targets to be reached. Increasing federal aid is not, of course, the only way to boost student performance. Alternative approaches include increased state educational aid to school districts, increased school district efficiency, and higher school property taxes. Because property taxes are constrained in most states through property tax limits or strong political opposition, we focus here on the other two routes. In particular, we estimate the increases in state education aid and school-district efficiency that would be necessary to meet various student performance targets in the four states that we are examining.

MEETING NCLB STANDARDS THROUGH INCREASES IN FEDERAL AID

Our analysis allows us to calculate the percentage increase in Title I aid that would be necessary to reach various proficiency levels in each state. We calculate the spending needed to reach a given level, subtract current spending, and then divide this amount by current Title I aid. This yields the required increase in Title I aid, assuming that state aid and school-district efficiency remain constant.

Our results are presented in Table 2.10 (pages 62–63). In New York, where proficiency levels are already very high, a 70 percent proficiency standard could be reached in the average district with only a 9 percent increase in Title I aid. The comparable required increase ranges from 185 percent in Kansas to 1,413 percent in California to 1,510 percent in Missouri. These numbers are not typos. To reach even 70 percent proficiency, Title I aid to the average district in Missouri would have to be about sixteen times as large as it is now. (Two times as large corresponds to a 100 percent increase, so sixteen times as large corresponds to a 1,500 percent increase.) Moreover, even in New York, a 600 percent increase in Title I aid would be required to bring the average district to 90 percent proficiency.

This table also shows that the required changes in Title I aid vary by type of district, but not in any clear-cut manner. These results depend not only on the current distribution of Title I aid per pupil, which tends to be relatively high in large cities, but also on the current distribution of other revenue sources, including state aid. We find that the required increase in percentage terms for large cities is not relatively large in California and Kansas; it is relatively large, however, in New York and Missouri. Rural, non-metro districts require relatively large-percentage increases in Title I aid in every state except Missouri.

Table 2.9 Change in Title I Aid from 2001–2006 as a Share of Change in Required Total Spending and Change in Spending for Children in Poverty by Census School-district Type

| | Proficiency Rates of | | | Proficiency Rates of | | |
| | California | | | New York | | |
Title I Increase as % of Required Spending Increase	70%	80%	90%	70%	80%	90%
Total state	8.8	5.4	4.3	95.3	41.1	16.7
Census district type:						
Large central cities	4.9	3.9	3.3	93.1	12.3	5.3
Medium cities	14.2	9.2	7.8	91.5	67.0	3.8
Urban fringe of large cities	8.1	4.0	2.9	100.0	95.5	57.3
Urban fringe of medium cities	4.9	2.5	1.7	100.0	94.5	31.8
Large town	—	—	—	100.0	100.0	6.5
Small town	11.9	3.1	1.8	96.3	64.0	13.0
Rural metro	6.0	3.1	2.2	100.0	84.7	21.2
Rural non-metro	4.4	3.4	1.7	99.4	97.6	25.8

Title I Increase as % of Required Spending Increase to Support Children in Poverty

Total state	10.6	6.8	4.8	95.4	42.4	19.9
Census district type:						
Large central cities	5.7	4.6	3.9	93.2	13.3	5.7
Medium cities	14.4	9.5	6.1	92.5	67.2	5.7
Urban fringe of large cities	11.6	6.6	4.7	100.0	96.0	63.6
Urban fringe of medium cities	8.8	5.6	4.6	100.0	94.9	43.3
Large town	—	—	—	100.0	100.0	15.0
Small town	13.8	6.3	3.9	96.5	65.3	15.2
Rural metro	7.7	5.0	3.5	100.0	85.3	24.0

Table 2.9 Change in Title I Aid from 2001–2006 as a Share of Change in Required Total Spending and Change in Spending for Children in Poverty by Census School-district Types (continued)

Title I Increase as % of Required Spending Increase	Proficiency Rates of Kansas			Proficiency Rates of Missouri		
	70%	80%	90%	70%	80%	90%
Total state	50.1	28.2	6.6	3.3	2.5	2.1
Census district type:						
Large central cities	20.7	11.9	8.6	2.2	2.0	1.8
Medium cities	100.0	66.5	3.1	2.7	2.3	2.0
Urban fringe of large cities	70.8	42.9	9.2	4.0	2.4	1.7
Urban fringe of medium cities	80.3	79.6	17.5	3.4	2.8	2.5
Large town	10.5	4.9	3.3	3.5	2.8	2.4
Small town	47.3	18.4	3.1	2.6	2.2	1.9
Rural metro	53.4	24.4	8.2	3.2	2.7	2.4
Rural non-metro	78.8	43.6	5.6	3.8	3.3	2.9

Title I Increase as % of Required Spending Increase to Support Children in Poverty					
Total state	55.6	33.6	22.1	5.1	4.3	3.8
Census district type:					
Large central cities	21.9	14.1	10.7	2.7	2.4	2.2
Medium cities	100.0	66.5	51.1	6.9	5.7	4.9
Urban fringe of large cities	73.6	58.1	41.0	4.1	3.5	3.0
Urban fringe of medium cities	81.1	80.2	79.8	6.2	5.3	4.7
Large town	20.5	8.0	5.3	6.8	5.6	4.8
Small town	49.5	14.6	7.1	4.3	3.7	3.3
Rural metro	69.1	31.1	18.7	8.1	6.9	6.0
Rural non-metro	92.7	56.6	26.7	5.7	4.9	4.4

Note: Entries are pupil-weighted averages. Title I aid for 2001 and 2006 is based on data from the U.S. Department of Education. Title I aid for 2001 is adjusted to 2006 dollars using the CPI for urban consumers. The spending increase is based on estimated spending to reach the specified proficiency rates compared to actual spending in 2005 (2004 in Kansas). Calculated only for districts with an increase in Title I aid. For cases where the share is negative or greater than 100, it is set to 100.

Table 2.10 Required Percent Increase in Title I Aid for Districts to Reach Proficiency Targets

	California Proficiency Rates of			New York Proficiency Rates of		
	70%	80%	90%	70%	80%	90%
Total Title I aid budget	968.79	1,350.73	1,730.21	10.36	158.67	587.17
Average district	1,413.09	1,951.45	2,493.29	9.00	85.81	599.82
Census district type:						
Large central cities	685.11	1,014.12	1,325.71	65.70	366.46	757.01
Medium cities	961.89	1,378.16	1,810.73	0.39	134.26	666.68
Urban fringe of large cities	1,046.10	1,566.65	2,117.62	17.72	59.13	337.53
Urban fringe of medium cities	1,663.07	2,153.55	2,643.31	0.00	43.53	644.61
Large town	—	—	—	0.00	4.56	439.47
Small town	871.32	1,236.56	1,588.59	7.74	93.94	519.39
Rural metro	2,219.57	2,921.64	3,617.09	3.02	115.09	666.75
Rural non-metro	1,656.31	2,288.37	2,900.88	13.65	103.89	772.87

	Kansas			Missouri		
Total Title I aid budget	146.1	339.5	638.4	1,820.3	2,186.1	2,522.5
Average district	185.1	449.1	778.8	1,510.2	1,764.1	1,998.1
Census district type:						
Large central cities	227.3	342.4	450.2	2,229.7	2,474.3	2,699.1
Medium cities	287.4	416.8	850.9	1,531.7	1,803.4	2,052.9
Urban fringe of large cities	172.5	434.6	819.2	2,478.8	2,983.6	3,452.4
Urban fringe of medium cities	62.5	343.1	747.2	1,218.0	1,445.5	1,654.5
Large town	161.2	339.2	529.3	2,486.8	2,916.6	3,311.4
Small town	155.7	349.4	592.3	1,065.4	1,227.6	1,376.6
Rural metro	195.1	445.8	743.9	1,915.5	2,244.1	2,546.1
Rural non-metro	189.9	578.9	1,071.2	1,333.6	1,542.7	1,735.2

Note: Entries are simple district averages. Calculated by taking projected spending to meet proficiency targets minus actual spending in 2005 (2004 in Kansas) and divided by per-pupil Title I aid in 2006. Spending is adjusted up to 2006 dollars using the CPI for urban consumers. If the change in spending is negative, it is set to zero.

Meeting NCLB Standards Through Increases in State Aid

In this section we estimate the increase in state education aid that is needed to reach various student performance standards, holding constant Title I aid, local property taxes, and school-district efficiency. Empirical evidence from evaluations of past Title I aid increases suggests that districts may substitute property tax reductions for the increase in aid.[75] Moreover, some studies find that increases in state aid lead to reductions in school-district efficiency.[76] Thus, our estimates of required state aid increases may understate the magnitude of the aid increases needed to reach high student proficiency rates. Table 2.11 (pages 66–67) reports the difference between the required spending to meet the proficiency targets and present spending relative to present state operating aid per pupil.

Not surprisingly, the size of the required state aid increases is linked directly to the share of students meeting the state's proficiency standards before the implementation of NCLB. The average districts in Kansas and in New York require only a small aid increase to reach 70 percent proficiency, but increases above 20 percent are needed to reach 90 percent proficiency. The large central cities in New York, on the other hand, require a 44 percent increase to reach 80 percent proficiency and a 94 percent increase to reach 90 percent proficiency. Because the large districts contain a large share of the state's pupils, a 90 percent proficiency rate in every district would require a 55 percent increase in the state aid budget. The total state aid budget in New York is adequate to support a 70 percent proficiency rate in all districts, but the funds would need to be targeted more heavily to high-poverty urban school districts than they are in the present formula.

While New York and Kansas may be able to support NCLB standards with modest state aid increases and better-targeted aid distribution, this is not the case for Missouri. In fact, the average district in Missouri would require a doubling of state aid to reach a 70 percent proficiency standard and an increase of 134 percent to reach 90 percent. The total state aid budget would need to increase 123 percent to reach 70 percent proficiency and 170 percent to reach 90 percent proficiency. Because of poorly targeted state aid in Missouri, the large central cities would require aid to increase by 2.5 to 3 times. Districts in California will require aid increases of 37 percent for 70 percent proficiency and 59 percent for 90 percent proficiency. State aid increases of this magnitude are unrealistic, but they highlight the magnitude of the problem faced by states like Missouri and California, where a relatively low share of students are currently classified as proficient.

Meeting NCLB Standards through Improvements in School-district Efficiency

Recall that spending equals costs divided by efficiency. We can observe current spending and we can forecast the spending required to meet a NCLB standard assuming efficiency does not change. Then we can calculate the percentage change in efficiency that is required so that spending necessary to meet the NCLB standard is equal to the sum of current spending, assuming no increase in state aid or Title I aid (Table 2.12, pages 68–69).[77]

Because New York and Kansas had high proficiency rates before NCLB, most districts require little to no efficiency improvements to reach 70 percent student proficiency. For a 90 percent proficiency rate, the median district would require an increase in efficiency of 8 percent in New York and 14 percent in Kansas, and one quarter of the districts in these states would require improvements of 18 percent or more. Much larger efficiency improvements would be needed in large cities, particularly in New York. In contrast, most districts in Missouri and California would require substantial improvements in efficiency to meet even the 70 percent proficiency target. The median district would require an increase of 28 percent in California and 43 percent in Missouri. One-quarter of the districts would need to improve efficiency by at least 49 percent in California and 54 percent in Missouri. For a 90 percent proficiency standard, the median district in California and Missouri would need efficiency increases of 48 percent and 55 percent, respectively, and a quarter of the districts would require improvements of over 66 percent (Table 2.13, pages 70–71).

6. Who Should Be Held Accountable?

NCLB is an educational accountability system in which penalties are imposed on schools when they do not meet student performance targets. In this section we evaluate the fairness and effectiveness of this arrangement.

Table 2.11 Required Percent Increase in State Aid for Districts to Reach Proficiency Targets with No Title I Aid Increase

	California Proficiency Rates of			New York Proficiency Rates of		
	70%	80%	90%	70%	80%	90%
Total state aid budget	38.4	49.2	59.6	0.7	20.6	54.7
Average district	37.4	48.4	59.1	0.4	3.7	23.2
Census district type:						
Large central cities	38.2	49.3	59.8	6.9	43.7	94.4
Medium cities	34.4	44.6	54.6	0.0	11.9	50.5
Urban fringe of large cities	28.2	37.6	47.0	0.7	3.3	16.6
Urban fringe of medium cities	46.8	58.7	70.1	0.0	1.7	19.6
Large town				0.0	0.3	26.3
Small town	29.2	39.9	50.2	0.6	5.7	27.4
Rural metro	40.6	53.1	65.2	0.1	3.9	26.0

	Kansas			Missouri		
Total state aid budget	7.1	13.5	21.4	122.8	147.5	170.4
Average district	6.1	13.3	21.7	100.6	117.7	133.6
Census district type:						
Large central cities	20.1	30.1	39.4	251.2	280.8	308.0
Medium cities	8.3	12.6	21.1	152.4	178.7	202.8
Urban fringe of large cities	4.3	9.4	16.1	136.1	172.3	207.3
Urban fringe of medium cities	2.0	6.5	13.1	61.2	72.6	83.1
Large town	7.5	16.0	25.0	215.0	247.2	276.8
Small town	8.3	16.2	24.9	102.8	118.3	132.5
Rural metro	6.5	14.4	23.4	79.0	91.8	103.5
Rural non-metro	3.3	9.0	16.2	95.2	109.6	122.8

Note: Entries are simple district averages. Calculated by taking projected spending to meet proficiency targets minus actual spending in 2005 (2004 in Kansas) and divided by per-pupil state aid in 2005. If the change is spending is negative, it is set to zero.

Table 2.12 Required Increase in Efficiency for Districts to Reach Proficiency Targets With No Title I Aid or State Aid Increase

	Proficiency Rates of California			Proficiency Rates of New York		
	70%	80%	90%	70%	80%	90%
Percentile:						
5th	0.0	1.6	8.6	0.0	0.0	0.0
25th	13.0	21.8	30.2	0.0	0.0	0.0
50th	28.0	38.1	47.6	0.0	0.0	7.6
75th	49.0	60.7	71.8	0.0	0.0	17.7
95th	87.6	102.3	116.3	1.8	22.6	44.6
Average district	33.8	43.8	53.6	4.5	7.9	17.8
Census district type:						
Large central cities	36.8	47.6	57.8	4.1	21.7	43.5
Medium cities	32.1	41.8	51.2	0.0	4.7	18.0
Urban fringe of large cities	26.4	35.4	44.3	0.4	1.2	4.0
Urban fringe of medium cities	42.7	53.8	64.3	0.0	0.8	7.8
Large town	—	—	—	0.0	0.2	13.0
Small town	26.5	36.3	45.7	0.3	2.8	13.1
Rural metro	33.4	43.6	53.5	0.1	1.8	11.7
Rural non-metro	37.9	48.4	58.6	0.1	1.1	8.5

	Kansas		Missouri		
Percentile:					
5th	0.0	2.2	13.9	22.1	22.8
25th	0.0	8.2	31.5	37.3	42.6
50th	1.2	14.0	42.5	48.8	54.6
75th	6.3	19.7	53.6	60.4	66.6
95th	16.2	30.9	78.9	86.8	94.1
Average district	3.9	14.6	44.4	50.8	56.7
Census district type:					
Large central cities	15.3	29.8	70.1	77.6	84.6
Medium cities	6.9	15.3	36.6	42.7	48.2
Urban fringe of large cities	3.7	13.7	35.6	41.5	47.0
Urban fringe of medium cities	1.9	12.1	30.9	36.7	42.0
Large town	5.8	18.4	40.0	46.2	51.9
Small town	4.2	15.0	43.6	49.9	55.8
Rural metro	3.9	14.5	39.3	45.5	51.1
Rural non-metro	3.3	14.2	43.2	49.5	55.3

Note: Entries are simple district averages. Calculation of efficiency increases are discussed in the text. If the change in efficiency is negative, it is set to zero.

Table 2.13 Required Percent Increase in Federal Title I Aid With Different Increases in Efficiency and State Aid

Range of State Aid Increases	Proficiency Target of 70% Possible Efficiency Increases			Proficiency Target of 80% Possible Efficiency Increases			Proficiency Target of 90% Possible Efficiency Increases		
	5%	15%	25%	5%	15%	25%	5%	15%	25%
California:									
5%	618.6	358.1	201.5	915.4	567.2	340.8	1,249.2	811.7	514.3
15%	396.9	211.8	109.9	626.8	360.1	200.0	893.4	543.8	323.0
25%	247.0	122.7	48.5	415.4	221.7	114.1	623.8	355.6	196.8
New York:									
5%	2.4	0.8	0.4	86.5	14.5	3.0	339.0	168.9	77.0
15%	1.1	0.6	0.1	54.1	7.1	1.3	262.6	129.4	45.0
25%	0.9	0.3	0.0	23.8	2.5	1.0	210.5	94.6	15.2

Kansas:									
5%	31.2	7.0	0.0	102.3	19.8	4.4	234.6	54.5	13.3
15%	11.6	0.6	0.0	29.0	6.6	0.0	81.4	17.7	3.7
25%	3.7	0.0	0.0	13.2	1.0	0.0	29.2	6.7	0.2
Missouri:									
5%	1,339.2	699.3	311.1	1,679.1	991.6	490.3	1,998.4	1,268.8	688.4
15%	1,146.9	535.9	212.1	1,485.7	804.0	349.0	1,804.6	1,076.8	525.5
25%	957.2	393.8	143.3	1,292.8	642.7	246.5	1,611.2	889.1	385.5

HOLDING SCHOOLS OR SCHOOL
DISTRICTS ACCOUNTABLE

As discussed above, school districts set their property tax rate, and both district and school policies influence school-district efficiency. Property tax rates usually face severe limits. Thanks to property tax limits, school districts have no control over their property tax rate in California and limited control in Kansas.[78] Property taxes are already very high in New York. As a result, the only route widely available to schools and school districts is to increase their efficiency. By all accounts, this is easier said than done.

As shown earlier, large efficiency increases would usually be needed for school districts to meet the NCLB targets in their state with no new resources. This is not true in the average district when the state already has a high proficiency rate (New York) and the proficiency target is low (70 percent); even in this case, however, it is true in districts with a high concentration of disadvantaged students.

There is no evidence that efficiency increases of the required magnitude are possible. No study of which we are aware documents widespread efficiency changes anywhere close to this magnitude. In our analysis, declining school-district spending over time, controlling for all the factors in our cost model, could be interpreted as an indication of increasing efficiency.[79] Following this interpretation, we find that, in the average district, efficiency increased at an annual rate of about 2 percent in Kansas, 1 percent in Missouri, and 5 percent in New York.[80] These changes are obviously far below the changes needed to reach the NCLB standards in states, such as Missouri and California, with a relatively low proficiency rate. Efficiency improvements uncovered by a few studies of accountability systems also fall far short of the improvements needed for these states to reach NCLB standards.[81]

In our opinion, these results demonstrate that the NCLB accountability system is fundamentally flawed. In formal terms, this system expects schools and school districts to make huge and entirely unprecedented changes in the efficiency with which they deliver math and English test performance. It is as if the federal government provided a modest subsidy to all college football programs with the stipulation that the football coach must be fired if he does not win the national championship within a certain number of years. When the expectations in an accountability system are so unreasonable, they undermine morale, encourage cheating, and generally are not effective.

Perhaps more important, the NCLB accountability system is profoundly unfair across schools and school districts. Districts facing relatively high educational costs, which are predominantly districts with a relatively high concentration of disadvantaged students, must, through no fault of their own, spend more than other districts to obtain the same performance (or the same performance increase). NCLB does provide more money to schools with more disadvantaged students, but as shown earlier, this extra money falls short of the extra costs that these schools must pay in order to meet performance targets. As a result, the NCLB accountability system expects a much higher efficiency improvement from schools with a high concentration of disadvantaged students than from other schools.

The problem here is not with the objective, namely the same performance from every school, regardless of the level of disadvantage among its students. Instead, the problem is the failure of NCLB to adequately recognize that this objective cannot be met unless schools are given the funding they need to deal with cost factors that are outside their control, such as concentrated poverty. Indeed, the design of the NCLB accountability system almost guarantees that sanctions will be imposed on schools with high concentrations of disadvantaged students; despite the link between school poverty rates and Title I, high-poverty schools do not receive the funds that they need to meet state targets in any of the states that we examine. As a result, the only legitimate way for these schools to meet NCLB performance targets is through unprecedented improvements in their efficiency.[82]

HOLDING STATES ACCOUNTABLE

Another way to interpret NCLB is that it requires schools, school districts, and their states to work together to meet the NCLB standards. States may be able to help school districts become more efficient—by helping them to identify programs that work, for example—but little is known about the effectiveness of this approach. A more direct way for states to influence school-district performance is through increases in state education aid. As shown above, however, the magnitude of the necessary funding increases is very large in most cases—far larger than state elected officials are likely to approve.

In our view, this analysis exposes additional weaknesses in the NCLB accountability system. Sanctions are not imposed directly on states, even though states control the most direct method—additional aid—for reaching performance standards. Nevertheless, states must deal with the consequences of sanctions imposed on their schools, and they may want to minimize those consequences by boosting state aid. Given the magnitudes involved, however, no state is likely to increase state aid enough to ensure that all its schools have the funds they need to meet performance standards. Moreover, the standards themselves are set by the state, so the state can minimize the short-run impact of the NCLB accountability system on both its school districts and its aid budget by lowering its standards. As discussed earlier, the available evidence indicates that several states are following this strategy, which undermines NCLB's objective of boosting student performance. If a 100 percent proficiency standard is ever literally imposed, states will be able to hold off sanctions on their school districts only by combining lower standards and larger state aid budgets.

Finally, it should be noted that NCLB is not fair across states. Even if all states had exactly the same performance standards, some states would have to spend more money than others to reach them. Because Title I does not adequately account for the added costs of reaching standards in some districts, it also does not account for the added costs of reaching standards in some states, and therefore treats high-cost states unfairly. As Liu has demonstrated, key provisions of the Title I aid formulas lead to significant disparities in aid distribution across states.[83]

HOLDING THE FEDERAL GOVERNMENT ACCOUNTABLE

A third way to look at NCLB is that because it is a federal mandate, it should be fully funded by the federal government. As shown earlier, the increase in Title I funding that accompanied the passage of NCLB falls far short of the increase in spending needed to meet NCLB performance targets, particularly in states with stringent accountability systems. In this section we examine the legal case for federal government accountability; we also explore the federal contribution that would be required to meet NCLB objectives under various circumstances.

The Legal Case for Federal Responsibility. In April 2005, in
Pontiac School District v. Spellings, nine school districts, along with
the National Education Association and other plaintiffs, filed suit
claiming that NCLB was an underfunded mandate and requesting the
federal district court to rule that states' obligations under NCLB were
limited to those that could be accomplished with available federal aid.
Later in the year, the State of Connecticut filed a suit asserting similar
claims. In this section we briefly examine these lawsuits and the legal
principles on which they are based. We then evaluate the implications
of these lawsuits for the debate concerning reauthorization and the
extent of federal responsibility for helping states meet the requirements
of NCLB. A more detailed discussion of the legal basis of the lawsuits
appears in Appendix 2.C.

State and local governments have brought two lawsuits challenging the extent to which the Department of Education can interpret
NCLB as imposing underfunded mandates. Plaintiffs in both suits
have centered their claims on Section 9527(a) of the NCLB, which
reads, "Nothing in this Act shall be construed to authorize an officer
or employee of the Federal Government to mandate, direct, or control
a State, local education agency or school's curriculum, . . . or mandate
any state or any subdivision thereof to spend any funds or incur any
costs not paid for under this Act."[84] The suits assert two claims in
common: (1) that section 9527(a) limits state obligations to implement
NCLB-mandated reforms only to those that are fully funded by federal
aid; and (2) that if NCLB is interpreted to impose additional obligations on the states, then it is unconstitutional because it exceeds the
limits of Congress's conditional spending power as defined by *South
Dakota v. Dole.*

With respect to the claim based on Section 9527(a), both parties appear to have good arguments. Section 9527(a) was enacted
as part of a 1994 reauthorization of the ESEA and it was carried over without change under NCLB.[85] The 1990s were a time
of considerable concern about unfunded mandates, and plaintiffs
present strong arguments from legislative history that Congress, in
fact, intended section 9527(a) to prevent the ESEA (and other legislation containing that provision) from imposing unfunded mandates on state and local governments.[86] On the other hand, section
9527(a) was carried over into NCLB unchanged and with little
or no debate, arguably unnoticed.[87] Further, the Department of
Education presents persuasive arguments that interpreting 9527(a)

as plaintiffs contend is not congruent with other sections of the statute.[88]

The constitutional claim arises because Congress enacted NCLB on the basis of its power under the "spending clause" of Article I, Section 8, of the U.S. Constitution. That clause allows Congress to condition a state's receipt of federal funds upon its meeting certain obligations. While Congress is *not* required to provide sufficient federal funding to cover the states' costs of meeting the statutory conditions, its "conditional spending power" is subject to certain constitutional limitations.[89] One of the constitutional requirements is that the statutory conditions must be imposed "unambiguously" so that states understand the conditions when exercising their choice whether to accept the federal funding.[90] In this case, the constitutional argument centers on whether section 9527(a) introduces sufficient ambiguity that states, in accepting federal funding, were not on clear notice of their obligation to use their own funds to comply with the act's requirements if federal funds were insufficient.

As of this writing (June 2008), neither litigation is concluded. In *Connecticut v. Spellings*, the district court entered judgment denying plaintiffs' claims and that judgment has been appealed. In its opinion, however, the district court stated explicitly that it was not addressing the merits of the claims based on section 9527(a) and the limits of Congress's conditional spending power. Instead, it simply found that, because Connecticut was currently in compliance with NCLB requirements and was not threatened with federal sanctions, these claims were premature.

In *Pontiac School District*, the district court disagreed with plaintiffs' interpretation of section 9527(a). It concluded that Congress had, in fact, intended states to bear some of the cost of implementing NCLB requirements and dismissed both of plaintiffs' claims.[91] On appeal, however, by a 2-1 majority, a three-judge panel of the United States Court of Appeals for the Sixth Circuit reversed the district court's decision to dismiss and remanded the case back to the district court.[92] Unlike the district court, the panel declined to authoritatively interpret the statute. Instead, the majority rested its decision on the constitutional claim, holding that "the Spending Clause requires a more clear statement from Congress before States and local education agencies can be required to expend their own funds in order to comply with federal guidelines."[93] In May 2008, however, the Sixth Circuit Court vacated the panel's decision and judgment and granted the department's motion for rehearing en banc. As a result, the appeal will now be heard and decided by all of the justices of the Sixth Circuit Court.

As the previous paragraphs suggest, the ultimate outcome of these suits remains uncertain. Nevertheless, these suits raise a couple of issues relevant to the debate concerning reauthorization of NCLB. First, the suits have squarely raised the issue of whether, and to what extent, Congress intended NCLB to impose underfunded obligations on the states. Further, the suits highlight the importance of developing a clearer understanding of the costs of complying with its mandates. Reauthorization provides Congress an opportunity to revisit and address these difficult but very important issues more explicitly and with the benefit of the additional information, experience, research, and debate generated by initial efforts to implement NCLB.

Second, these suits demonstrate yet another way in which NCLB has changed the balance of power and the dynamics of education policy. Previously, education policy was debated in school districts, state legislatures, and state courts. Now, an important share of the policy dialogue has shifted to interactions between state and federal departments of education concerning approval of state plans and waivers from NCLB requirements. This brings into the policy process. not only the federal bureaucracy, but also federal courts, as these suits illustrate. NCLB appears to have shifted the debate substantially from state legislators, courts, and departments of education to federal ones.

7. Conclusions and Policy Recommendations

The No Child Left Behind Act created a new school accountability system at the federal level and increased federal funding for education. This chapter uses education cost functions to estimate the spending required to support NCLB standards in California, Kansas, Missouri, and New York and compares this spending with the funding available through NCLB.

Our central results are (1) that NCLB leaves a funding gap between the spending required to meet NCLB standards and the additional federal aid associated with NCLB, (2) that this funding gap is much larger in states with low proficiency rates (California and Missouri) than in states with high proficiency rates (Kansas and New York), and (3) that this funding gap is larger in school districts with high concentrations of disadvantaged students than in other districts. We also explore three alternative routes for closing this gap: increased federal funding, increased state aid, and increased school-district efficiency. We find that to meet a target of 80 percent proficiency (our middle target) in the average district, federal Title I aid would have to increase between 86 percent (New York) and 1,951 percent (California), or state aid would have to increase between 4 percent (New York) and 118 percent (Missouri), or school district efficiency would have to increase between 8 percent (New York) and 51 percent (Missouri). This target could obviously also be met with some combination of these three types of changes. Even in the highly unlikely case in which state aid and efficiency both increase by 25 percent, Title I aid would need to go up three to five times for proficiency rates to reach 90 percent in states with relatively low rates of student proficiency (Missouri and California). If more realistic increases in state aid and efficiency are assumed (5 percent), federal aid would have to increase two to three times even in states with relatively high student proficiency rates, such as New York and Kansas.

NCLB was up for reauthorization in 2007 but serious consideration of NCLB was delayed until after the 2008 presidential election. Based on the analysis in this chapter, we believe the debate about reauthorization and reform of NCLB should focus on four key issues.

The first issue is that the current design of NCLB places schools and school districts in an untenable position. Many schools cannot meet 80 or 90 percent proficiency on state tests—let alone 100 percent—without outside financial help, even if they could figure out a way to make unprecedented improvements in their efficiency. A 100 percent proficiency target may be a good political slogan, but it cannot be the basis for a reasonable school accountability program. Some combination of a lower proficiency target and more funding is needed. One could say that the U.S. Department of Education has implicitly acknowledged this lesson by basing sanctions on a more flexible definition of AYP. This, however, is only a temporary fix; a reauthorization of NCLB in its current form would still require all schools to reach 100 percent proficiency by 2014.

Moreover, the combination of equal standards and sanctions for all schools combined with only a modest amount of extra funding for schools with high educational costs implies that sanctions are based in part on factors outside schools' control. This arrangement is profoundly unfair. In our view, it would not be appropriate to "solve" this problem by setting lower standards for high-cost schools, which tend to be schools with high concentrations of disadvantaged students. Instead, we believe that this serious fairness problem can be addressed by moving all schools away from a 100 percent proficiency target—a target that is particularly hard on schools with high costs—and by altering NCLB funding mechanisms so that the funding individual schools receive is more in line with the extent to which they face higher costs because of concentrated disadvantage among their students.

As shown in this chapter, NCLB improved interdistrict equity by putting heavier emphasis on Targeted Grants, but Title I funding per child in poverty still varies widely across schools, districts, and states.[94] Moreover, the Title I aid formulas include factors that significantly weaken the targeting of aid to high-poverty school districts; these factors include state per-pupil expenditures, absolute student counts, and minimum-aid and hold-harmless provisions. Simplifying the Title I distribution formulas and strengthening their linkage to educational costs would make it possible to fill a portion of existing funding gaps without increasing the Title I budget.

A second key issue is that the NCLB accountability system does little to encourage school districts to eliminate intra-district inequities in educational funding. In particular, the so-called comparability loophole implies that districts can continue to receive full Title I funding even when they staff some of their neediest schools with their most inexperienced teachers. We believe that the NCLB accountability system could be improved not only by eliminating the comparability loophole, but also by rewarding districts that allocate their resources so as to account for educational costs and to minimize variation in student performance across their schools.

A third key issue for the reauthorization debate is the role of the states. In our view, NCLB should be reformed so that states are rewarded for setting high standards and for helping to fund them. Rewards for high standards could be based on an analysis of the relationship between state standards and national tests.[95] States with higher standards could be given lower proficiency targets and/or they could be given more federal aid. These steps would directly address the serious problem of the current design of NCLB encouraging, if not requiring, states to lower their standards. States also should be given financial rewards for implementing an education financing system that accounts for cost factors outside districts' control. This type of reward would require a system for rating state education finance systems, such as the "poverty funding gap" developed by the Education Trust.[96]

The final key issue is whether the Title I funding currently provided by the federal government is sufficient given the stringent requirements and severe sanctions built into NCLB. A full resolution of this issue will depend, of course, on a resolution of the legal issues discussed earlier. In the meantime, our analysis indicates that a significant increase in federal funding, particularly if it were focused on the higher costs associated with disadvantaged students, would bring the NCLB accountability system more in line with best practices and would significantly reduce the unfairness in NCLB as it currently stands. Even assuming a 15 percent increase in state aid and efficiency, federal Title I aid will have to more than double in urbanized states with relatively high student proficiency rates, such as New York, and increase five to ten times in states with low proficiency rates, such as Missouri and California, to meet a 90 percent proficiency target. We think that federal aid increases would be a step in the right direction, but even doubling or tripling federal funding would leave many states far from a 90 percent proficiency rate, let alone the 100 percent rate called for by NCLB. If federal funding is not increased substantially, then it becomes even more important to move away from a 100 percent proficiency requirement, to better align existing Title I funds with educational costs, and to reward states with education finance systems that account for the relatively high costs of disadvantaged students.

APPENDIX 2.A
DATA SOURCES AND MEASURES

The cost function estimates in this chapter are based on data for three pre-NCLB years (1999–2000 to 2001–2) for school districts in Kansas and Missouri plus either two years (Kansas) or three years (Missouri) after the passage of NCLB. Data for California was available only for two post-NCLB years (2004 and 2005). The state education departments in each state supplied most of the data: California Department of Education (CDE), Kansas State Department of Education (KSDE), Missouri Department of Elementary and Secondary Education (MDESE), and New York State Education Department (NYSED). This section is organized by major category of variables, and summary statistics are reported in Table 2.2 and Tables 2.B.1 to 2.B.4 in Appendix 2.B.

DISTRICT EXPENDITURES

The dependent variable used in the cost function is inflation-adjusted district operating expenditures per pupil.[97] For California, we constructed a broad measure of operating expenditures, which included personnel compensation, books and supplies, services, and other operating expenses. Excluded are transfers of direct costs to other funds, tuition, pupil transportation, facilities acquisition and construction, facilities rents and leases, and debt service.[98] In Kansas, our measure includes expenditures for six functional areas: instruction, student support, instructional support, school administration, general administration, operations and maintenance, and other.[99] Our measure for Missouri includes total instructional and support spending minus total capital outlay, debt service, special education, transportation, and several revenue categories.[100] For New York we used total expenditures minus transportation, tuition, debt service, and other undistributed spending (e.g., pensions).[101]

STUDENT PERFORMANCE

In all four states our measure of student performance is based on the share of students reaching proficiency on math and English language arts (or the equivalent) exams for one grade in elementary school, one in middle school, and one in high school. For Kansas, proficiency scores are for fourth, seventh, and tenth grades for math and for fifth, eighth, and eleventh grades for reading. For Missouri, proficiency rates are for third, seventh, and eleventh grades for communication arts and fourth, eighth, and tenth grades for math. In New York the exams were given in fourth and eighth grades and during high school. New York calculates proficiency for NCLB differently than the other states. Performance is divided into four levels. If a student reaches no higher than level 2 this is counted as 100; if they reach either level three or four, this is counted as 200. The final performance index goes from 0 to 200. To make this index roughly comparable to the other states we divided it by 2.

Student Enrollment

For California, we use total enrollment. The enrollment measure for Kansas is enrollment from first to twelfth grades plus half of total enrollment in kindergarten and prekindergarten programs. For Missouri we construct a rough measure of average daily membership by averaging enrollment in September and January. New York calculates a measure of average daily membership, which attempts to measure all students being educated at district expense.[102]

Student Need

Cost functions usually include student-need measures for child poverty, limited English proficiency (LEP), and special education. The poverty measures used most often in state aid formulas are the percentage of students receiving a free lunch or a subsidized lunch. We used the percentage of K–12 free lunch students for Kansas, percentage of K–6 free lunch students in New York, and the share of K–12 free and subsidized lunch students in California and Missouri. We chose the poverty measure used in state aid formulas, because we expected that this measure is more apt to be audited. While the reliability of these measures has been challenged, especially for secondary students, they generally track fairly closely with the child poverty rate produced by the Census Bureau.[103]

The lack of a consistent definition of, and data collection method for, LEP students in each state makes it difficult to develop comparable measures across states. We experimented with several LEP measures in the cost model for each state. Only in California is the coefficient on the LEP measure statistically significant from zero. In California, we used the share of students classified as English learners (EL) based on data from the language census.[104]

Measures of special education students are problematic because of the potential for districts to overclassify special education students, particularly those with mild disabilities, in order to increase state aid.[105] For states where information was available on the share of students by the severity of the disability (California and New York), we used the share of special education students with moderate to severe disabilities. In New York, we include students who are in settings outside of their regular classroom 60 percent or more of the time or are being served entirely in a separate location. In California, we used the number of students who are outside of a regular classroom at least 80 percent of the time as a share of total enrollment.[106] For Missouri and Kansas, only information on the share of total special education students was available. For Kansas, the special education variable was not statistically significant so it was dropped from the final regression model.

TEACHER SALARIES

To develop a comparable salary measure across districts, data on individual teachers are used to predict what teacher salaries would be in each district if teachers had average experience and education. Specifically, the natural logarithm of a teacher's salary is regressed on the logarithm of their total experience and an indicator variable (0–1) for whether the teacher had a master's, doctorate, or law degree (Kansas) or had a graduate degree (Missouri and New York). For Missouri and New York, we limited the teachers used in the calculation to those with five years or fewer of experience, because their salary is more apt to reflect variation in the underlying cost of hiring comparable teachers, not differences in teacher contract provisions.[107] The large share of very small districts in Kansas prevented us from selecting only inexperienced teachers in the calculation of adjusted salaries. For California, data on individual teacher salaries is not available, so we used the minimum salary on teacher salary schedules in each district from CDE. Teacher salaries are also adjusted for inflation.[108]

OTHER COST FACTORS

In California and Missouri a sizable number of districts do not serve a full range of grades. Because costs of serving students may vary across grade levels, we have included indicator variables in the cost model. In Missouri there are K–12, K–8, and K–6 districts; we include in the cost model indicator variables for whether the district served all grades (where K–8 districts, or K–6 districts are the omitted category). California has K–12 districts, elementary districts, and high school districts; in the cost model we include indicator variables for elementary districts or high school districts (where K–12 districts are the omitted category). In California we also took into account possible cost impacts of short-run enrollment change on spending per pupil, defined as enrollment change over a three-year period. Because increases and decreases may have different impacts on costs, we included measures for both.[109] For Kansas, in order to reflect potential short-run adjustment costs associated with consolidation, we include a measure of whether a district has consolidated between 2000 and 2004.[110]

EFFICIENCY INDICATORS

Fiscal capacity variables included in the cost models include income, property wealth, and state aid. The income variables include median household earnings from the 2000 census (California) or per-pupil adjusted gross income (Kansas, Missouri, and New York). Property wealth is an estimate of the market value (New York) or assessed value (Kansas and Missouri) of all real property in a school district. Property value data are not available for California. The aid variable is per-pupil state aid (New York) or per-pupil state aid relative to income (California, Kansas, and Missouri).[111] In California, a large share of state education aid is provided in the form of categorical grants; therefore we include a measure of the share of state aid as categorical grants.

In addition, voters might have more incentive and capacity to monitor operations in school districts with relatively more college-educated adults, more elderly residents, and a larger share of households that own their own homes. Measures of these variables came from the 2000 census. We would also expect that efficiency could be influenced by the "tax price" that voters pay for additional education services. The higher the price, the more likely voters are to monitor district operations. A key part of the tax price is called the tax share and is typically measured by the median housing price divided by per-pupil property values.[112] Median housing value comes from the 2000 census. Proposition 13 in California significantly constrains local school districts' use of property taxes; instead, some counties vote to implement a tax on the number of parcels; the inverse of the number of parcels is the tax price for the parcel tax.[113] Because of the highly centralized and constrained education finance system in California, we include several other efficiency-related variables in the cost model—the percentage change in the revenue limit since 1975 and the population migration rate.[114]

Appendix 2.B
Statistical Methodology and
Cost Function Results

In this section, we discuss the statistical methodology used in the analysis and cost-function estimates.

Statistical Methodology

We estimate the cost function using a multiple-regression method, which has been commonly employed in economics and public policy research. This method estimates the relationship between an independent variable (e.g., student poverty rate) and the dependent variable (e.g., per-pupil spending), controlling for the impact of other variables in the model on the dependent variable (e.g., efficiency-related factors). In specifying the functional form of the empirical cost function, we use one of the most common cost functions employed in empirical research, a constant elasticity (or Cobb-Douglas) function. In a constant elasticity function, both the dependent and all the independent variables are expressed in natural logarithms. We modify this in several ways. Variables that are already in percentage terms (e.g., percentage of students receiving free lunch) or variables expressed as 0 or 1 (e.g., whether a district is a K–12 district) are not expressed as natural logarithms.

We have taken several steps to assure that the statistical estimates from the multiple-regression models are accurate. First, we have included in the cost model several efficiency-related factors to account for relative efficiency differences across school districts. Second, the standard errors in multiple regressions can be biased when a panel data set is used, because the errors are not statistically independent of each other. We use a method to correct standard errors for clustering at the district level (multiple observations for the same district). In addition, to account for possible correlation of standard errors across time, dummy variables are included in the model for the year of the data (omitting the dummy variable for one year).

Third, standard multiple-regression methods are based on the assumption that unobservable factors, such as unique district characteristics, influence only the dependent variable, not the independent variables. If this is not true, then the regression estimates can be biased (so-called endogeneity bias). Student performance targets, and teacher salaries, are potentially set simultaneously with district spending, as part of the annual budgeting process, so all of these variables may be influenced by the same unobservable factors. To account for the potential endogeneity of these variables, we employ a statistical procedure used frequently in economics research: two-stage least squares (2SLS) regression. This approach involves the selection of exogenous "instruments" to isolate the exogenous component of the endogenous variables. Ideally, instruments should be strongly related to the endogenous variable but not independently related to the error term of the regression.

The process for selecting a set of instruments involved two steps: (1) select potential instruments on theoretical grounds and (2) use statistical tests to select the strongest subset of instruments. Research on teacher labor markets has determined that the cost of living and amenities (such as urban location) of an area, as well as student characteristics in a district, are likely to affect teacher mobility decisions and the salaries required to attract teachers to work in a district.[115] As confirmed in decades of research on education production, the socioeconomic characteristics of students are strongly related to student performance.[116]

To screen out inappropriate sets of instruments, we use several common statistical tests to evaluate instruments. First, a "weak instrument" test was used to identify instruments that are strongly correlated with teacher salaries and the performance measure[117]. The weak instrument test is a partial F-statistic for the instruments in the first-stage equation, which for multiple endogenous variables is replaced with a Cragg-Donald F statistic. The Cragg-Donald statistic is compared to a set of critical values developed by Stock and Yogo, which vary with the number of endogenous variables and instruments, and the maximal level of acceptable bias of the 2SLS estimator compared to OLS regression.[118] The instruments used for California and New York have bias between 5 percent and 10 percent of OLS, for Missouri the bias is between 10 percent and 20 percent, and for Kansas the bias is between 20 percent and 30 percent. When the instruments are considered weak, other methods are available for estimating the model, which are more robust. We estimated the cost models using one of these methods and found that the results did not change significantly.[119] Second, an overidentification test[120] was used to examine whether the instruments are exogenous. The results of the overidentification tests indicate that the instruments used for the cost function for each state are not significantly correlated with the error term of the second-stage equation; thus, they can be used as instruments.

Based on theory, we would expect that comparable private sector salaries, urbanization, and student socioeconomic characteristics should be related to teacher salaries and student performance. To assure that these factors are exogenous, we have used the average of these characteristics for other school districts in the same labor market area. For California, instruments included a measure of private sector wages in the labor market and for other districts in the same labor market, median house values, the share of LEP students, the share of subsidized lunch students, the share of African-American students, and the percentage of urban population in the district. For Kansas, instruments include for other districts in the same labor market, the share of free lunch students, per-pupil income, enrollment, and the share of households with single mothers; we also use the maximum share of free lunch students in adjacent districts. In Missouri, instruments include a measure of private sector wages in the labor market and for other districts in the same labor market, enrollment, the share of Hispanic students, and the share of African-American students. For New York, instruments include for other districts in the same labor market area, the child poverty rate, the share of LEP students, the share of the population that is Hispanic, and the share of the population that is African-American.

Cost-function Results

Tables 2.B.1 to 2.B.4 present results of the cost function estimated for school districts in each state. Most of the independent variables are expressed in relative terms (either per pupil or as a percentage) and their regression coefficient can be interpreted as an elasticity—the percent change in per-pupil spending associated with a 1 percent (or percentage) change in an independent variable (holding the other variables in the model constant). These tables also include descriptive statistics for variables in the model in their unlogged form.

In general, per-pupil spending has the expected relationship with the independent variables in the cost functions, and the coefficients are significantly different from zero. Student performance and teacher salaries are positively related with spending, and their coefficients can be interpreted as the percent change in spending associated with a 1 percent change in student performance or teacher salaries, holding other variables in the model constant. Also consistent with expectations, higher student needs—such as poverty, LEP status, or disabilities—is associated with more spending. Cost-function estimates for all states indicate significant economies of size. In Kansas and Missouri, districts with over 2,500 students are estimated to spend 50 percent to 80 percent less per pupil than districts with under 100 students. For California districts with over 5,000 students are estimated to spend 40 percent less than districts with under 250 students, while in New York this spending difference is only 15 percent. The relatively small economies of size in New York are probably due to the small number of districts with enrollments below 250 students. Most of the efficiency variables have the expected sign and some are significantly different from zero.

Table 2.B.1 Cost-function Estimates and Descriptive Statistics for California School Districts (2004–2005)

Variables	Coefficient	t-statistic	Mean (2005)	Standard Deviation (2005)
Intercept	-1.18181	-0.50	—	—
Performance measure	0.56617	4.78*	46.6	15.5
Cost variables:				
Teacher salaries	0.69852	2.70*	$35,521	$3,383
% free and subsidized lunch students	0.00562	4.91*	48.0	26.1
% limited-English students	0.00324	5.03*	18.4703	18.5171
% special education students	0.01281	2.41*	1.4018	1.0394
% 3-year enrollment change if positive	-0.07888	-13.54*	0.1042	0.5855
% 3-year enrollment change if negative	-0.37691	-5.33*	-0.0364	0.0799
Elementary district (1= yes)	-0.14599	-10.58*	0.5643	0.4961
High school district (1= yes)	-0.07106	-3.18*	0.0865	0.2812
Enrollment categories:				
250 to 500 students	-0.21555	-9.46*	0.1535	0.3607
500 to 1,000 students	-0.29605	-11.14*	0.1124	0.3161
1,000 to 1,500 students	-0.28766	-9.42*	0.0670	0.2502
1,500 to 2,500 students	-0.31865	-11.24*	0.1027	0.3037
2,500 to 5,000 students	-0.35241	-11.24*	0.1416	0.3489

5,000 to 15,000 students	-0.40291	-12.27*	0.1827	0.3866
Over 15,000 students	-0.41052	-10.76*	0.1211	0.3264
Efficiency-related variables:				
Median household earnings	-0.00036	-0.01	$24,175	$9,077
Total aid/income ratio	2.74524	9.95*	0.0386	0.0355
Categorical Aid as % of total operating revenue	0.34766	4.33*	0.2989	0.0905
Inverse of local tax share (number of parcels)	0.17774	12.98*	6.9421	8.0130
Population migration rate (2000)	0.00246	4.17*	19.8052	8.6966
% change in revenue limit since 1975	0.09204	5.39*	0.5328	0.4270
Year indicator variables:				
2004	0.08150	4.47*	—	—
Sample Size	1,850		925	

Note: Estimated with linear 2SLS regression with the log of per-pupil operating spending as the dependent variable. Performance and teacher salary variables are treated as endogenous variables. Robust standard errors are used for hypothesis testing (controlling clustering at district level). The performance index, teacher salaries, number of parcels, and median earnings are expressed as natural logarithms. * indicates statistically significant from zero at 5% level.

Table 2.B.2 Cost-function Estimates and Descriptive Statistics for Kansas School Districts (2000–2004)

Variables	Coefficient	t-statistic	Mean (2004)	Standard Deviation (2004)
Intercept	-1.99801	-0.49	—	—
Performance measure	0.47189	2.13*	71.8	7.9
Cost variables:				
Teacher salaries	0.66475	2.02*	$39,427	$2,950
% free lunch students	0.00542	2.88*	26.7	11.3
Consolidated districts (1 = yes)	0.21243	2.25*	0.007	0.1
Enrollment categories:				
100 to 150 students	-0.12718	-1.78**	0.040	0.197
150 to 250 students	-0.23449	-3.19*	0.110	0.314
250 to 500 students	-0.36282	-4.94*	0.301	0.459
500 to 1,000 students	-0.43111	-5.59*	0.254	0.436
1,000 to 1,500 students	-0.51676	-6.59*	0.087	0.282
1,500 to 2,500 students	-0.57308	-7.57*	0.087	0.282
2,500 to 5,000 students	-0.56084	-7.10*	0.060	0.238
5,000 to 15,000 students	-0.50646	-6.35*	0.030	0.171
Over 15,000 students	-0.57563	-5.48*	0.017	0.128

Efficiency–related variables:

Per-pupil income	0.13274	3.82*	$87,950	$31,021
Per-pupil property values	0.07622	2.93*	$57,065	$43,629
Total aid/income ratio	0.78494	2.36*	0.079	0.105
Local tax share	-0.00526	-0.19	1.6150	0.8783
% of adults that are college educated (2000)	-0.00503	-2.54*	17.97	6.75
% of population 65 or older (2000)	-0.00231	-1.24	16.84	5.47
% of housing units that are owner occupied (2000)	-0.00138	-0.84	88.59	5.66
Year indicator variables:				
2001	-0.01383	-1.30	—	—
2002	-0.00544	-0.40	—	—
2003	-0.05134	-1.62	—	—
2004	-0.09301	-1.86**	—	—
Sample Size	1,463		299	

Note: Estimated with linear 2SLS regression with the log of per pupil operating spending as the dependent variable. Performance and teacher salaries are treated as endogenous variables. Robust standard errors are used for hypothesis testing (controlling clustering at district level). The performance index, teacher salaries, per pupil income, per pupil property values, and local tax share are expressed as natural logarithms. * indicates statistically significant from zero at 5% level. ** indicates statistically significant from zero at 10% level.

Table 2.B.3 Cost-function Estimates and Descriptive Statistics for Missouri School Districts (2000–2005)

Variables	Coefficient	t-statistic	Mean (2005)	Standard Deviation (2005)
Intercept	-8.01604	-1.92**	—	—
Performance measure	0.32470	1.83**	25.6	7.2
Cost variables:				
Teacher salaries	1.36616	3.66*	$27,460	$3,290
% free and subsidized lunch students	0.00550	3.75*	46.1	16.0
% special education students	0.00198	1.65**	16.7	4.9
K–12 districts (1= yes)	0.11391	3.74*	0.9	0.3
Enrollment categories:				
100 to 150 students	-0.15969	-3.12*	0.047	0.211
150 to 250 students	-0.31873	-4.65*	0.132	0.339
250 to 500 students	-0.47467	-6.28*	0.203	0.403
500 to 1,000 students	-0.59681	-6.86*	0.238	0.427
1,000 to 1,500 students	-0.68113	-7.10*	0.093	0.291
1,500 to 2,500 students	-0.75541	-7.11*	0.089	0.285
2,500 to 5,000 students	-0.82272	-6.91*	0.085	0.280
5,000 to 15,000 students	-0.82756	-6.20*	0.041	0.198
Over 15,000 students	-0.79915	-6.96*	0.021	0.145

Efficiency–related variables:

Per-pupil income	0.19305	4.77*	$63,962	$35,112
Per-pupil property values	-0.00742	-0.22	$61,631	$41,074
Total aid/income ratio	1.34201	4.06*	0.059	0.062
Local tax share	-0.08901	-3.35*	1.2348	0.4863
% of adults that are college educated (2000)	0.26404	0.91	0.13	0.08
% of population 65 or older (2000)	-0.32683	-1.49	0.15	0.04
% of housing units that are owner occupied (2000)	-0.16991	-1.75**	0.77	0.08
Year indicator variables:				
2001	-0.00137	-0.10	—	—
2002	-0.01425	-0.61	—	—
2003	-0.03139	-1.10	—	—
2004	-0.05870	-1.98*	—	—
2005	-0.04191	-1.24	—	—
Sample Size	3,068		516	

Note: Estimated with linear 2SLS regression with the log of per-Pupil current spending as the dependent variable. Performance and teacher salaries are treated as endogenous variables. Robust standard errors are used for hypothesis testing (controlling clustering at district level). The performance index, teacher salaries, per-Pupil income, per-Pupil property values, and local tax share are expressed as natural logarithms. * indicates statistically significant from zero at 5% level. ** indicates statistically significant from zero at 10% level.

Table 2.B.4 Cost-function Estimates and Descriptive Statistics for New York School Districts (2000–2005)

Variables	Coefficient	t-statistic	Mean (2005)	Standard Deviation (2005)
Intercept	-8.43774	-2.03*	—	—
Performance measure	1.39681	2.32*	86.6	6.0
Cost variables:				
Teacher salaries	0.67462	3.32*	$54,922	$8,895
% free lunch students	0.00731	4.82*	30.9	19.7
% special education students	0.01412	2.34*	2.7	1.6
Enrollment categories:				
250 to 500 students	-0.04951	-0.67	0.079	0.269
500 to 1,000 students	-0.10154	-1.36	0.166	0.373
1,000 to 1,500 students	-0.10274	-1.39	0.191	0.394
1,500 to 2,500 students	-0.11713	-1.56	0.196	0.397
2,500 to 5,000 students	-0.12339	-1.63	0.211	0.408
5,000 to 15,000 students	-0.15625	-2.04*	0.120	0.325
Over 15,000 students	-0.10374	-0.69	0.010	0.101

Efficiency-related variables:

Per-pupil income	0.05578	1.59	$148,370	$124,444
Per-pupil property values	0.23366	3.48*	$712	$1,704
Per-pupil aid	0.10997	2.26*	$4,445	$2,140
Local tax share	-0.08925	-1.57	0.0047	0.0059
% of population 65 or older (2000)	-0.01395	-0.06	14.24	3.65
% of housing units that are owner occupied (2000)	-0.12879	-1.19	75.70	11.19
Year indicator variables:				
2001	0.10253	4.48*	—	—
2002	-0.23183	-2.74*	—	—
2003	-0.22615	-2.72*	—	—
2004	-0.26573	-2.67*	—	—
2005	-0.24612	-2.42*	—	—
Sample Size	3,980		674	

Note: Estimated with linear 2SLS regression with the log of per-pupil operating spending as the dependent variable. Performance and teacher salaries are treated as endogenous variables. Robust standard errors are used for hypothesis testing (controlling clustering at district level). The performance index, teacher salaries, per-pupil income, per-Pupil property values, per-pupil state aid, and local tax share are lexpressed as natural logarithms. * indicates statistically significant from zero at 5% level.

Appendix 2.C
Legal Challenges to NCLB

Legal Context

Article I of the U.S. Constitution creates the federal legislative branch and empowers it to make laws. Section 8 of Article I sets out specific powers of Congress, including such well-known powers as the power to "regulate commerce . . . among the several states," to "raise and support armies," and to "declare war," as well as the power to "make all Laws . . . necessary and proper for carrying into execution the foregoing Powers." The Tenth Amendment, however, provides, "The powers not delegated to the United States by the Constitution, nor prohibited by it to the states, are reserved to the states respectively, or to the people." The extent to which this constitutional structure enables the Congress to regulate in areas outside those enumerated in Section 8 and that are traditionally regulated by the states, such as education, has been and remains under debate.[121]

As a result, in the case of NCLB and most legislation concerning education,[122] Congress attempts to influence policy indirectly, enacting legislation by virtue of the power granted under the "spending clause" of Article I, Section 8. That clause authorizes Congress to "pay the debts and provide for . . . the general welfare of the United States." The Supreme Court has traditionally construed Congress's power under the spending clause broadly. Under it, Congress may authorize funds to promote policy objectives in substantive areas where it cannot regulate directly, and it may condition receipt of federal funds upon states' taking actions that Congress could not otherwise require.[123]

Nevertheless, Congress's power under the spending clause is not unlimited. In the leading case of *South Dakota v. Dole*, the Court recognized five limitations:

1. "the exercise of the spending power must be in pursuit of 'the general welfare'"

2. the conditions must be imposed "unambiguously . . . , enable[ing] the States to exercise their choice knowingly, cognizant of the consequences of their participation"

3. conditions "might be illegitimate if they are unrelated 'to the federal interest in particular national projects or programs'"

4. "other constitutional provisions may not provide an independent bar to the conditional grant of federal funds" and

5. the "financial inducement offered by Congress [may not] be so coercive as to pass the point at which 'pressure turns into compulsion.'"[124]

THE LITIGATION

In April 2005, nine school districts, the National Education Association, and eight state education associations sued the U.S. Department of Education in federal district court (*Pontiac School District v. Spellings*). Plaintiffs' complaint divided NCLB mandates into five categories—curriculum and instruction; annual data collection, grading, and reporting; enabling schools and districts to achieve AYP; improvement measures applicable to schools and districts that do not make AYP; and teacher and paraprofessional qualifications—and set out estimates of costs to meet NCLB requirements in each category. Comparing these costs to federal aid provided under NCLB, plaintiffs asserted that the cost of meeting NCLB mandates exceeded federal funding in each category.

On the basis of these facts, plaintiffs presented two claims, one statutory and one constitutional, both centered on section 9527(a) of the NCLB. Section 9527(a) reads in full: "GENERAL PROHIBITION. Nothing in this Act shall be construed to authorize an officer or employee of the Federal Government to mandate, direct, or control a State, local education agency, or school's curriculum, program of instruction, or allocation of State or local resources, or mandate any State or any subdivision thereof to spend any funds or incur any costs not paid for under this Act."[125] Plaintiffs argued that this clause limits any conditions that states must meet to receive NCLB funds to those that can be implemented using only federal dollars. The Department of Education, in contrast, interpreted NCLB as requiring states to comply with all of its statutory mandates, regardless of whether federal funding was sufficient to pay for them, in order to receive any NCLB funds.

In their statutory claim, plaintiffs contended that the department's position was contrary to section 9527(a). Plaintiffs' constitutional claim invoked the second of *Dole*'s four limitations on congressional spending power: the requirement that the conditions must be imposed "unambiguously . . . , enabling the States to exercise their choice knowingly, cognizant of the consequences of their participation." Plaintiffs asserted that the Department of Education's interpretation violated the spending clause by changing one of the statutory conditions under which the states and school districts had chosen to accept federal funds.

The district court disagreed with plaintiffs' interpretation of section 9527(a) and dismissed both of their claims. The district court reasoned that the inclusion of the phrase "officer or employee of the Federal Government" limited the reach of section 9527(a). Under this reading, the law merely prohibited "federal officers and employees from imposing additional, unfunded requirements beyond those provided for in the statute."[126] The court reasoned that section 9527(a) could not reasonably be read as prohibiting *Congress* itself from imposing unfunded mandates on the states; by passing a statute containing this elaborate set of requirements, Congress had clearly done so. Because it interpreted section 9527(a) as allowing congressional imposition of an unfunded mandate, the district court did not have to determine whether or to what extent federal funding under NCLB fell short of covering the costs of compliance.

Plaintiffs appealed the court's dismissal of their claims to the Court of Appeals for the Sixth Circuit. By a 2-1 majority, a three-judge panel of the appellate court reversed the district court's decision and remanded the case to the district court for further proceedings.[127] The majority did not address plaintiffs' statutory claim or the meaning of section 9527(a). Instead they rested their decision on plaintiffs' spending clause claim. After examining the text of the act, its legislative history, and statements by the previous secretary of education, the majority concluded, "Congress has not 'spoke[n] so clearly that we can fairly say that the State[s] could make an informed choice' to participate in the Act with the knowledge that they would have to comply with the Act's requirements regardless of federal funding."[128] The court continued, "Of course, if that ultimately is what Congress intended, the ball is properly left in its court to make that clear."

The panel's decision was short-lived, however. In May 2008, a majority of the Sixth Circuit's fourteen regularly sitting judges granted the department's motion for rehearing en banc and vacated the panel's decision and judgment. The appeal is once again pending and will now be decided by the entire court.

In August 2005, the State of Connecticut filed a second suit, asserting statutory and spending clause claims similar to those raised by the *Pontiac* plaintiffs. Connecticut, however, raised additional constitutional arguments. Connecticut contended that the department's threats to withhold all Title I funding as well as additional funding were "so harsh and unrelated to the conditions upon which the State accepted the funds that they violate the *Tenth Amendment*."[129] Connecticut also asserted two claims under the Administrative Procedure Act (APA), a generic statute that establishes procedures for administrative agencies to follow in implementing federal legislation and authorizes judicial review of agency action. Connecticut claimed that the secretary abused her discretion in failing to grant its requests for waivers of certain NCLB requirements and by denying requested amendments to its plan.

The district court dismissed both Connecticut's section 9527(a) claim and its constitutional claims. The court reasoned that because the parties agreed that Connecticut was currently in full compliance with NCLB requirements and because the secretary had taken no enforcement action against Connecticut, these two claims were not sufficiently developed for judicial review. The district court emphasized, however, that its dismissal of these claims did not in any way constitute a judgment of their underlying substantive merit. The district court later denied plaintiffs' APA claims as well, and plaintiffs have appealed this judgment.

STANDARDS-BASED REFORM: A POWERFUL IDEA UNMOORED

Lauren B. Resnick, Mary Kay Stein, and Sarah Coon

INTRODUCTION

No Child Left Behind is the current expression of a twenty-year drive to use a "standards" strategy to steer American education toward higher levels of achievement and greater equity.

The idea, as it developed over the last two decades of the twentieth century, was that a standards-based system could combine the positive aspects of centralized curriculum guidelines with the individuality and energy of the American local-control system. Standards and assessments would be set by public entities such as states, but the details of curriculum, teaching, and professional development would be left to districts and schools. Student performance accountability systems, rather than detailed regulations, would structure the priorities of schools and districts and press them to make the changes necessary to deliver effective teaching to all of their students. Broadly, the goals of the standards movement, beginning in the late 1980s, were to promote both equity and excellence in education. In this chapter, we begin with an overview of these goals, tracing the societal conditions that gave rise to them and how they became entwined with the standards movement. Next, we provide a step-by-step history of the events leading up to NCLB, focusing on both the tension between national and local control and the maneuvering to resolve that tension. In the third section, we return to the two overarching goals of excellence and equity and ask if they were accomplished, and at what cost. We close with a set of recommendations for adjusting our standards-based efforts to improve American education.

EDUCATIONAL EXCELLENCE
IN A SHRINKING WORLD

The public and political energy for what was to emerge as the "standards agenda" came from two separate streams of thinking, both centered on American competitiveness but born in two different eras that overlapped just enough to form an alliance between the scientific/intellectual community and the business community.

In 1983, during the Reagan administration, at what seemed the height of the cold war, thae National Commission on Excellence in Education issued a report titled *A Nation at Risk*. This report called for higher levels of academic achievement, especially in mathematics and science (but by implication in literacy as well) for American students. The report brought national attention to the poor performance of U.S. students on international, as well as national, assessments in mathematics and science. *A Nation at Risk* warned, "The educational foundations of our society are presently being eroded by a rising tide of mediocrity" and called for a nationwide system of standardized tests to resist the tide. In its words: "Standardized tests of achievement . . . should be administered at major transition points from one level of school to another, and particularly from high school to college. These tests should be administered as part of a nationwide (but not Federal) system of State and local standardized tests."[1]

A Nation at Risk attracted significant attention to education and spurred a variety of reforms including efforts to raise the quality of teachers, to increase the supply of teachers, and to create more challenging career opportunities for teachers. Despite the renewed attention to education, however, unequivocal benefits were slow to appear. In 1990, the National Assessment of Educational Progress (NAEP) reported some increase in math scores, but the average was still far below what was to become the nation's target of "proficient" performance. Reading scores showed no progress at all.

By 1990 the Berlin Wall had fallen, the cold war had ended, and the defense-preparedness argument for educational improvement, with its origins in Sputnik, was no longer convincing to many. But rising concerns about global competitiveness and the intellectual capacity of the American workforce had motivated the increasing involvement of the business community in education. The earliest hints of the now highly visible "flattening" of the earth—the process of sending jobs requiring literate and numerate workers "offshore"—was just becoming visible to the public. The apparently highly efficient Japanese economy heightened fears of challenges to American prosperity. Dire predictions were being made that apart from highly trained college graduate positions, only the most unskilled jobs would remain in the United States. The solution, many agreed, was higher levels of skill and knowledge among high school graduates, along with higher rates of high school graduation.[2]

At the federal level, newly elected president George H. W. Bush made it clear that he intended to become an "education president." In a June 1989 meeting of the Business Roundtable, which included some of the nation's most important business executives, Bush challenged the CEOs to work with governors and other state leaders to help improve schools in their respective states. Chairs of IBM, Xerox, and UPS, among others, accepted leadership positions in education task forces and commissions.[3]

Many governors, influenced in part by the business leadership in their states, had also become convinced that only improved levels of education could maintain (or in some states, raise) economic prosperity and the standard of living of their citizens. In September 1989, the president convened a two-day summit with the National Governors Association (NGA) to discuss school reform. Held in Charlottesville, Virginia, the summit was hailed by *Education Week* as only "the third such policy meeting ever called by a U.S. President."[4] Many states, particularly southern ones that were vying to create human capital in order to attract business, were introducing major education reforms of their own. Several of the "education" governors—including Bill Clinton, Richard Riley, Jim

Hunt, and George W. Bush—were to become visible figures in the national standards movement.

At the summit, a joint statement by President Bush and a bipartisan coalition of governors called for: (a) the establishment of a process for setting national education goals; (b) greater flexibility and enhanced accountability in the use of federal resources to meet the goals through both regulatory and legislative changes; (c) a major state-by-state effort to restructure the education system; and (d) annual reporting on progress in achieving those goals.

Within a year the National Education Goals Panel had been formed to promote (and perhaps oversee) the process. In the same time period, the president had convened the Education Policy Advisory Committee[5] to explore the feasibility of a national achievement test. Soon thereafter, with support from private foundations, the New Standards Project[6]—a consortium of state education officials, governors, educators, and scholars—had formed a coalition to identify benchmarks of educational achievement and, subsequently, assessments that states might use in judging student progress toward those benchmarks.

About this same time, the National Council of Teachers of Mathematics (NCTM) began to disseminate hundreds of thousands of copies of standards documents[7] for the improvement of K–12 mathematics education. Based on careful analysis of where the field of mathematics was headed, the increasing role of technology in mathematical thinking and reasoning, and predictions of the kinds of skills that workers would need in the twenty-first century, these standards—created in the 1980s with input from mathematics educators and a wide variety of stakeholders—provided a vision of *what* mathematics should be taught and *how*. These documents carried the endorsements of hundreds of professional organizations and played an important role in guiding states' work to set standards for improvement.[8]

The American education standards movement was underway. But many difficult questions still lay along the path to implementing a standards-based public education system for the nation. Two of the most difficult questions concerned how to ensure educational equity for the country's growing racial and ethnic minority populations, and how to implement any kind of national program in a country in which states—not the federal government—retained constitutional power over education.

EDUCATIONAL EQUITY: USING STANDARDS TO CLOSE GAPS IN EDUCATIONAL OPPORTUNITY

Calls for "equity" and "adequacy" had been heard in education circles since the *Brown v. Board of Education* U.S. Supreme Court decision in 1954. *Brown* had brought differences in educational opportunity between the races into national consciousness and specified desegregation of schools as a means to reducing these differences. Desegregation was meant to provide redress for the effects of segregation. Social scientists had begun to show how segregation had negative effects on the development of African-American children.[9] Desegregation was also understood to be a major tool for equalizing resources for learning by eliminating the subpar buildings, understaffed classrooms, and poor or outdated equipment and textbooks that characterized "separate but unequal" schools serving African-Americans. For the great civil rights movement of the 1960s and 1970s, education was second only to voting rights as a centerpiece of advocacy concerns.

Beginning in the mid-1970s, the fledgling NAEP had begun to report national achievement differences by race, ethnicity, and socioeconomic status, following the lead of a number of influential research studies such as the "Coleman Report"[10] on educational equality. NAEP showed large gaps in achievement between the races. Throughout the 1980s, African-American twelfth-grade students' scores in reading and math were about equal to those of white eighth-graders—and Latino students were not faring much better. As national attention to the "excellence" agenda rose, the achievement gap remained in the public eye. With the publication of NAEP results, students who had previously been "out of sight" began to be visible on a national and, in some cases, state level.

There was little agreement, however, about using test-based evidence to pursue the goal of equal opportunity to learn.[11] Minority-advocacy communities were slow to take up evidence of the "achievement gap" as a tool for improving educational opportunity. Advocacy leaders recognized the discouraging African-American/white achievement gap but worried that publicizing test-score differences would lead citizens at large to blame the students and their families, rather than mobilizing to provide better learning opportunities. Many were also worried about setting standards that would drive their students out of school.

In the 1970s, some minority advocates had actively resisted the use of test scores as criteria of educational achievement, evident in their reaction to the movement for minimum competency tests as criteria for high school graduation. Minimum competency tests were introduced in a few states in the 1970s as an attempt to give some academic meaning to high school diplomas. In keeping with their label as minimum, the tests generally demanded performances that many experts considered to be at most a middle-school level of competence in math and literacy. Yet they typically revealed massive differences among racial and economic groups. As one example, in October 1977, when Florida sophomores faced a functional literacy test that was a new requirement for a diploma, 78 percent of African-American students failed. The comparable failure rate for white students was only 25 percent.

Advocacy groups swung into action, calling the test requirement unfair because of unequal opportunities to learn the material tested. A Florida Supreme Court decision[12] called for suspension of the testing requirement for graduation until the state could show that students had been systematically taught the material that would be tested. A few years later, Florida's African-American students performed *much* better, particularly on the math section, with 69 percent of African-American tenth-graders passing.[13] The Florida high court then allowed the test-based requirement for graduation, and advocates began to switch their focus to providing more equal opportunities to learn.

Opportunity to learn was given fuel and focus by growing evidence of a curriculum *tracking* system in which most minority students were assigned to classes in which the "high cognitive demand" subjects were never taught at all. Sputnik had increased the popularity of tracking and gifted and talented programs in the 1950s, but throughout the following decades, sociologists and minority advocates had been documenting the ways in which early tracking of students became a self-fulfilling prophecy of low achievement. In 1990, using longitudinal data available for the first time through the National Science Foundation, a RAND study showed that low-income, minority, and inner-city students were disproportionately assigned to low-track classes. These assignments meant almost no opportunity for students to take the critical gatekeeping courses that would prepare them for science and mathematics study after high school.[14]

Mathematics was a focus of particular concern partly because of the National Science Foundation and National Academy of Science's insistence on its centrality, and partly because there was a clear sequence of courses in place in the "academic track" of American high schools. Tracking studies made it evident that minorities were largely not participating in this sequence. In fact, they were being "counseled out" of it by many high school advisers.

Starting in 1989, several visible efforts to undo the tracking tradition drew further attention to the problem and offered the vision of a possible solution. The Mathematical Sciences Education Board (MSEB) of the National Research Council released *Everybody Counts: A Report to the Nation on the Future of Mathematics Education*.[15] This 1989 report cited changing demographics as having raised the stakes for all Americans. "Never before have we been forced to provide true equality in opportunity to learn," the report concluded.

In 1990, the College Board launched the EQUITY 2000[16] program, aimed at the goal of having *all* American high school students take algebra by ninth grade. The goal of "algebra for all"—along with the 1989 *Curriculum and Evaluation Standards for School Mathematics*, published by the National Council of Teachers of Mathematics—had a large impact on the mathematics curriculum, leading states and districts to treat middle- (and even elementary) school curricula as preparation for ninth-grade algebra.

Visible efforts to de-track soon began to appear as well as efforts to demonstrate that students from impoverished backgrounds could learn to think and reason at high levels. One example is the QUASAR Project[17] under the direction of Edward Silver at the University of Pittsburgh's Learning Research and Development Center. QUASAR set out to examine the feasibility and effectiveness of providing a high-quality, demanding middle-school mathematics program for students attending schools in impoverished neighborhoods. After several years of program development, teacher professional development, and research in six urban middle schools, the QUASAR project demonstrated that, given the opportunity, students from high-poverty schools could learn to think, reason, and problem solve at high levels. Still, many school across the country that enrolled all or most students in algebra in ninth grade were, in the absence of any uniform standards for "algebra," changing the title but not much of the content of their courses.[18]

Increasing numbers of minority advocates who had been skeptical of a standards-and-test-based solution to creating greater learning opportunities began to change their views as legal cases in which constitutional challenges to state spending formulas began to stress *adequacy* of opportunity to learn rather than just equalization of expenditures. Plaintiffs often contended that funding provided by a state was inadequate to provide opportunities for students to meet even minimal learning standards. Responding to one such complaint, in 1989, the Kentucky Supreme Court essentially invalidated Kentucky's entire public school system and directed the state to reestablish its system on grounds that would ensure an adequate education to all of its students. The resulting Kentucky Education Reform Act[19] (KERA) mandated the creation of statewide goals for student performance and a statewide assessment matched to the goals. The Kentucky decision and the efforts to create a new performance-based system there marked a turning point in thinking about the potentially positive role of achievement standards in providing educational equity.

Throughout the 1990s, the equity aspects of the standards agenda became increasingly prominent. The achievement gap, along with concerns over weak high school diplomas in the face of global competitiveness, all contributed to the growing belief among governors, policy makers, business leaders, educators, and Americans in general that something had to be done to dramatically lift the quality of education for all American students. Equity joined excellence as the motivation for education reform. By the time NCLB was legislated in 2002, the equity-creating possibilities of standards and test-based accountability had become a centerpiece of the effort, and some equity-advocacy organizations were among its major supporters.

A BRIEF HISTORY OF STANDARDS-BASED EDUCATION REFORM

By 1989 it had become clear that the country was ready for something new in education. A new view of learning had developed, one that focused on understanding, and not only on a practiced fluency in retrieval of facts and procedures and that held out the promise of educating all students to be thoughtful and articulate citizens and workers.[20] The governors had embraced education reform as a major agenda and various organizations that represented state interests in education had put out position papers and sponsored meetings to discuss the excellence and equity agendas.[21] The business community was supporting the idea of new initiatives aimed at a more competitive workforce. The American Federation of Teachers, under the leadership of its president, Albert Shanker, was drawing the teachers' unions into a reluctant but irreversible coalition focused on raising educational achievement and increasing equity.[22]

Despite this convergence of opinion on the importance of raising student achievement, it was not at all clear how the United States could move *as a nation* to achieve this goal. The federal government did not directly control education anywhere—except in the District of Columbia. Education was a "reserved power" for the states, and in most states the power had by tradition been handed off to localities, although there was variation in this respect—southern states had traditionally kept more power centrally.[23] There were other centralizing approaches elsewhere, including New York's state-run Regents testing system and the California Department of Public Instruction's state curriculum frameworks. But these were exceptions in the general educational landscape.

NAEP had been founded with an explicit mandate to *not* provide breakouts of data by states or school districts. Data were to be provided only on the nation as a whole and on several large regions of the country. This had been a political compromise: All the states wanted to improve but were wary of direct, public comparisons with one another. Localities, as well, were not interested in being compared with one another and mostly didn't want their states, much less the federal government, telling them how to "keep school."

The dilemma faced by American education reformers was how to encourage higher demand and greater equity in a vast and varied national system with a strong tradition of local control. The answer that emerged was agreement on a standards-based system that left details of instruction to very local decision makers (individual teachers, schools, perhaps school districts) but set teachers' and schools' work within a context of publicly established criteria for what was to be taught and accountability for student learning. Ideas for such a system had been laid out in a widely read and discussed paper by Marshall Smith and Jennifer O'Day on systemic reform.[24] Smith and O'Day called for state standards, initially called curriculum frameworks, with linked accountability assessments that would judge how well *systems* (states, districts, schools) were doing at meeting publicly established educational goals. These ideas took on reality and a new form as the concept of standards-based education grew from a visionary ideal to a political reality.

The NGA Summit introduced the concept of national (not federal) educational goals but left the specifics to a small working group (in which Bill Clinton was the lead governor).[25] The group met for the first time in late October 1989 and quickly established six national goals. One month later, the NGA approved the goals. In January 1990 President Bush announced the goals in his State of the Union address:

- By the year 2000, all children in America will start school ready to learn.

- By the year 2000, the high school graduation rate will increase to at least 90 percent.

- By the year 2000, American students will leave grades 4, 8, and 12 having demonstrated competency in challenging subject matter including English, mathematics, science, history, and geography, and every school in America will ensure that all students learn to use their minds well, so they may be prepared for responsible citizenship, further learning, and productive employment in our modern economy.

- By the year 2000, U.S. students will be first in the world in science and mathematics achievement.

- By the year 2000, every adult American will be literate and possess the skills necessary to compete in a global economy and exercise the rights and responsibilities of citizenship.

- By the year 2000, every school in America will be free of drugs and violence and will offer a disciplined environment conducive to learning.

The National Education Goals Panel

To monitor the progress toward these goals, the National Education Goals Panel was created. Governor Roy Romer of Colorado became the panel's first chair. The Goals Panel quickly established advisory resource groups for each goal and began a process of reports and hearings that drew increased attention, fed by interest groups ranging from equity advocates to business leaders to educators themselves, who were basking in the unusual degree of public support for their enterprise. In *Measuring Progress Toward the National Education Goals*, released in March 1991,[26] the student achievement resource group made recommendations for how to use existing data (including NAEP, college entrance exam participation and scores, Advanced Placement test scores, and international comparison data) to begin tracking progress toward the math and science and student achievement goals. This group also recommended that the country develop a new national assessment system that would set national standards for student performance in key subject areas, while allowing clusters of states to develop their own tests to measure performance against the standards. It was recommended that NAEP be used, at least temporarily, to "monitor" the state tests but not be used to measure individual students. In adopting this concept, the Goals Panel included the possibility of creating a board that would oversee the standard-setting process and create a national "anchor" examination tied to common standards that could be used to calibrate results of state tests.[27]

In April 1991 Secretary of Education Lamar Alexander (who had been appointed by Bush at the very end of 1990, just as the Goals Panel was being formed) put forward a legislative proposal, called America 2000, that called for creating "world class standards and voluntary national exams to help parents assess how well their children's school is performing." Congress did not pass the America 2000 legislation (which also included several controversial proposals for parental choice and freedom from bureaucratic controls in running schools). But Congress did refer the goal panel's proposal for a standards and assessment system to a newly legislated National Council on Education Standards and Testing (NCEST),[28] whose charge was to provide advice on the desirability and feasibility of national education standards and a system of voluntary national tests.

The National Council on Education Standards and Testing (NCEST)

NCEST delivered *Raising Standards for American Education* to Congress and the Goals Panel on schedule in January 1992. Of the six original goals, NCEST focused on how to measure progress on goals 3 (fourth-, eighth-, and twelfth-grade achievement) and 4 (math and science). NCEST recommended that the Goals Panel establish a new National Education Standards and Assessments Council (NESAC) that would:

◆ Provide for and coordinate the development of voluntary national standards for content, student performance, and system performance

◆ Provide for the development, by states, of school delivery standards

◆ Certify content and student performance standards as world-class

◆ Provide for the development of a system of assessments for individual students that is aligned with national standards

◆ Develop assessments to monitor the performance of programs and systems consistent with national standards.

NESAC was also to provide research and development for "break the mold" assessments, issue quality guidelines for the development of assessments, and ensure the technical merit (i.e., validity, reliability, and fairness) of assessments. Further, it would certify that assessments were aligned with national standards and would establish procedures and criteria for achieving comparability among assessments.

The council's recommendations reflected the general uncertainty about the relation between states and the national government in the emerging standards movement. It did not specify a *federal* role, but it did recommend significant *national* engagement in education. It called for national content standards and even (individual) student performance standards. The latter was understood at the time to mean assessments for individual students—going well beyond what NAEP was authorized to provide. At the same time, in assigning to NESAC the role of "certifying" content and system performance standards, it seemed to suggest that the states, and not the federal government, would develop these standards. And it suggested several different guiding and supporting roles for the nation in assessment development, reflecting a divided view on whether there should be national tests. It did, however, seem to insist on some form of national oversight.

It is not completely clear in retrospect what "system performance" standards were meant to be, but NCEST's formulation clearly was a call for national criteria of how well education providers (states? school systems? schools?) ought to perform. This thrust would later emerge as school accountability criteria, the currently debated centerpiece of the No Child Left Behind Act (NCLB). At the same time, NCEST called for "monitoring" the performance of programs and systems and for some way of establishing comparability among different assessments—a role that would eventually fall to NAEP—thus recognizing that there would probably not be a single national test or set of tests. Curriculum and teaching, both key elements of the Smith and O'Day systemic reform proposal, were mentioned by NCEST only indirectly. They became "school delivery standards" and were clearly viewed as a responsibility and prerogative of states or localities, not the nation.

NCEST's recommendations provided the framework—and forecast the uncertainty—within which the standards agenda would evolve during the rest of the decade.

GOALS 2000 AND THE REAUTHORIZATION OF TITLE I

In March 1994 President Bill Clinton signed into law the Goals 2000: Educate America Act. Goals 2000 reaffirmed the original six National Education Goals and added two more, one dealing with teacher professional development and one dealing with parental involvement.

Goals 2000 tried to keep the national review of content standards and assessment alive, converting the National Educational Standards and *Assessment* Council (NESAC) to the National Educational Standards and *Improvement* Council. But the political press for state, not national, control of content and performance standards was so strong that NESIC was soon abandoned entirely.

The question of the time was whether there could be any national enforcement mechanism at all for a standards-based approach to educational improvement. The answer came with the October 1994 ESEA reauthorization, called Improving America's Schools Act (IASA, P.L. 103-382). IASA, like its predecessors, provided federal funding assistance for poor children and schools, but the 1994 reauthorization made standards and accountability an official policy. It tied federal resources to specific requirements of standard setting and testing. And it embraced an educational equity agenda even more ambitious than the agenda of ending segregated public schooling by setting a goal of common achievement expectations for all groups of children.

The 1994 IASA built on the fact that a number of state education agencies had already spearheaded standard-setting processes on their own. Among them, Texas, North Carolina, Kentucky, Delaware, Massachusetts, and Maryland all had been developing standards-based or standards-related reforms from the mid- to late 1980s or early 1990s. Florida, California, and several others had major state-initiated standards reforms in the early and mid-1990s. Many states, however, either had no official standards or allowed use of different, less demanding standards and tests for disadvantaged students. The new legislation halted this practice by making receipt of Title I (also called Chapter 1) funds depend on two key requirements:

◆ The requirement that states develop content and performance standards for all children in mathematics and science.

◆ The replacement of generic multiple-choice tests for Title I students with tests that were aligned to the standards, creating coherence between standards and assessments.

By tying locally valued federal funding to compliance with these requirements, IASA put some "teeth" into the standards mandate. States and localities could not—if they wanted to receive the federal funding assistance—use different standards and tests for different groups of students. In the words of Christopher Cross, the ESEA reauthorization in October 1994 "virtually forced states to make mandatory the standards, assessments, and curriculum changes that were 'voluntarily' contained in Goals 2000 by linking them with Title I funds."[29]

Except for an attempt (refused by Congress) to create voluntary national tests that states and localities could use, however, the
Democratic administration gave up on further attempts to directly
influence the quality of state standards and testing. And while IASA
called for states to develop school accountability standards based
on common standards and tests, there was little attempt to enforce
accountability practices. Instead, the administration put substantial
effort into support for states to create these policies in a way that
would encourage good teaching. Progress was slow in many states.
In others, the issue became embroiled in disputes over the educational and technical quality of tests. Nevertheless, by 2000, a study
by *Education Week* showed that almost every state was well on its
way, that scores were rising, and that teachers generally favored the
effort.[30] Some states—mostly in the South and Southwest—developed
test-based accountability systems that were to deeply influence the
shape of the next round of standards-based reform.

No Child Left Behind

Eight years after IASA, in 2002, the new Republican president,
George W. Bush, with bipartisan support in Congress, signed the No
Child Left Behind Act. NCLB was technically just the next round
of reauthorization of Title I. In fact, it left the basic standards and
assessment apparatus of the previous round more or less untouched.
That is, it required states to develop standards and tests but established no review or quality control at the federal level, except for
requiring states that accepted Title I money to participate in state-
level NAEP tests. This opened the way to public reporting of state-
to-state differences in the extent to which NAEP-defined levels of
achievement were being met. What is more, NCLB created a tight
federal framework for the school accountability aspect of the standards agenda. It did so with particular focus on the equity aspect of
the effort, by requiring that school-by-school test results in elementary and middle school be reported annually by:

◆ Major racial and ethnic subgroups

◆ Limited English Proficiency (LEP)

◆ Students with disabilities and

◆ Economically disadvantaged (students who receive free or reduced-price meals).[31]

To ensure that districts addressed those children who were not yet proficient, the law incorporated strict sanctions for schools where even one subgroup of the student population was failing to meet adequate yearly progress (AYP) requirements. A series of progressively more serious interventions are implemented for schools that fail to make AYP for two or more consecutive years. First, the school becomes identified for "improvement." In this stage, the interventions include developing an improvement plan and offering parents the choice to transfer their children to another public school, and providing supplemental services like free tutoring. If an identified school misses its targets for a second year, the district must take one of several "corrective actions," followed by "restructuring" if the school misses its targets for a third year.

It is these sanctions that are creating much of the current dissatisfaction with NCLB. Educators and communities—especially in schools accustomed to getting high marks for their educational programs for high-achieving students—are distressed that one "failing" subgroup marks the entire school as failing. The "assistance" that they are offered (and usually required to accept) by the states is rarely viewed as helpful, and the threat of being closed entirely, or "restructured" in a way that displaces teachers and administrators, is looming closer. Meanwhile, the probability of all students reaching a test-defined proficiency in 2014, now just six years away, seems so low as to make many wonder why they should stay the course.[32]

Table 3.1 traces the relative attention to the three key components of standards-based reform from the 1991 NCEST recommendations to the 2002 No Child Left Behind legislation. Dark-shaded boxes indicate components that were to receive substantial federal or national guidance (at least some form of national review). No shading indicates components that were required but would come under no form of national review.

In NCLB, as in IASA, content and student performance standards were left almost entirely to the states. The only "national" element left from the Goals Panel and NCEST recommendation was the use of NAEP to "monitor" state results. What had migrated to the center,

Table 3.1 Political History of Standards–based Reform

	1991 NCEST	1994 ESEA	2002 NCLB
Content Standards (Voluntary)	National No Review	States Required to Develop – No Review	States Required to Develop–
Student Performance Standards	National Tests (Voluntary)	States Required to Develop– No Review	States Required to Develop– No Review
Accountability	National "System Performance Standards" (Voluntary)	States Required to Create and Use Same Assessments for Title I and non-Title I Students	Strict Sanctions Defined Federally, Based on State Scores, Disaggregated Reporting

under surprisingly direct federal mandate, were the "system performance" standards, now specified for individual schools, with quite-stringent consequences for weak performance.

In sum, content and performance standards were initially to be a centerpiece of national attention but later became an unsupervised, state-overseen requirement. The states had to have content standards and student performance standards (which amount to assessments), but there would be no official review of their quality or demand level. By contrast, accountability criteria, which had at first been called for as "voluntary system performance standards" and then allowed to become state prerogatives, returned with NCLB as a national requirement.

RESULTS OF THE GRAND EXPERIMENT

Is there merit to the increasingly popular view that No Child Left Behind is failing? Or, are standards and assessments working, despite the pains of adjusting to a new system? As we have shown, our current version of the standards venture, No Child Left Behind, is mostly a continuation of the IASA formulation of 1994, with strong federal specification of accountability requirements and consequences added. So, although it is really too early to estimate the effect of NCLB in particular,[33] it is possible to examine the effects of the combined IASA and NCLB programs. We look first at student achievement indicators, then at the effects of the new way of working on the quality and satisfaction of the teaching force.

STUDENT ACHIEVEMENT: EQUITY

On the equity goal of the standards agenda, there is real progress to report: the achievement gap is shrinking. *Education Week*'s 2006 *Quality Counts at 10: A Decade of Standards-based Education* reported that "nationally, NAEP scores in 4th grade math have increased on average by 18.5 points on a 500 point scale, or nearly two grade levels, since 1992, near the start of the standards movement."[34] The report further indicated that gains for African-American and Latino fourth-graders had *increased more than the average* at 27.7 percentage points and 24.2

percentage points, respectively. Reading scores have not improved at the same rate, but there is evidence that the achievement gap is closing somewhat in reading as well. Figures 3.1 through 3.4 summarize the most recent national data available, showing average achievement levels on NAEP up through 2007 separately for whites, African-Americans, and Latinos.

Perhaps even more important than the narrowing gap is the fact that average fourth-grade African-American and Hispanic math performance is now well above the *basic* level. Reading scores are approaching that level more slowly. All told, though, the really troubling performances of the early 1990s, in which large numbers of our minority students seemed to be fundamentally illiterate or innumerate, have changed. It appears that the standards effort, including requirements for disaggregated test-score reporting, is having the hoped-for equity effects. We are teaching basic literacy and math to more and more of our elementary school children, and fewer and fewer are being left *way* behind.

Figure 3.1 Disaggregated NAEP Scores through 2007, Fourth Grade Mathematics

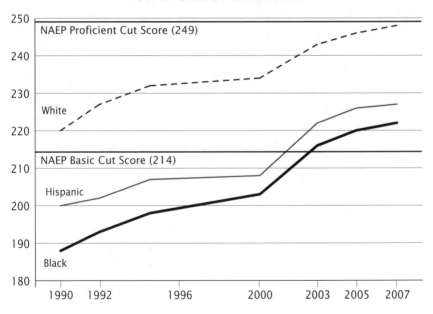

Source: U.S. Department of Education, Institute of Education Sciences, National Center for Education Statistics, National Assessment of Educational Progress (NAEP), NAEP Data Explorer, available online at http://nces.ed.gov/nationsreport-card. (Appendix 3.A for this chapter contains the numeric score data on which these graphs are based.)

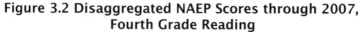

**Figure 3.2 Disaggregated NAEP Scores through 2007,
Fourth Grade Reading**

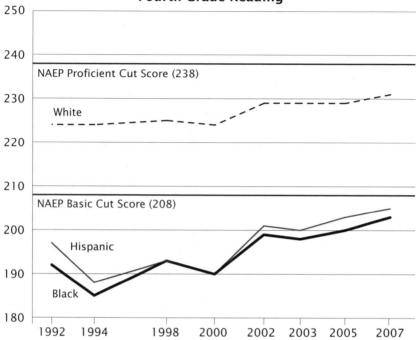

Source: U.S. Department of Education, Institute of Education Sciences, National Center for Education Statistics, National Assessment of Educational Progress (NAEP), NAEP Data Explorer, available online at http://nces.ed.gov/nationsreport-card. (Appendix 3.A for this chapter contains the numeric score data on which these graphs are based.)

Still, the achievement gap has not disappeared. It remains especially large if we compare the proportions of students meeting the more advanced proficient standard on NAEP. There is still a large equity problem to solve. The big new challenge facing educators, and the country at large, is extending these promising gains into middle and high school, and pushing everyone toward the proficiency mark, rather than settling for basic levels of educational performance.

STUDENT ACHIEVEMENT: EXCELLENCE

Meeting this challenge will require much more attention to real academic excellence for all American students than the current ver-

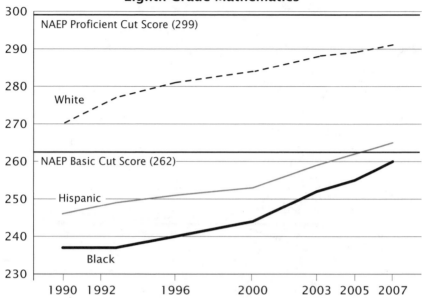

Figure 3.3 Disaggregated NAEP Scores through 2007, Eighth Grade Mathematics

Source: U.S. Department of Education, Institute of Education Sciences, National Center for Education Statistics, National Assessment of Educational Progress (NAEP), NAEP Data Explorer, available online at http://nces.ed.gov/nationsreport-card. (Appendix 3.A for this chapter contains the numeric score data on which these graphs are based.)

sion of standards-based education has supported. Although students' scores on state tests have improved since the introduction of IASA and throughout the period of NCLB, few are meeting the standards of excellence to which we aspire. Although increasing numbers of students have been certified as proficient, the tests intended to measure proficiency have come under fire. At the heart of the issue is the fundamental question of whether the state tests measure what they are intended to measure.

Several alignment studies discussed below have examined the match, or quality of relationship, between a state's standards and its tests. Although their methods differ, generally these studies have found that most state tests are not well aligned with their own standards. In some extreme cases, studies have found that alignment between state standards and tests is so weak that the standards from one state more closely match the tests used in another state. And the alignment is systematic. Based on a five-state review of

**Figure 3.4 Disaggregated NAEP Scores through 2007,
Eighth Grade Reading**

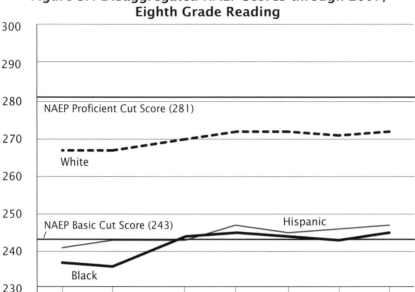

Source: U.S. Department of Education, Institute of Education Sciences, National Center for Education Statistics, National Assessment of Educational Progress (NAEP), NAEP Data Explorer, available online at http://nces.ed.gov/nationsreportcard. (Appendix 3.A for this chapter contains the numeric score data on which these graphs are based.)

English and mathematics standards and tests, researchers found that "the most challenging standards and objectives are the ones that are undersampled or omitted entirely . . . [and those] that call for high-level reasoning are often omitted in favor of much simpler cognitive processes."[35]

State tests often fail to measure adequately the cognitive complexity or "depth of knowledge" described in state standards. For example, in an analysis of eighth-grade mathematics standards and tests in one state,[36] it was found that the tests generally neglected more complex topics and cognitive demands included in the standards, such as solving nonroutine problems. Another study of mathematics standards[37] found that most states failed to adequately measure the "depth of knowledge" described in their standards. In short, most state assessments are cognitively impoverished.[38] Although a new view of learning informed the beginnings of the standards-based assessment,[39] it has been buried under an avalanche of traditional tests in recent years.

Separate from the quality of *what is* tested is another concern about how cut scores are established—that is, how well do students have to perform on the test to be rated *basic* or *proficient*. Figure 3.5 shows the results of a study that compared state proficiency criteria with NAEP criteria in thirty-two states.[40] Only eight states met NAEP's basic cut scores in reading and none were able to meet the NAEP proficient cut score.[41] The results were similar in grade 8 reading, with about half the states meeting the basic and none of the states meeting the proficiency standard.

The states' standards for mathematics fared only slightly better (see Figure 3.6). Of thirty-three states, all but six met the NAEP basic cut score and two met the NAEP proficiency cut score for grade 4. But the overall performance of states is not even close to

Figure 3.5 NAEP Score Equivalents of State Proficiency Standards (Grade 4 Reading)

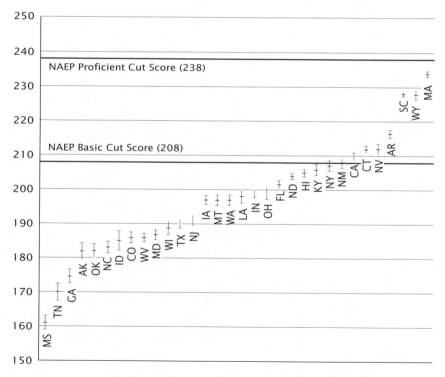

Source: U.S. Department of Education, Institute of Education Sciences, National Center for Education Statistics, National Assessment of Educational Progress (NAEP), 2005 Reading Assessment, and National Longitudinal School-Level State Assessment Score Database (NLSLSASD).

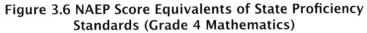

Figure 3.6 NAEP Score Equivalents of State Proficiency Standards (Grade 4 Mathematics)

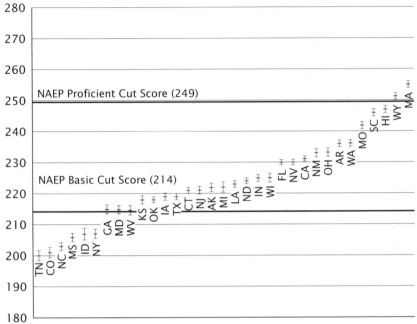

Source: U.S. Department of Education, Institute of Education Sciences, National Center for Education Statistics, National Assessment of Educational Progress (NAEP), 2005 Reading Assessment, and National Longitudinal School-Level State Assessment Score Database (NLSLSASD).

meeting the all-students-proficient goal, using the NAEP criterion as a benchmark.

The generally low level of expectations that are embodied in state tests is further illustrated by Figure 3.7, which plots the relationship between states' reported percentage proficient in grade 4 reading and their average NAEP scores. The more students a state reported as proficient in reading, the lower their average NAEP score was on the state-by-state NAEP. This suggests that states that are declaring high percentages of student proficiency may be "attaining" that proficiency by setting low student performance standards.[42]

Studies of state-designed high school graduation tests also do not paint a flattering portrait. For example, in 2004 the American Diploma Project examined the graduation tests that six states (educating nearly one-quarter of the students in the nation) had put

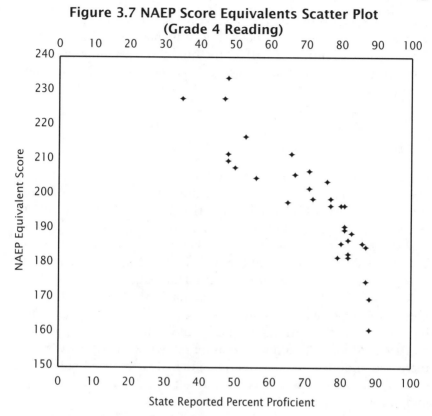

Figure 3.7 NAEP Score Equivalents Scatter Plot (Grade 4 Reading)

Source: U.S. Department of Education, Institute of Education Sciences, National Center for Education Statistics, National Assessment of Educational Progress (NAEP), 2005 Reading Assessment, and National Longitudinal School-Level State Assessment Score Database (NLSLSASD).

into place.[43] They found that the tests mainly cover material that is part of the early secondary school curriculum, that the cut scores required to pass the tests reflected modest expectations, and that the tests measured only a fraction of the knowledge and skills that colleges and employers consider essential. What is more, students who have completed high school and met college entrance requirements often find college work to be inordinately challenging.[44]

If we look beyond student performance on state tests, then, the nation does not appear to be doing very well at meeting the excellence goals laid out at the beginning of the 1990s. Neither IASA nor NCLB set a national standard of excellence, and the resulting pattern is now clear: we do not have a serious national standard of excellence. NCLB placed high "stakes" on low-demand tests. And because high-stakes tests inevitably influence education practice, the system is beginning to affect the quality of teaching in a direction *opposite* to what was intended as the standards movement began.

EFFECTS OF ACCOUNTABILITY ON TEACHING

The effects of high-stakes, low-level tests on instructional practice have been quite widely documented by now.[45] Most studies show that state tests have led to a noticeable increase in the amount of instructional time devoted to the tested subjects and a corresponding drop in non-tested subjects. For example, the Center on Education Policy (CEP) found that "eight out of ten districts who reported increasing time for English Language Arts did so by at least 75 minutes per week, and more than half did so by 150 minutes or more per week." Similarly, "among districts reporting adding time for mathematics, 63% added at least 75 minutes per week, and 19% added 150 minutes or more per week. Most districts that increased time for ELA or mathematics also reported substantial cuts in time for other subjects, including social studies, science, art and music, physical education, recess, or lunch."[46]

Even within the tested subjects, it appears that test-based accountability may be narrowing what is taught. In many urban school districts, teachers are emphasizing test preparation over other aspects of their districts' official curriculum.[47] As end-of-year testing dates approach, teaching time is spent on test practice. In one district that we have studied intensively, elementary students stop reading and discussing grade-level appropriate books and instead spend time digesting brief passages, accompanied by multiple-choice test items that mimic the ones that appear on the state tests. District leadership supports this practice because the tests carry heavy consequences.

Tests have come to have even more influence as school districts, enacting the currently popular theory of "data-based education management," have introduced periodic "interim" tests. These are intended as diagnostic, "formative" assessments, but often they are more geared to predicting state test results than to measuring where students need help on the intended curriculum. As the accountability requirements become more urgent, *the tests are becoming the curriculum.*

It should not be a surprise that tests are influencing what is taught and how time is spent. Indeed, in the theory of standards-based education, assessments are *meant* to influence and guide curriculum. Public examinations have effectively played that role in other countries. In the theory of examination-based "steering" of education practice, however, there was an expectation that the assessments would provide models of expected student performance that went well beyond collections of quick responses to short questions. It was assumed that new forms of "performance" assessment would be used in which students composed relatively extended pieces of writing, explained the reasons for their mathematical solutions, and the like.[48] Under those conditions, "teaching to the test" could have positive, expanding effects on what, and how, students learned.

In addition to perhaps negatively affecting the quality of *what* is taught, NCLB's particular accountability mechanism of "adequate yearly progress" may be unintentionally affecting *who* is taught most intensively. Teachers have been shown to concentrate on students who are *almost* proficient, ignoring most of the others who are judged to be well above the proficiency mark and those who are far below it. Schools and school systems have become adept at helping teachers make these adjustments. In some large school districts, a "practice" version of the state test is given a couple of months before the official test date. The bulk of the attention in succeeding weeks is given to students who score below proficient, and this is done—as we have already noted—by teaching as directly as possible the material that is expected on the "real" test. For observers of the schools, as for those who live and work in them, the whole system seems to be turning schools into "test-score factories."

All of this is apparently affecting the motivation and satisfaction of teachers and so could, if not corrected, have long-term negative effects on the quality of the teaching force, especially in the most challenging schools. Educators fear the negative publicity and sanctions that accompany low test scores under NCLB and rarely see the "assistance" offered by states as likely to be helpful. Teachers report that they are overwhelmed by what has been proven to be an unrealistic expectation (100 percent proficiency by 2014) and regret the loss of independence, creativity, and "teachable moments" in their classrooms.[49] As reports about the increasingly negative culture of teaching continue to appear, some experts suspect that the current challenge of attracting and retaining good teachers may grow worse[50] unless our testing and accountability systems are revised to promote high-quality content and instructional practices rather than preparation for low cognitive demand testing.

CONCLUSION: REDESIGNING THE STANDARDS SYSTEM

Standards-based education was an imaginative effort to harness the power of alignment without diminishing local control. The two major pieces of legislation (IASA and NCLB) that transformed the vision of standards into a national policy envisaged a coherent system in which accountability for results would be based on well-defined standards and assessments that clearly embodied new expectations for learning. By political design these laws left the "meat" of the standards and accountability sandwich to schools and districts. NCLB added test-based accountability requirements on the assumption that the assessments could bear the weight and that real improvement in outcomes would result. What has happened, however, is that the capacity of the schools to dramatically improve education has been quickly outpaced by the much faster moving introduction of tests and accountability systems. This has created a virtual hijacking of standards and education by narrow tests.

We need a plan that will recover the original intent of the effort. Our analysis suggests that both "sides" of the sandwich need revision: we need better standards and assessments, along with a redesigned accountability system that motivates positive effort rather than strategies for avoiding negative consequences.

STANDARDS AND ASSESSMENTS

Much of the negative impact of NCLB derives from the narrowness of the tests for which educators are held accountable. In standards *theory* the way to fix this problem would be to revisit the standards, perhaps providing greater national guidance in the form of "model" standards. Our own view, however, is that the nation has already tried this approach and found it ineffective. The National Council of Teachers of Mathematics, for example, has developed several successive sets of standards over the past two decades that have garnered positive reviews in many quarters but have not significantly affected the kinds of tests used for accountability by states.

We could also provide better national guidance on standards by reinstating the original intention, as expressed in the 1992 NCEST report, of national reviews of state standards. But unless states were required to revise standards in accordance with these national reviews, this is unlikely to be effective. Several organizations (Achieve, the American Federation of Teachers, the Fordham Foundation) have provided regular reviews of state standards. Many states have conducted one or more revisions of their standards in response to these reviews. But most state tests remain only weakly aligned with these revised standards. And some of the revised standards specify so much detailed content that they actually discourage any form of testing other than the decomposed and decontextualized short answer and multiple-choice tests that now dominate in student accountability testing.

Nor would new sets of standards developed by consortia of states—an early idea that is now being revived for consideration—necessarily have any impact on the tests that states use for accountability purposes. We know this because even states whose standards are ambitious, specific, and span the range from basic facts and procedures to conceptual understanding and creative problem solving mostly use tests that look more like the standardized tests of the 1980s than the adventurous performance assessments that were being tried out in the mid-1990s.

The unhappy truth is that our present system is not in practice a standards-based system. It is a test-driven system. The tests are unmoored and floating free. They will continue to do so until we develop a political and technical process that relinks them. What might this look like?

A first point is that tests and standards must be linked *from the start,* and at every step along the way. Probably the best way to achieve such linkage is to have the people who develop and approve the standards also provide detailed assessment specifications. These specifications should include both the types of tasks to be used in the assessment and examples of student work that "meets the standard."

These examples would go well beyond counting up how many individual test items the student correctly answered.[51] If the standard setters agree that open-ended performances in which students develop solutions, write explanations, or evaluate potential strategies are the best way to assess the standard, then provision for such performance tasks will need to be made. In other words, standard setters, not test developers, should certify the content validity of assessments, and they should do so by actually examining the proposed assessment tasks—not taking the word of technical specialists who provide checklists and matrices of which standards have been "covered" in their tests.

A standard-setting process of this kind would have the power to guide teaching toward the *thinking curriculum,* rather than away from it, as is happening as today's tests become the de facto curriculum. Such a standard-setting process was what many of the early advocates of a standards system were envisaging.[52] The power of assessment to guide and shape instruction, to set understandable targets for teachers and students alike, could then begin to be realized.

Fortunately, there are major technical advances in testing and assessment research on which we can build as we reclaim the standards. In the early 1990s, when the standards movement was beginning to take shape, advocates of the standards-based system insisted on a major distinction among norm-referenced and criterion-referenced tests. The distinction had been developed by major testing and measurement scholars (e.g., Glaser[53]) and was widely accepted by testing specialists. Norm-referenced tests were those that distinguished among test takers, placing them on a scale that compared them to one another rather than to an absolute standard of what students ought to know. IQ tests are norm-referenced. So is the SAT. And so are the standardized tests still widely used in education. Criterion-referenced tests were those that aimed to assess each individual against an absolute standard of what people should know. Criterion-referenced, sometimes called "standards-referenced," tests became the goal in the early 1990s.

Today's state tests use the language of criterion referencing, describing students as above or below a proficiency mark. But most of them continue to define proficiency simply in terms of cut scores —the number of items that a student has answered correctly. And, as we have said, the items on the tests mostly favor specific bits of knowledge over deep understanding or the complexities of problem solving. At the same time, by insisting on a form of accountability reporting that asks only how many students have reached the proficiency mark, schools are unable to show the authorities progress that students are making toward proficiency, even if they are still below the cut point. As we have shown earlier in this chapter, most of the gains that American education has made as a result of the standards movement have been in the range between basic and proficient levels of performance. Yet these are mostly invisible to students, parents, and the political authorities responsible for education policy. This is why there is so much interest in the potential for shifting from an absolute standard of proficiency to a value-added approach to accountability testing—one in which schools will be judged on how much progress *toward* proficiency students have made each year rather than just how many students have reached the mark.

Value-added accountability will do much to make the system seem more fair to teachers, and probably to students and parents as well. It will not by itself, however, solve the problem of unmoored and mostly fact-oriented tests. Indeed, some current approaches to value-added assessment would call for a norm-referenced approach to validating tests and so could make it harder to keep the positive aspects of criterion referencing—the ability of tests to provide true and proper targets for instruction.

Developments in the science of learning and of testing (psychometrics) over the last decade and a half offer the promise of an assessment system that will not, in the future, have to choose between criterion and norm referencing. The new idea is to create a graduated set of goals for instruction that describe a *learning progression*: an ordered sequence of goals that a student would be expected to meet if she or he were to be successful in a well-conducted instructional program. There might be three to five major goals to meet in each subject each year. Students would not have to be tested on all of the yearly goals at one time. Instead, assessments on a particular goal could be administered after instruction on that goal had been completed. The test could be much richer and more complex than is possible with current end-of-year tests. And it could serve simultaneously as a test-of-record for the accountability system and a diagnostic or *formative* assessment, picking out students who need additional work on a given goal.

Cognitive and psychometric scholars will be quick to point out that only a few well-researched learning progressions exist at the moment. And in fact there are probably very few progressions that are independent of the sequence in which topics are taught in the curriculum. One could, for example, teach ordinary fractions first and decimals a year or two later, as we do in the United States. Or one could reverse the order as schools in France and other European countries do. These different teaching sequences will entail different testing sequences: the steps of the "ladder of achievement" will be different depending on the curriculum sequence used.

To apply the logic of learning sequence measurement, therefore, will inevitably implicate curriculum. To take advantage of the fast-developing measurement opportunities, which are well-founded in research on how students learn complex cognitive content, we will need to stop pretending that curriculum is totally off limits to standard-setting. Yet in a country as large as the United States, with its appreciation for local choice in educational matters, it may be necessary to develop and try out several (but not fifty) alternative sequences in each key subject matter.

Such a large-scale program would need to be federally funded. It would be beyond the means of fifty individual states to mount the kind of research, development, and field-testing that a learning progression approach to assessment would call for. Thus, we would recommend—along with an aggressive national R&D undertaking—a voluntary approach to adoption of the new learning progression assessments, allowing, but not requiring, states and districts to use them, at least in the early years. During this period we assume that NAEP would continue to be administered on a state-by-state basis, thus providing a national monitor on the effects of the new program.

A REDESIGNED ACCOUNTABILITY SYSTEM: FROM STICKS TO CARROTS

Redesigning assessments to better represent the learning outcomes that we really value will do much to counter the current disaffection with NCLB within the education profession and by many citizens. But something else is needed. It is extraordinary that in a culture that in other domains values incentive-based work and risk taking, we have created for education an accountability system that is almost entirely negative. It is really not surprising that teachers, principals, and district leaders are turning to test practice as a substitute for deep curriculum engagement as the testing date nears. Schools can lose prestige, students, and eventually their very existence on the basis of accountability test scores. There is almost nothing that they can gain by taking the risk of teaching a high-end, high-demand curriculum to all of their students.

The formal accountability system of NCLB is loaded against risk taking. It does not even offer much in the way of "carrots" for initial levels of learning gains. It is a "sticks" system that punishes schools for failure but barely sees and rarely rewards their successes. There are virtually no "carrots."

We do not believe that the creators of NCLB meant to punish educators. Rather, they assumed that the generally low performance of our schools was mainly a result of educators failing to do something that they already knew how to do. They assumed, that is, that our low achievement results derived mainly from low expectations for students, and that if we raised expectations and made it painful not to meet them, things would change for the better. What we are now learning is that just changing expectations will not automatically solve the problem. Most educators are probably already doing the best that they can. We need an accountability system that will change capacity for educating everyone. That calls for a new look at motivation for learning, by adult individuals and the organizations they work in.

Decades of research on human motivation tell us that effective motivation requires a judicious mix of reward and punishment. Punishment alone, especially when the goal appears unreachable, leads people to "game" the system, to cheat, or, if they can, to not participate at all. We have seen all of these reactions by educators. None of them builds capacity for teaching children more effectively.

What might an accountability system that added appropriate "carrots" look like? We can only speculate at this time, but we can offer some ideas to work from. First of all, not unlike the current "stick" system, the new system probably needs to include a graduated set of incentives. So, for example, at a first level schools might be named in a publicly promoted and celebrated list of schools that are making progress if more students than in past years are reaching proficiency or even achieving basic levels of academic success, or if value-added scores reach a certain level. At an intermediate level, schools might receive some significant financial reward for success-fully participating in tested and proven forms of professional devel-opment that upgrade the quality of the teaching force in the school and are linked to the curriculum being taught.

For the very highest level of recognition as "good-to-great" schools, it will probably be necessary to go beyond paper submis-sions and provide for site visits to candidate schools during which classes can be observed, students and perhaps parents interviewed, and the overall quality of the education that the school offers be evaluated. Only some schools would be candidates for this recogni-tion, and the evaluation visits could be conducted periodically rather than yearly, thus keeping costs of the system down and keeping the incentive value of recognition up.

Models for this kind of practice exist in the education "inspection" systems of other countries and in the accreditation system that we use in America for higher education and private schools. We are propos-ing that it be viewed as the "capstone" level of a positive incentive system that can be used side by side with a reworked "sanctions" system and expanded forms of assessment. Title I law revised along these lines might well result in major strides in both excellence and equity and thus regain the professional and popular support that it once had.

Appendix 3.A Numeric Score Data for Figures 3.1 through 3.4, Disaggregated NAEP Scores through 2007

4th Grade Math	White	Black	Hispanic
1990	220	188	200
1992	227	193	202
1996	232	198	207
2000	234	203	208
2003	243	216	222
2005	246	220	226
2007	248	222	227

4th Grade Reading	White	Black	Hispanic
1992	224	192	197
1994	224	185	188
1998	225	193	193
2000	224	190	190
2002	229	199	201
2003	229	198	200
2005	229	200	203
2007	231	203	205

Continued on next page

Appendix 3A continued

8th Grade Math	White	Black	Hispanic
1990	270	237	246
1992	277	237	249
1996	281	240	251
2000	284	244	253
2003	288	252	259
2005	289	255	262
2007	291	260	265

8th Grade Reading	White	Black	Hispanic
1992	267	237	241
1994	267	236	243
1998	270	244	243
2002	272	245	247
2003	272	244	245
2005	271	243	246
2007	272	245	247

Source: U.S. Department of Education, Institute of Education Sciences, National Center for Education Statistics, National Assessment of Educational Progress (NAEP), NAEP Data Explorer, available online at http://nces.ed.gov/nationsreportcard.

4.

School Choice beyond District Borders:
Lessons for the Reauthorization of NCLB from Interdistrict Desegregation and Open Enrollment Plans

Jennifer Jellison Holme and Amy Stuart Wells

Over the last fifty years, school choice policies in the United States have come in many shapes and sizes, reflecting a wide array of goals and assumptions about the benefits of offering families more choice in education. For instance, in the 1960s and early 1970s, hundreds of public and private alternative schools were established, providing a more progressive, child-centered pedagogy than traditional schools. By the late 1970s and early 1980s, school choice options in the form of magnet schools and voluntary transfer plans became popular mechanisms for accomplishing school desegregation. The central goal of this "voluntary desegregation" was greater educational access and opportunities for African-American and Latino students while allowing all families more say in the type of schools that their children attended.[1]

More recently, in the last fifteen to twenty years, school choice policy has been promoted and widely expanded, based primarily on theories of market forces as mechanisms for improving academic performance in public schools.[2] Ignoring the many schools of choice established in the prior eras, leaders of this political movement claim that deregulated, market-driven choice policies break up the public education "monopoly" that allows educators to ignore students' needs. The lack of competition for students and the public funds allocated for their education is seen as the greatest weakness of the public education system. Over the last two decades, arguments for laissez-faire, free market school choice policies have fueled political movements to establish more charter schools, interdistrict open enrollment choice plans, and vouchers for private schools. The central goal of these programs is to insert market mechanisms into public education, forcing schools to compete for students, and, so the theory goes, lifting all boats.

This framework for rationalizing school choice policies provided the context within which the No Child Left Behind (NCLB) legislation was written, passed, and signed into law in 2002. Reflecting the popular free market ideology of the last two decades, NCLB also includes school choice policies as a mechanism to force failing schools to improve so that they can compete for students or risk "going out of business." More specifically, NCLB requires a school that is not meeting its state definition of adequate yearly progress (AYP) for two consecutive years to allow its students to choose any non-failing public school that has room for them.

At the same time, reflecting the more complicated political compromises out of which it grew, NCLB is more than just a competitive school choice policy. In fact, the most visible purpose of the complex federal law is to require that states, districts, and schools help all students achieve to high standards. In this way, NCLB has been promoted primarily in terms of its focus on "educational excellence" and what some would call "equity," because of the stress it places on the need for *all* students to achieve at high levels. Still, despite Congress's effort to provide increased competition as well as greater excellence and equity through NCLB, the equity promise of this legislation remains unfulfilled, particularly in relation to the school choice component of the law.

Indeed, the central argument of this chapter is that NCLB's use of school choice as a competitive mechanism to lift the educational boats of all children—even those from poor and racially isolated communities—comes up short as an equity measure for two important reasons. First of all, because it mandates school choice within a single district, NCLB is weak in creating cross-district choices and thus rarely helps children from isolated poor communities gain access to schools with more resources and fewer burdens. Second, the laissez-faire nature of NCLB's school choice provisions—in contrast to its highly regulated testing and accountability requirements—places most of the burden of gaining access to better schools on the families themselves and thus does little to guarantee students' meaningful access to better schools.

The end result of these two defining factors is that few children have worthwhile school choice opportunities under NCLB. Data on the first five years of NCLB implementation reveal that on average, across districts, less than 1 percent of students—only thirty-eight thousand out of four million—who were enrolled in schools that did not meet AYP for two straight years were able to transfer to a higher-performing school.[3] In fact, at best, NCLB has given a tiny percentage of the children attending low-achieving public schools limited school choices, most of which are only marginally higher performing than the schools they left.[4]

Meanwhile, as NCLB has failed to provide meaningful school choices to the most disadvantaged students in poor school districts, a dwindling number of the older, equity-minded school choice policies, including voluntary interdistrict school desegregation plans that allow students to cross school-district boundaries, are still in existence. These programs, operating under the radar screen of the market-based school choice political frenzy of the last two decades, have been providing meaningful alternatives to students in failing schools and serving as reminders of reasons—aside from competition—for providing choice to students. Below we compare such equity-minded, cross-district, choice-oriented school desegregation plans to more recent interdistrict free market school choice policies known as open enrollment plans; we make the case that policy makers might want to look back to an earlier era of school choice policies for solutions to the failures of current policies.

There is ample evidence that the voluntary interdistrict school desegregation plans have been more successful at providing educational opportunities to poor students of color in failing neighborhood schools. They do this through regulations that assure the historical victims of discrimination have the most choice and that school officials facilitate that choice across separate and unequal school districts via guaranteed access, outreach, recruitment, and transportation. And yet, while the social science evidence is clearly in favor of interdistrict voluntary school desegregation and against free market open enroll-ment plans, these findings have done little to put a damper on political enthusiasm for the latter or resistance to the former.

Meanwhile, in 2007 the U.S. Supreme Court made such interdis-trict voluntary integration plans much more difficult—although still not impossible—to construct with its decision in the Louisville and Seattle school desegregation cases. In these cases, a majority of the justices ruled that school districts, unless they are under a court order to desegregate, cannot consider the racial classification of individual students as they assign them to schools.

Still, even with the political and legal winds blowing against inter-district desegregation cases, we argue that these equity-minded volun-tary desegregation plans are worth revisiting as policy makers begin to contemplate the many reasons why the market-based, competitive model of school choice policies is intellectually and empirically bank-rupt. Yet, at the same time, the older, equity-minded school choice programs created as part of an effort to desegregate schools, and thus serve those historically marginalized in public schools, remain models of what NCLB could accomplish for students in failing schools through choice provisions of another, less competitive sort.

WHY NCLB SCHOOL CHOICE PROVISIONS PROVIDE LITTLE CHOICE

Under the NCLB legislation, school districts are required to provide students in schools labeled "in need of improvement" according to their state's measure of adequate yearly progress (AYP) for two consec-utive years the opportunity to transfer to a higher performing school, with transportation provided or with transportation costs reimbursed through federal funding for Title I, compensatory education. As stated in the NCLB legislation itself, the school district, or "local educational agency," shall, no later than the first day of the school year following the year in which a failing school has been identified as such, "provide all students enrolled in the school with the option to transfer to an-other public school served by the local educational agency."[5]

NCLB also states that the local educational agency shall give prior-ity to "the lowest achieving children from low-income families" for these choice options, although there are no guidelines to assure this happens.[6] And in circumstances in which districts lack available space in non-improvement schools, NCLB calls for the creation of "cooperative agreements" between districts to allow interdistrict transfers.[7]

As a result of these requirements and options, at the time that NCLB was passed, many pundits predicted that districts would be inundated with a flood of transfer requests and that the challenge was going to be how to handle them.[8] Yet, in reality, the number of students who have requested school transfers under the NCLB choice requirements has been extremely low. While there is no comprehensive national data on school choice transfers under NCLB, surveys and case studies by the federal government and independent researchers have shown that very few students who were eligible for transfers have enrolled in non-failing schools. For example, according to the U.S. Department of Education (DOE), less than 1 percent of eligible students actually participated in NCLB school choice in both the 2002–3 and 2003–4 school years.[9]

Furthermore, several additional surveys of school districts with large populations of poor students of color suggest that the transfer rates are very low—consistently less than 6 percent of eligible students. For instance, according to a 2006 study by the Council of the Great City Schools (2006), in the 2005–6 school year, just 2.1 percent of all students eligible for transfers in thirty-six urban school districts surveyed actually requested transfers, and only 1.7 percent actually moved to another school.[10] Similarly, the Citizens' Commission on Civil Rights found that in 2002–3, just 2.4 percent of eligible students were able to transfer to better-performing schools; the following year, that percentage increased to only 5.5 percent.[11] And finally, a Harvard Civil Rights Project study of NCLB in ten predominantly poor school districts found that less than 10 percent of eligible students in each district actually requested a transfer. In fact, in seven of the ten districts studied, less than 2 percent of the eligible students requested transfers.[12]

Many observers attribute the low participation rate in NCLB-sanctioned school choice to the unwillingness of officials in school districts with many failing schools to adequately inform parents of other options or to make enough choices available.[13] Yet, our review of the research on school choice policy, racial segregation, and inequality suggests that the true failure of NCLB choice lies in the limitations of the policy itself. More specifically, we argue that there are two central reasons for this lack of school choice under NCLB.

First, the lack of meaningful interdistrict options in NCLB means that the reality for most students in failing public schools is that their choices are limited to schools in the same poor and racially segregated school districts in which they reside. Such districts more often than not have many failing schools and few seats in a limited number of non-failing schools.

In fact, the demographic trends in many metropolitan areas over the past thirty years have resulted in high concentrations of poverty in "inner-city" urban communities and, increasingly, in poor and racially segregated "inner-ring" suburban school districts. Thus, in both poor urban and poor suburban communities children attend separate and unequal public schools, shut off by political boundaries from the opportunities available in more affluent school districts.[14]

And while NCLB encourages the expansion of choice options for students in poor districts through cooperative agreements between lower- and higher-performing districts, the legislation neither requires nor provides funding for those kinds of arrangements; as a result, they have been rare, and many students who live in high-poverty, segregated districts end up with few if any real choices.

Second, as with most laissez-faire or free market school choice policies of this era, the burden of securing a seat in a non-failing school under NCLB is placed almost entirely on the student and parent, while the decision of which (if any) students to accept from failing schools is made by officials in the non-failing schools. Unlike the most successful voluntary school desegregation programs we discuss below, there is no mandate for—or commitment to—taking students from low-achieving schools on the part of these higher achieving school districts. Thus, in a strictly market-oriented system poor students of color routinely lack access to better schools.[15]

Clearly, the status quo is not working. It is time to reconceptualize the school choice policies within NCLB. In examining the research on these two types of cross-district school choice programs, we conclude that if policy makers want to provide students in failing schools with meaningful choice through NCLB, they need to, first and foremost, construct a choice policy that assures that more students cross school-district boundary lines, which divide the world of public education into haves and have-nots. At the same time, they need to rethink the competitive free market model as the best way to structure more equal opportunities for students who have had the fewest opportunities. Research on both equity-minded, interdistrict school desegregation programs and free market, interdistrict, open enrollment school choice laws strongly suggests that more, not less, regulation of, and/ or incentives for, the receiving schools, is needed to assure meaningful choice and access for disadvantaged students. In addition, more outreach, information, and support, particularly transportation, are needed to help parents choose new and better schools for their children.

Moreover, these two key aspects of meaningful school choice policy that are missing from NCLB are intertwined and interconnected. In other words, school choice policies that are going to be most successful in helping students escape poor schools and districts will need to be more cooperative and supportive, as opposed to competitive and laissez-faire. They must bring educators and local officials together across dividing lines to work toward common causes, and they must assure that families are provided the necessary scaffolding to cross the deep divisions between communities.

THE PROBLEM OF WITHIN-DISTRICT CHOICE IN HIGH-POVERTY SCHOOL DISTRICTS: THE LOW SUPPLY OF NON-FAILING SCHOOLS

Once it became clear that the NCLB student transfer rates were well below predictions, observers, especially supporters of the deregulated choice provision in NCLB, began blaming officials in districts with high numbers of failing students.[16] Yet we argue that simply blaming low transfer rates under NCLB on district officials is not fair given what we know about the larger context of schools and the societal inequality reflected in the educational system.[17] For instance, the concentration of poverty in this country and the correlation between student achievement and such poverty clearly contributes to the lack of choice that students in failing schools have. As Clotfelter has demonstrated statistically, the more likely a school district is to have one or more failing schools under NCLB, the less likely that district is to have many non-failing schools and the closer its non-failing schools will be to not meeting AYP.[18] In fact, the U.S. Department of Education and other researchers have documented cases in a number

of districts in which the "better performing" schools were not significantly better—at least in terms of test scores—than the so-called
failing schools.[19]

For example, the 2006 DOE report found that in their national
sample of case study districts, many officials in urban districts
with large numbers of failing schools were forced to offer choices
of schools that themselves were just one year away from being targeted for program-improvement status. An earlier U.S. Government
Accountability Office (GAO) study also found that in districts with
"high proportions of Title I schools, the majority of the schools
offered as transfer options were often demographically similar
to those attended by students eligible for transfer. Specifically, the
schools offered as transfer options served many poor students and
had high minority populations."[20]

Not surprisingly, this "supply problem" is most acute in urban
core districts with large numbers of failing schools.[21] Indeed, the 2006
U.S. Department of Education evaluation showed that, although
urban districts house just 36 percent of the nation's Title I schools,
two-thirds of all schools identified for improvement were in those
districts. According to the Citizens' Commission on Civil Rights,
in many urban school districts "the number of schools in need of
improvement is so large that there literally are not enough successful
schools from which to choose."[22]

Researchers and journalists have reported on dozens of districts—particularly urban and inner-ring suburban districts—that
were unable to accommodate the transfer requests that they received
due to the lack of available space in better-performing schools.
According to a case study of Los Angeles Unified, for example, the
district granted only 175 of the 513 requests—34 percent—that it
received for transfers in 2003–4, and Chicago granted less than 5
percent of requested transfers that same year.[23] Similar problems
have been noted in Detroit as well.[24]

Meanwhile, in some districts, reporters found that there were literally no schools that were *not* identified as failing at particular grade
levels. For example, in Providence, Rhode Island, and Richmond
County, Georgia, all the schools at some grade levels were deemed
as failing; thus, there were literally no schools that were eligible to
accept transfers.[25] These problems were predictably most severe
in large urban school districts, although some problems were also
found in remote rural districts with no other schools available to

receive transfers or where distances between schools were too far for students to travel.

Even when districts have a mix of failing and non-failing schools, officials often fear that placing too many students from failing schools into the schools that are meeting AYP requirements—often just barely—would lead to overcrowding and lower achievement rates for all students in non-failing schools.[26] As a result, many districts deny student transfers, in violation of the law—and under the threat of lawsuits—because of limited capacity in schools making AYP. In San Diego, for instance, only six of the district's twenty-three middle schools were not categorized as in need of improvement; thus, these non-failing schools lacked the capacity to handle all the transfer requests from the other schools.[27]

Many policy analysts have viewed this "low supply" problem of too few non-failing schools in high-poverty districts as a technical problem that requires a technical solution, such as modifying NCLB choice regulations to ensure district compliance. According to the U.S. secretary of education, Margaret Spellings, when she learned of the low rates of eligible student transfers through the 2006 Department of Education report, "We want to ensure that districts are living up to their responsibilities to notify parents about their options in a timely and easy to understand way. And there are a number of steps we can take to enforce these provisions, including withholding federal funds."[28]

Reflecting the market metaphor of NCLB, the focus of U.S. Department of Education officials has been on creating more "supply" but still within the limited confines of the existing legislation. For instance, in 2004 the Department of Education issued regulations stating that a district's lack of capacity is not an excuse for denying students choices under NCLB (34 C.F.R. 200.44[d]). Subsequent non-regulatory guidelines issued by the department encourage districts to "create" capacity: "If an LEA does not have sufficient capacity in its schools that are not identified for improvement (or as persistently dangerous) to accommodate the demand for transfers by all eligible students, the LEA must create additional capacity or provide choices of other schools."[29]

According to this federal document, suggestions for creating additional capacity in non-failing schools include reconfiguring classrooms, redrawing attendance zones, adding portable classrooms, or creating new charter schools or distance learning programs. More recently, the Aspen Institute's Commission on NCLB also suggested technical solutions to the capacity problem by recommending that schools making AYP be required to offer 10 percent of their seats for students from NCLB choice-eligible schools; they also suggested that districts audit schools to ensure space that is made available.[30]

Yet proposals that conceptualize the failure of NCLB choice as a simple technical problem fail to acknowledge not only the limited capacity within high-poverty school districts, but also the reality that students have little incentive to transfer out of their home schools for what may only be marginally better educational opportunities.[31] We argue, therefore, that neither the supply nor the demand problems of NCLB choice are a function of simple district recalcitrance, but rather the products of severe inequality and racial and social-class segregation across district boundaries. Furthermore, the failure of federal policy makers to recognize the complex relationship between demographic shifts, growing poverty concentration, district boundaries, and student achievement will inevitably leave NCLB choice a hollow and unfulfilled promise.

WHEN "ALLOWING" INTERDISTRICT CHOICE IS NOT ENOUGH: THE HIGH BARRIERS BETWEEN INCREASINGLY SEPARATE AND UNEQUAL SPACES

As we noted earlier, while NCLB does not prohibit interdistrict transfers—in fact, the law "encourages" cross-district choice—it offers no incentives for school districts with few or no failing schools to enter into agreements with high-poverty districts that lack capacity to provide better choices for their students. As a result, such arrangements have been extremely rare.[32] In fact, the 2004 GAO report on the implementation of NCLB's school choice provision noted that "where districts lack other schools to offer as transfer options, districts are required, to the extent practicable, to make transfer agreements with neighboring districts, but we are not aware of any locations where such interdistrict transfers have occurred."[33]

These agreements between districts were no more common several years into the implementation of NCLB choice, according to a 2006 U.S. Department of Education evaluation. This report found that during the 2003–4 school year, a very small percentage of the fifteen case-study districts had instituted these agreements and that they were quite unpopular among receiving districts. In addition, this report found that only 9 percent of 1,179 school districts that offered Title I choice and had responded to a national survey reported negotiating transfer agreements with neighboring districts. The DOE report concluded that "data suggested that currently these options are not attractive to receiving districts or parents."[34] The DOE report, however, contained little information about the details of these rare interdistrict agreements, and unfortunately no research to date has evaluated these plans either in terms of their implementation or the outcomes for students.

Clearly, then, in spite of efforts by some urban district administrators to find open space in neighboring districts, the bulk of NCLB choice is limited to within-district choice. These de facto intra-district restrictions on choice under NCLB, when overlaid on growing between-district segregation by both income and race, essentially shut students in poor school districts out of better-performing schools. Meanwhile, given the growing inequality across school-district lines, school choice simply for the sake of choice means very little unless these policies can enable student transfers out of impoverished schools and spaces.[35]

THE CHANGING NATURE OF EDUCATIONAL INEQUALITY. In the early part of the twentieth century, before millions of whites moved from cities to suburbs, school segregation tended to be within districts. In other words, fifty years ago individual school districts had, on average, more diverse—racially, ethnically, and socioeconomically—student populations, even as these students were often segregated from one another into separate schools within their home districts. The form and structure of school segregation has evolved over time: white families fled large urban school districts between 1950 and 1980 and enrolled their children in separate suburban school districts. In fact, the vast majority of school segregation—84 percent as of 2000—is now *between districts*.[36] As a result, lower-income students of color are now less likely to be segregated from more affluent white students within the same district; these two student populations are now more likely to be enrolled in schools in different districts altogether.

This spike in between-district segregation is reflected in broader demographic analyses that show that, while racial segregation has decreased by only a small amount since its peak in 1970, social-class segregation has in fact increased at the local, neighborhood level. In other words, a new layer of social-class segregation has been laid down on the ongoing racial segregation, leading to a situation in which poor families of color are the most isolated of all.[37] For example, one analysis of state, regional, and neighborhood level census data found that in the metropolitan areas studied, "The net increase in neighborhood-level class dissimilarity between 1970 and 2000 was about 30 percent."[38] The study concludes, "As rich and poor families came to inhabit the same regions, states, and metropolitan areas, therefore, they simultaneously moved into different neighborhoods."[39]

According to the sociologist Saskia Sassen, the global economy helps explain this phenomenon.[40] She writes that so-called global cities such as New York, San Francisco, and Chicago are home to "producer service" firms that rely heavily on a bifurcated workforce of well-educated and well-paid professionals on one end of the spectrum and, on the other, poorly educated, poorly paid hourly workers, who support the professionals by cooking, cleaning, and catering to their needs. These two classes of codependent employees must live in the same metropolitan areas, in close proximity to their shared work sites. They rarely live in the same local neighborhoods or municipalities, however, or send their children to the same schools. Increasingly, the well-paid professionals are living either in high-cost gentrified areas of the cities or in outer-ring suburbs or exurbs, where well-paid jobs are found in shiny new office parks. Meanwhile, the poorly paid workers are living in the high-poverty pockets of the cities or in the inner-ring, working-class suburbs where they can commute into the city or out to the office parks.[41] This so-called donut effect—with poor people and people of color surrounded by more affluent white residents on both sides—caused by changing housing patterns and socioeconomic segregation that these changes breed, has lead to increasing the concentrated poverty within particular communities and among particular racial/ethnic groups, especially Latinos.[42]

Related to this donut effect, researchers have discovered that while concentrated poverty was largely confined to inner cities in the 1990s, by 2000 this concentrated poverty had spread into "first" or "inner-ring" suburbs—the older, inner-ring suburbs bordering central cities, which currently house 20 percent of the nation's residents.[43] These inner-ring suburbs have the fastest growing rates of black, Latino, and (in some instances) Asian residents and a corresponding decrease in white residents, as well as rapidly growing rates of immigration. In the nation's one hundred largest metropolitan areas, these first-suburbs also have had significant increases in the percentages of residents living in concentrated poverty between 1990 and 2000.[44]

Many of these suburbs house separate school districts, and the demographics of the public schools reflect—and oftentimes portend—demographic changes happening within the local communities.[45] This is particularly true in the more "fragmented" metropolitan regions in the Northeast and Midwest, which contain a larger number of smaller, self-contained school districts that encompass separate and unequal geographic units. These trends have been reflected in district- and school-level segregation in recent years, as an increasing number of suburban school districts that were racially diverse are now experiencing the white and middle-class flight that the urban districts experienced several decades ago.[46]

Taken together, these data regarding ongoing racial segregation, coupled with an increase in social-class segregation at the community level and the growth in low-income families in inner-ring suburban communities, shed light on the "spatial" and "supply" problem of NCLB choice. Looking across metropolitan areas, we see that poverty and its negative effects on school districts reflect such high levels of segregation by race and class that the poorer districts simply lack more than a handful of "better-performing schools." In fact, according to the U.S. Department of Education, while only 41 percent of Title I schools in the United States were in the highest-poverty districts, 73 percent of program improvement schools were in those districts.[47]

Understanding these demographic shifts affecting poor school districts within and just beyond city limits explains the need for broader, metropolitan-wide solutions to reoccurring patterns of racial and social-class segregation. In fact, it is quite clear that unless NCLB choice options facilitate the student transfer across boundary lines that distinguish separate and unequal school districts, they will do little to create more meaningful choices.

THE LAISSEZ-FAIRE NATURE OF NCLB SCHOOL CHOICE PROVISIONS: FALSE PROMISES FOR POOR, ISOLATED STUDENTS

Policymakers who want to expand access to high-performing schools need to modify the scope and framework of NCLB school choice options to include more affluent suburban districts *and* assure more meaningful access for disadvantaged students in

better-performing schools. As we noted above, the existing NCLB legislation encourages districts to set up interdistrict transfer programs
"to the extent practicable." Yet it is the laissez-faire, market-driven
nature of the policy that places far too much of the burden of making
these transfers happen on the shoulders of disadvantaged families
with children in low-performing schools or on officials in the districts
that these students want to flee. Either way, it is clear that these are
not the actors with the "market" power or the ability in most cases
to make these transfers happen; thus, for the most part, they do not
occur. According to Lewin, "Absent regulation, uncontrolled school
choice, such as that mandated in the NCLBA, will simply become
another mechanism by which we maintain our system of separate
and unequal public schools."[48]

Without concrete incentives for the more affluent and higher-performing school districts to participate, they are unlikely to do this on
their own. In fact, many parents and officials in urban and first-sub-
urban districts have been outright rejected in their efforts to get more
affluent suburban districts to open up spaces for students from failing schools. As the 2004 Citizens' Commission on Civil Rights study
found, "some districts around the country with inadequate numbers
of high performing schools asked neighboring districts if they would
take transfers under NCLB from schools in their districts, but they
got negative responses."[49] The study also found that many poor districts did not even ask better-performing districts to accept interdistrict
transfers because they assumed that their requests would be denied.

Local and regional newspaper articles across the country illustrate the CCCR report's findings. For example, in Providence, Rhode
Island, more than a dozen middle school parents requested a suburban
middle school enroll their children because all the middle schools in
Providence had been deemed failing; they were turned away.[50] Lancaster,
Pennsylvania, school-district officials were also turned down when they
asked suburban school districts to open up slots for their students after
they themselves had run out of space in their non-failing schools.[51]
Suburban districts proved equally resistant to accepting transfer students from Pennsylvania's Chester Upland School District—in which
all schools were deemed in need of improvement.

Clearly, a more systemic, proactive approach to providing students
in failing schools and districts with meaningful options to transfer to
higher-achieving schools needs to be developed. Perhaps what the free
market advocates of school choice policies did not realize is that some

students are—or are perceived to be—harder to educate than others because they come to school at a disadvantage, in particular due to their social-class backgrounds. What the students bring with them, beyond their per-pupil funding, is also subject to the laws of supply and demand, which are defined in the eyes of those in a position of power—for example, those who control access to high-achieving schools. What incentive do school districts have, under a strictly competitive, free market framework, to take on students who may well, at least in the short run, harm their positioning in the race for the highest test scores? In a policy era in which schools and districts are regularly ranked according to test scores in local newspapers, what incentives do higher-performing schools have to welcome low-performing students? In other words, do competitive school choice models that lack any incentive or support for districts to take students from failing schools create better schools for all students or do they lessen the chances for students deemed to be less competitive?[52]

There is ample social science evidence, discussed in more detail below, that laissez-faire school choice policies such as interdistrict open enrollment choice plans, voucher programs, and charter schools create opportunities for schools of choice to select students from local communities who are privileged to some degree—in terms of their parents' education, involvement in their education, or social networks, and so on—relative to other students in their neighborhood public school.[53] At the same time, these free market school choice policies have failed to improve student achievement, even after the choice schools have selected students and successfully denied access to more troubled students or those with special education needs.[54]

More equity-minded and less competitive school choice policies might include provisions to improve the schools left behind in the poor districts, which serve those students who cannot or do not wish to transfer out; furthermore, these policies may even attract students from more affluent districts to dynamic urban or inner-ring suburban schools. Some, but not all, of the interdistrict school desegregation plans that we highlight below have offered such meaningful school choices for several decades now.

As we show in the following sections, in which we discuss the type of infrastructure created to support interdistrict school desegregation, many parents and students require a supportive infrastructure to make meaningful choices of schools across many miles and district boundaries. For instance, agencies that conduct outreach and counseling to families sending their children to schools far away are critical to the success of such school choice plans, as is free round-trip transportation.

Laissez-faire choice policies do not create meaningful choice or competition because for the market to actually work, each family would need to gather information on dozens of districts and perhaps hundreds of potential schools and then individually negotiate access to their schools of choice at the same time that they arrange for their own transportation—even if the cost of that transportation will be reimbursed. Such a process of market consumption would be overwhelming even for the best-resourced family with time and money to spare. For poor families who regularly lack both spare time and money, it is an absurdity.[55]

Furthermore, there is some evidence that the students "left behind" in schools eligible for NCLB choice have *already* been left behind not only by housing segregation but also by existing choice policies. For example, the 2006 report of the Council of the Great City Schools found that all but five of the thirty-six districts it studied already offered students some form of choice.[56] As a result, students who remain in NCLB choice-eligible schools may well be those least likely to take advantage of choice options in the first place.[57] Creating more supportive policies with outreach and recruitment may well be essential to school choice assuring all students are taught to high standards under NCLB.

The Potential (and Perils) of Interdistrict School Choice: Different Goals, Different Designs, and Different Outcomes

In the first section of this chapter, we argued that the existing NCLB school choice provisions are simply not enough to help even a small percentage of students in failing schools because they impose de facto limits on students' choices of schools within high-poverty districts and are far too laissez-faire in their design to support meaningful student access to non-failing schools. In this second section we examine two forms of school choice that are both designed to overcome the first shortcoming of NCLB choice by providing cross-district choices to students. They are starkly different, however, in relation to the second limitation.

For this chapter, then, we have reviewed the research on the two most popular types of interdistrict school choice policies: interdistrict open enrollment and interdistrict desegregation. Through our comparative analysis of these two types of plans, we show how interdistrict policies have the potential to increase student achievement and address inequality as long as they are carefully designed—not in a laissez-faire manner, but in a way that assures more access and opportunities to those who have historically had the least, namely low-income students of color.

Through this analysis we are able to underscore a central argument of this chapter and school choice research in general: "design matters" in school choice policy. As we will show, the fundamental differences in the goals and thus the details of these two vastly distinct interdistrict choice policies have shaped dramatic differences in their outcomes for students. These disparate goals, designs, and outcomes offer extremely important lessons to policy makers in their reauthorization of the school choice provisions of NCLB.

INTERDISTRICT OPEN ENROLLMENT AND INTERDISTRICT DESEGREGATION: CONTRASTING HISTORIES, IDEOLOGIES, AND GOALS

While interdistrict desegregation and interdistrict open enrollment plans are similar in theory— they both offer students choices of schools outside their home districts—they are dramatically different in origin, and thus in their central purpose and intent. Indeed, each of these two different types of interdistrict policies grew out of distinct historical circumstances, and, as a result, they embody dissimilar visions of the nature of educational inequality and opportunity.

INTERDISTRICT OPEN ENROLLMENT PLANS: THE LAISSEZ-FAIRE APPROACH TO CHOICE AND ITS UNEQUAL OUTCOMES. Interdistrict open enrollment plans are a product of the 1990s policy efforts to improve public education by subjecting schools to competitive market forces. These market-based choice policies rest on the assumption that "the incentives and dynamics of the marketplace must be brought to bear if we are to effect real change in our education system."[58]

During the 1990s, as policy makers placed growing faith in the ability of market forces to transform public education, many states passed interdistrict "open enrollment" choice policies that allowed students to transfer between school districts. These policies were explicitly intended to "encourage competition among districts as a means of fostering improvement in public schools, and to provide families with increased flexibility in their educational choices."[59]

While these policies are not designed specifically to expand opportunity for disadvantaged students in urban schools, advocates of market-based school reform claim that they are implicitly about that by using market forces to liberate students from the low-performing schools and thus spurring educational improvement by forcing schools to compete for clients.

These programs, implemented via state legislation, are far more pervasive than the interdistrict desegregation plans described below: as of 2007, nearly all fifty states had interdistrict open enrollment policies on the books, with most of these laws passed in the last fifteen years. Between 1993 and 2003 (the most recent year that data are available), the number of states with interdistrict choice legislation grew from 14 to 42 (plus Puerto Rico), and enrollment in these plans grew from 208,000 in 1993–94 to more than 487,000 students in 1999–2000—more than the number of students enrolled in charter schools and voucher programs combined that year.[60] By the early twenty-first century, nearly half of all school districts in the country—43 percent—had students transferring out to another district through open enrollment plans, while nearly half—46 percent—accepted students from other districts.[61]

These policies do, in theory, have the potential to grant disadvantaged students in low performing urban districts access to higher performing schools in other school districts. But the research evidence that we present below indicates that these policies have had, thus far, the opposite effect. In other words, open enrollment plans have allowed more advantaged students to transfer to relatively more advantaged school systems, thereby exacerbating inequality between school districts.

VOLUNTARY INTERDISTRICT SCHOOL DESEGREGATION PROGRAMS: SCHOOL CHOICE POLICIES WITH AN EQUITY AGENDA. In contrast to the laissez-faire nature of the open enrollment school choice policies, the handful of interdistrict school desegregation programs that exist across the country were designed explicitly to provide greater educational opportunities for students of color trapped in low-achieving schools in poor and segregated school districts. Indeed, in St. Louis, Missouri; Boston, Massachusetts; Hartford, Connecticut; Rochester, New York; the mid-Peninsula section of the San Francisco Bay area, California: Milwaukee, Wisconsin; Indianapolis, Indiana; and Minneapolis, Minnesota (see Table 4.1), elementary and secondary school students have been crossing school-district boundaries—in some cases for forty years now—in an effort to both improve educational equity and bring students together across color and class lines.[62]

What most starkly differentiates voluntary interdistrict school desegregation programs from more recently implemented laissez-faire school choice policies such as interdistrict open enrollment plans, therefore, is that the desegregation plans are skewed in favor of students who are disadvantaged because of their race/ethnicity and/or social class and are guided by the goal of ensuring that these students have access to better schools. In other words, while open enrollment plans are designed to force schools to compete for students—at least those students with the resources and ability to choose new schools—interdistrict desegregation plans are designed to remedy the harms of past discrimination against communities of color and to help the most disadvantaged students cross racial and social class boundaries to attend schools with more resources and opportunities.

Overall, these unique cross-district desegregation programs are small in scale—serving somewhere between five hundred and ten thousand students each—compared to the number of potential students who could benefit from such interdistrict school choices in these metropolitan areas. Furthermore, in almost all of these programs, the number of students served has dwindled over the years, as political and legal support for interdistrict school desegregation has waned, despite evidence that such plans provide more choice and meaningful educational opportunities to disadvantaged students than the newer, market-oriented open enrollment choice plans described above. Several of these interdistrict desegregation plans are on the verge of extinction if the federal government or another major funder does not intervene in the near future.

Yet, part of the "political problem" with these desegregation programs in the current context is that they are clearly distinct from the more popular free market school choice policy counterparts, particularly the open enrollment interdistrict choice plans. In fact, their common mission of correcting past wrongs through concrete, equity-minded tactics stands in direct opposition to a reliance on laissez-faire market forces. Meanwhile, this shared sense of mission and focus on equity across these eight voluntary interdistrict programs is noteworthy because they have disparate legal and policy origins.

For instance, Milwaukee's Chapter 220 program, Indianapolis's Marion County Integration plan, and St. Louis's Voluntary Transfer program were all initiated via federal school desegregation cases in which judges found that urban school officials and/or state governments had violated the Fourteenth Amendment rights of African-American students. Still, such federal court orders that remedy urban school-district segregation with interdistrict desegregation plans are anomalies in light of the Supreme Court's 1974 ruling in the *Milliken v. Bradley* case. In this ruling, the Supreme Court stated that suburban school districts could be ordered to participate in interdistrict school desegregation plans only if they themselves were found guilty of creating the cross-district segregation that defines every metropolitan area across the country. This is a difficult legal hurdle to clear when urban/suburban segregation is created and maintained as much by housing policies and real estate practices as it is by school districts. Therefore, the three interdistrict desegregation programs put in place by federal courts in Milwaukee, Indianapolis, and St. Louis all got around these legal obstacles in creative ways that are not widely replicable. Furthermore, in light of the U.S. Supreme Court ruling in the Louisville and Seattle cases in the summer of 2007, these legal hurdles have become even greater. Still, we argue that even these challenges are not necessarily insurmountable if such policies were to be created via federal legislation as we discuss below.

With limited options available for interdistrict transfers via federal court cases and with the growing cross-district segregation we discussed above, other more recently established interdistrict plans were derived from desegregation cases brought in state courts, where state constitutional guarantees of an adequate education apply. As a result, the state-ordered interdistrict transfer plans in Hartford and Minneapolis—the Project Choice program and The Choice Is Yours program—are both interdistrict school desegregation cases *and* fiscal equity cases. In other words, these cases address both the need for the most disadvantaged students in poor urban school districts to have school choices beyond their district boundaries and the need for a more equitable distribution of resources and opportunities across these same boundaries in order for states to maintain their constitutional guarantees to all students. The other interdistrict school desegregation plan derived from a state court case—the Tinsley Transfer plan in the Palo Alto area—was strictly focused on desegregation because California had already implemented a fiscal equity remedy through a separate case.

And still two additional interdistrict plans discussed in this chapter—the Boston Metropolitan Council for Educational Opportunity (METCO) program and the Rochester Urban-suburban Interdistrict Transfer program—came about without court orders at all, but rather through the efforts of advocates and state and local officials who were trying to avoid court cases. Ironically, these two programs are the oldest and longest-standing programs.

In fact, regardless of whether these programs were court ordered, they all require support from state policy makers and officials—support that could be garnered via federal support for such state-level efforts. As we explain in the next three sections of this chapter, "state support" for interdistrict school desegregation—whether coerced via a court order or brought about through the political process—has at least three critical components: guaranteed access for transferring students, outreach to families eligible for choice, and free and easily available transportation across school-district boundaries. Each of the eight programs we review in this chapter varies in terms of how much support they have from their state governments on these three critical components. The larger and most successful plans have had strong state support in each of these areas. The plans that have not been as successful thus far need more state support in one or more of these areas.

DIFFERENCES IN DESIGN: HOW DISPARATE GOALS LEAD TO DISPARATE SUPPORTS FOR DISADVANTAGED STUDENTS ACROSS CHOICE PROGRAMS

The differences in the historical roots, ideologies, and goals of interdistrict open enrollment and voluntary interdistrict desegregation plans have led to fundamental differences in the design of the two types of policies and supports for disadvantaged students. For instance, because the interdistrict school desegregation plans embody a mission of correcting past wrongs by guaranteeing the most choice to students who have the least, these plans are designed to facilitate a shift in power from those with resources to succeed in the free market to those who have been disadvantaged in that market due to discrimination, segregation, and lack of economic and political resources. Simply put, desegregation plans redistribute opportunities while free market open enrollment plans reinforce many of the existing market-based inequalities. This distinction can make all the difference in the world.

INEQUITABLE BY DESIGN: HOW INTERDISTRICT OPEN ENROLLMENT CHOICE LAWS CURRENTLY STRUCTURE OPPORTUNITY. Because open enrollment policies grew largely out of a belief that competition would lead to improved outcomes for all students, they have very few supports built in for disadvantaged students in the areas in which social science research suggests it is critical to give such students and families an advantage in the choice process. In this section of the chapter we examine several aspects of the design of such interdistrict open enrollment choice programs to illustrate these fundamental differences between them and their school desegregation counterparts. Most important, we explore the issues of student access, parental information, transportation, monitoring, and incentives to ensure suburban district participation. In each of these areas, the market-based open enrollment plans come up short in assuring choice for those who historically have had the least.

Unfettered Choices via Interdistrict Open Enrollment Plans Lead to Unequal Participation: Few Preferences for Disadvantaged Students or Restrictions against Segregation. One of the most clear-cut distinctions between interdistrict school desegregation and interdistrict open enrollment choice laws is the extent to which they contain provisions that give preferences to particular subgroups of students or restrictions about which types of students can transfer. For the most part, the open enrollment choice programs are open to whoever wants to and is able to participate. The exceptions to that rule are two states—Kentucky and Louisiana—that designed their interdistrict choice programs specifically to serve students in low-performing schools.[63] Minnesota's open enrollment law, as we explain below, is now interwoven with an interdistrict choice program aimed at low-income students in the city of Minneapolis— The Choice Is Yours program. Thus, in Minneapolis only, the open enrollment program is targeted at poor students, who are supposed to be given preference for admission by suburban districts. Still, nonpoor students can also transfer out to the suburbs, and many do.

Meanwhile, in the other thirty-eight states plus Puerto Rico, no such restrictions are placed on participation. In fact, some states, such as Georgia, explicitly permit receiving school districts to establish "admissions requirements" for interdistrict transfer students in a manner that actually lessens the opportunities of poorer and more disadvantaged students. Indiana and Missouri also permit districts to charge transferring students tuition—a provision that will bar many low-income families.

While most open enrollment laws require interdistrict choices to be in compliance with existing desegregation orders where they exist, just five states—Arkansas, California, Ohio, New Jersey, and Wisconsin—explicitly prohibit transfers that adversely affect the racial balance of the sending or receiving districts. Florida's law, meanwhile, contains less forceful language, requiring that each district's choice plan contain provisions to maintain racial and economic balance. Iowa's law mandates that preferences be given to transfers that would facilitate voluntary desegregation plans. Yet, it is unclear whether even these limited equity provisions are being monitored or enforced, or what impact the Supreme Court's decision in the Seattle and Louisville cases will have on the states' ability to enforce them.

Thus, by and large, the vast majority of the interdistrict open enrollment choice laws have few if any mechanisms to foster the participation of disadvantaged students. As a result, as our review of the research below demonstrates, disadvantaged students and students of color are the least likely to choose.

No Incentives, No Participation: The Social Construction of "Capacity" in Suburban Districts Equals Limited Choices for Urban Students via Open Enrollment Plans. The potential of interdistrict open enrollment choice to create opportunities for students in troubled schools and districts has been limited in many states by provisions allowing districts to refuse to accept transfers. In other words, while most state open enrollment choice laws mandate that districts cannot *prevent* students from transferring out, they do not require districts to *accept* students who want to transfer in.[64] In fact, state open enrollment laws provide few incentives for middle-class or affluent school districts to participate. After all, these policies were not designed with the explicit goal of opening up opportunities for poor students of color.

The more competitive nature of these school choice policies makes it less likely that the neediest students will gain greater access to high-performing schools. NCLB accountability pressures likely play an additional role, as the districts have even less incentive to serve students who may have lower levels of academic performance. Why, in such a highly competitive environment with a heavy focus on student "outcomes" simply defined as test scores, would many schools or districts choose to accept students with lower test scores and more disadvantage?

To make matters worse, many districts have large financial incentives to reject interdistrict transfers. For instance, while open enrollment laws generally allow for the per-pupil funding from the student's home district to transfer with them, few provide any meaningful financial incentives for affluent suburban districts with higher per-pupil funding to accept the harder-to-serve students from poorer districts. Thus, some of these laws actually make it costly for districts to accept out-of-district transfers—and thus even less likely that districts would accept more disadvantaged students. In fact, because of these laissez-faire funding formulas, these laws are skewed against students from poorer districts trying to gain access to more affluent schools.

As a result, our review of the literature suggests that middle-class and affluent suburban school districts that are adjacent to poorer districts are most likely to deny requests from interdistrict transfer students. Michigan's law, for example, allows suburban districts to avoid accepting students from urban schools by declaring themselves closed to interdistrict transfers, by forging their own agreements with other nearby districts, or by limiting the number of spaces that they make available to out-of-district transfers. Indeed, in the Detroit metropolitan area, most suburban districts have refused to accept transfers from Detroit city schools, either by declaring themselves closed or by making very few seats available.[65]

In Michigan's other metropolitan areas—Grand Rapids and Flint—suburbs bordering the large-city school districts have formed their own interdistrict choice agreements with neighboring suburbs, but not the urban districts. Overall, "as district family income and home value rise, the probability of participation in open enrollment declines."[66] Thus, higher-spending districts have little financial incentive to accept out-of-district transfers from lower-spending districts because students bring only their home-district per-pupil allotment with them.[67]

Similarly, Ohio's interdistrict open enrollment choice law also allows suburban districts to decide not to participate. As of 1998, when the state's Legislative Office assessed this plan, all the suburban districts immediately adjacent to the state's large urban districts had—with only one exception—exercised this option, refusing to accept interdistrict transfers via the open enrollment law. According to the Ohio Legislative Office, "Interdistrict open enrollment does not necessarily expand educational opportunities for poor and minority children from large urban areas."[68]

Such is the outcome when policies are framed in terms of competition and a race to the top for schools and districts. And yet, we know from years of experience with interdistrict school desegregation programs that there are alternative ways of looking at relationships between schools and districts that may spawn greater cooperation and good will on the part of more privileged districts to provide greater access to students from failing schools. Indeed, as we demonstrate below, when the goals of education and school choice policies are framed in terms of assistance and supporting all children, as opposed to competition between schools and districts for students and dollars, opportunities for the most disadvantaged students are expanded.

Few Supports for Disadvantaged Students in Open Enrollment Plans: Lack of Information and Transportation. Not only do most interdistrict open enrollment choice laws lack any regulations or incentives to facilitate the participation of disadvantaged students, they also lack a key tool for access: provisions for transportation. Indeed, less than one-fourth of the open enrollment laws make provisions for transportation for low-income families. Of the forty-three states (including Puerto Rico) with interdistrict choice laws that were not designed specifically for desegregation purposes, only two require transportation assistance for all students, and only seven require that low-income families specifically be provided some form of transportation assistance. One state—Kentucky—requires that students in low-performing schools get transportation assistance regardless of whether the transferring students are low income.

Furthermore, even when transportation "assistance" is provided, in each of these states it comes in the form of a reimbursement for out-of-pocket transportation costs. In other words, most laws require parents to come up with the means to transport their own child, which creates a significant barrier for parents who either do not own a car, own only one car, or cannot afford to pay, upfront, the high fuel costs. These provisions also exclude students whose parents do not have the time or flexible work schedule needed to transport their child. These state reimbursement policies also create barriers to low-income families and non-English speakers who may lack access to the information about how to navigate the reimbursement application process.[69] These policies certainly affect the ability of lower income students to participate. For example, the study of interdistrict choice in Georgia found that just one-fourth of districts provided transportation to out-of-district students—this same analysis also found a dramatic underrepresentation of African-American students in the program.[70]

In addition, few state open enrollment laws contain requirements to inform parents of the interdistrict choice options. While it is unknown how many laws require parents to be informed, even if such requirements are in place it is difficult to know whether these provisions are being monitored or enforced. Few of these laws allocate additional monies to the states to administer these programs; thus, funding for information programs is not generally available. As a result, even those states with information requirements are unlikely to be able to disseminate information widely, or to target the hard-to-reach lower-income or non-English-speaking populations.

Ironically, while U.S. Secretary of Education Margaret Spellings accuses school districts with many failing schools of not informing parents of options to transfer their children into the few non-failing schools in those districts, she has not, apparently, argued that suburban school districts or states should be more proactive in informing students in poor, failing schools about transfer options to other, higher-achieving school districts under open enrollment laws. The obvious question for policy makers is why, when a policy is framed in terms of competition, would a school district advertise a program that would bring in lower-achieving students whose test scores could, quite likely, make it less competitive according to the narrow criteria—test scores—used to judge it? In this way, these open enrollment program designs stand in dramatic contrast to the voluntary interdistrict desegregation plans discussed below.

HOW INTER-DISTRICT SCHOOL DESEGREGATION PLANS SHAPE ACCESS TO HIGH-ACHIEVING SCHOOLS. Because voluntary interdistrict desegregation plans grew out of the civil rights movement and were crafted with both the recognition of the spatial dimensions of educational inequality and the explicit goal of correcting intergenerational inequalities, they look entirely different in their design from open enrollment plans. These programs are not about competition but about expanding opportunities and encouraging educators and their constituents to think more broadly about the interconnectedness of local communities across spaces within a metropolitan area.

As a result, these interdistrict desegregation plans are characterized first and foremost by a strong and central state role in terms of funding, technical support, and concrete incentives to ensure the participation of suburban school districts, as well as the key provisions of outreach, information, and transportation.

Student Access across District Lines: Carrots and Sticks for Suburban Districts. Across the eight voluntary interdistrict desegregation plans we examined for this review, we see that state oversight and support of these programs is critical. In several cases state *requirements and/or incentives* directed at suburban school districts by court orders and/or state legislation to accept transfer students from urban schools were critical. In addition to such requirements—or in lieu of them—the *financial support* these districts receive from their states has proven critical to the success and stability of these programs.

Requirements and/or Incentives. Of the six interdistrict school desegregation programs prompted by federal or state court orders (all but the Rochester Urban-Suburban Interdistrict Transfer plan and the Boston METCO program), state laws or regulations were created to implement these orders in the targeted metropolitan areas. Between the court orders and the state laws and requirements that resulted from them, the suburban school districts in these six metro areas really had no choice initially but to accept student transfers from urban and/or poor suburban school districts.

For instance, in St. Louis, under the federal court order of 1983, sixteen suburban school districts were required to accept African-American transfer students from the city and to increase their black enrollment to at least 15 percent but not more than 25 percent of their total student population. Furthermore, these sixteen suburban districts were not allowed to "deny admission to African-American students from the city because of grades or test scores."[71]

In Milwaukee, Wisconsin, a state law known as "Chapter 220" was passed in 1976 prior to the settlement agreement in the federal school desegregation case. This law authorized school districts in Wisconsin to enter into agreements to provide for the voluntary interdistrict transfer of students to promote racial and cultural integration. Then, under the 1987 federal court settlement agreement, eighteen suburban school districts outside Milwaukee signed on, vowing to make a good faith effort during the next five years to fill a certain number of seats—specified by a goal calculated by their total enrollment—with Chapter 220 transfer students from the city.[72]

Perhaps the most prescriptive and regulatory of these interdistrict school desegregation programs has been the Indianapolis-Suburban Township Desegregation plan, which is now being phased out after a final settlement agreement in 1998. Basically, the original 1981 settlement agreement in the Indianapolis school desegregation case mandated that African-American students who lived in certain sections of the city transfer to designated suburban schools.[73] The original court order of 1975 paired particular areas of the city with specific suburban schools and then stated that the Indianapolis Public Schools were "ordered and adjudged" to transfer a set number of "Negro students" to these suburban districts. The suburban school districts were likewise ordered to "accept such transfer students and enroll them accordingly."[74]

Thus, while there is variation in how coercive the court orders were in these six cases, they all helped to pave the way for interdistrict transfers to occur. More important, in the case of the Rochester Urban-suburban Interdistrict Transfer program and the Boston METCO program, there were no court-ordered "sticks" to force the suburban school districts to accept urban transfer students at all. The Boston METCO plan was inspired by the Massachusetts Racial Imbalance Act and the state funding that came with it. The Rochester transfer plan, the oldest such program in the country, was started voluntarily by one suburban school district, and subsequent state legislation was passed to support it.

What is extremely important, however, about these two longest-running programs in Boston and Rochester is that they grew out of the 1960s and were not at all couched in competitive, market-oriented terms, but rather in an ideology of greater equality and equal educational opportunity. In both examples, the suburban school districts were persuaded to participate by both state-funded incentives and a strong sense of good will—that this was the right thing to do given the inequality and segregation in their metro areas. They could also have been concerned that they would end up, down the road, being defendants in interdistrict school desegregation cases if they did not act preemptively (this was especially the case in Boston's suburbs).

But the point here is that state laws—sometimes prompted by court orders and sometimes not—can serve as both carrots and sticks to either encourage or require suburban school districts to become involved in these programs. One of the reasons why state government support is so critical is that, at least initially, most suburban school districts need to be either encouraged, coaxed, or mandated to participate in these urban-suburban transfer programs.[75] When they do so, however, they do not sign on because they are buying into a competitive model of school choice, but rather because they are persuaded or required to participate in a program that tries to expand educational opportunities for the most disadvantaged students.

It is obvious that this way of framing and promoting interdistrict school choice policies is more meaningful and effective for high-achieving suburban school districts. Evidence of this finding lies in the fact that although most of the states that house these eight interdistrict desegregation programs have open enrollment laws, the suburban districts that participate in the desegregation-oriented transfer programs are far less likely to take black or Latino transfer students through regular open enrollment plans. In Massachusetts, for instance, the suburban districts adjoining Boston have opened up seats for interdistrict transfers only through the state's long-established interdistrict desegregation plan, METCO, as opposed to the more recently constructed open enrollment program. In fact, the same suburban districts that take METCO students have voted not to participate in the interdistrict open enrollment choice program, even though the per-pupil funding they would receive under open enrollment would be higher.[76]

Financial Support. Whether state lawmakers are coerced into supporting interdistrict school desegregation plans via court orders or they are inspired to pass laws such as Massachusetts's Racial Imbalance Act—or some combination of the two—state funding is the most critical form of support for these programs beyond the requirements placed on districts to accept transfer students. In all eight of these programs, state funding pays for all or part of the per-pupil tuition or incentive payment for receiving school districts, as well as the cost of transporting transfer students to their suburban schools. In fewer cases, states have paid or still do pay for school improvement costs for the urban schools left behind, student recruitment and outreach centers, and ongoing counseling for students who transfer across district lines.

Clearly the two largest costs of these programs are the incentive payment or per-pupil funding for the receiving districts and transportation. The incentive payments for the suburban school districts come in four different and unequal forms (also see Table 4.1):

1. The equivalent to the receiving district's average per-pupil cost for educating their resident students

    ◆   This was the original model for the St. Louis Voluntary Interdistrict Transfer plan, in which each district receives its per-pupil amount.

    ◆   In the Chapter 220 plan, the suburban districts still receive one full FTE for each Milwaukee student who transfers in.

    ◆   Suburban districts' funding via the Indianapolis-Suburban Township plan was approximately equal to their total per-pupil funding level.

2. The equivalent of the sending urban district's per-pupil funding, or a portion thereof

    ◆   Through the Tinsley Transfer plan in the mid-Peninsula section of the San Francisco Bay area, the suburban school districts receive 70 percent of the Ravenswood Elementary School District's per-pupil funding for each student from that district that they enroll.

    ◆   In the Rochester Urban-Suburban Transfer plan, the suburban districts receive the Rochester Public Schools' per-pupil funding amount for each city student who transfers into one of their schools. This funding level is often close to or greater than the per-pupil spending in the suburban districts.

3. The average amount of state funding (with or without compensatory funding) per student across the state

◆   In the future, the St. Louis suburban school districts will each
    get the state funds for each transfer student (or $8,000 in
    2008).

◆   Through the Minneapolis The Choice Is Yours program, the
    suburban school districts are provided with the per-pupil state
    aid for each transferring student, as well as any state or fed-
    eral compensatory funding that student is entitled to receive.

4. A set amount of money

◆ $2,500 per student transferring from Hartford to a suburb
    through the Project Choice program.

◆ $3,700 for each student who transfers from Boston to a sub-
    urb via the METCO program.

Of these four models, the first is usually the best financially from
the receiving suburban school district's perspective. It is worth noting
that the three programs funding suburban school districts in that way
were all derived under federal court orders. Meanwhile, the plans that
resulted from state court cases—Hartford, Minneapolis, and Tinsley—
vary dramatically in terms of how suburban school districts are com-
pensated, as do the two legislation-initiated programs of Boston and
Rochester. What is most interesting perhaps is that the Hartford and
Boston programs, which provide the suburban school districts the
smallest financial incentives via relatively meager set payments per
transfer students, are different not only in terms of their origins—a
state court case versus a piece of state legislation—but also in terms
of the willingness of suburban districts to participate. Although the
Boston METCO plan would clearly benefit from suburban districts
opening up their doors to more students, that long-running program
currently enrolls more than twice the number of students as the court-
ordered Hartford Project Choice program. It appears that the way in
which the policy is presented to suburban school districts matters as
well as the financial incentives. This is a story about how competition
within the field of education is not always the best method for getting
school districts to do the right thing. This suggests that participation on
the part of suburban school districts in meaningful transfer programs

for low-income students of color may not simply be about the money, although the money helps them justify their participation to their constituents. But at the same time, framing their choice to participate in terms of the need for greater diversity in their districts as well as the need to be part of a larger, metropolitan-wide community may prove to be more successful.

Meanwhile, as we discuss in more detail below, in all eight of these interdistrict school desegregation programs, the states pay for all or, at the very least, a large portion of the cost of transportation to and from school for the transfer students. The estimated costs of such services can be quite high—more than $2,000 a year—depending on the distance traveled.

And then there is the issue of each state's willingness to provide this critical financial support of these programs, especially after court mandates end. In some contexts, perhaps most notably in St. Louis, the state's role in financing these programs was strongly resisted by state policy makers, some of whom built successful political careers by publicly opposing the urban-to-suburban transfer plan. Despite this resistance, the state of Missouri, which was found guilty of discriminating against black students for many years, has been forced by a federal court order to pay several billion dollars for the transfer plan since its inception in 1983.

Yet, over time, in places where state legislatures were originally forced to pay for these programs via court orders, these costs are eventually incorporated into state budgets and become part of the state education funding formula. Thus, even when court-ordered settlement agreements end, as in Milwaukee in 1993 and more recently in Minneapolis, some state legislatures will continue to support these programs. In Minneapolis, however, this is possible, ironically enough, because of that state's open enrollment law, which provides some of the infrastructure for The Choice Is Yours program. In fact, in many ways The Choice Is Yours program is highly unique in that it is a targeted version of an open enrollment choice program, which gives priority to low-income students to participate in open enrollment. Yet, because it is not a race-conscious policy, as we discuss below, a disproportionate number of white students use the policy to escape poor urban schools.[77] At the same time, however, the larger non-targeted, open enrollment plan, which The Choice Is Yours program is a part of, suffers from the same shortcomings and problematic outcomes as other laissez-faire open enrollment plans. It is the mission and the goals of The Choice Is

Yours program, derived from a state court case, that make it special and successful at helping the most disadvantaged students.

In other cases, such as Indianapolis, the end of a court order meant a gradual phaseout of an interdistrict school desegregation plan due to a lack of state funding. In St. Louis, the fate of the inter-district transfer program has historically been tied to the longevity of its court order, through which a second settlement agreement was created in 1999. But with that 1999 agreement, due to expire in 2008, a new compromise was reached in the summer of 2007, just before the U.S. Supreme Court ruled in the Louisville and Seattle cases. Indeed, thirteen of the sixteen suburban school districts in St. Louis County voted to continue accepting new transfer students absent a court order and the additional per-pupil state subsidies it provided them. In the future, the suburbs will simply receive the equivalent of the per-pupil state aid funding for each transfer student—about $8,000—which in all cases is less than the full per-pupil funding they were used to receiving.

We are not implying that these programs have escaped intense political pressure at the state level, including fierce resistance from those who think that state funds would be better spent in other ways. In fact, in the last fifteen to twenty years, the funding for most of these programs has been cut or remained constant and the number of total students served has declined. Yet at the same time, the fact that several of these programs are now more than thirty and even forty years old and have survived some of the most politically conservative eras in our country's history speaks to the durability of the mission and goal of equity as a political rationale for funding and supporting school choice plans. For instance, in Massachusetts and New York, where there were never court orders to mandate the two interdistrict transfer programs in Boston and Rochester, supporters of these two programs lobby their state legislators to continue to fund them, and they have each added more participating school districts over time.

Either way, whether created by court order or a political process, state support is important for meaningful cross-district integration to occur. At a 1982 conference of educators and officials from five states with interdistrict desegregation programs, participants stressed the critical need for state government involvement in these programs.[78] Furthermore, over time in many of these places, state legislators, even in Missouri, have become more supportive of these programs, despite the fact that federal courts have become less so.

Outreach, Recruitment, and Coordination. In addition to the carrots and sticks necessary to assure local school-district participation in interdistrict student transfer programs, evidence from these eight programs suggests that some form of outreach, recruitment, and coordination of the cross-district transfer process makes that practice much easier for families and students and assures that more children have access to suburban schools. And if there is ongoing counseling and diversity training available for both transfer students and suburban school teachers, many of the most difficult aspects of having students attend schools far from their homes—physically and culturally—can be ameliorated. These sorts of infrastructural supports are rarely if ever available to students transferring through open enrollment programs.

For instance, the St. Louis Voluntary Interdistrict Desegregation plan has always had a state-funded central office—the Voluntary Interdistrict Coordinating Council, which was replaced by the Voluntary Interdistrict Choice Corporation (VICC) as part of the 1999 settlement agreement—to help recruit, place, and counsel African-American students from the city who transfer to suburban schools. This centralized office assures that the transfer students are not being denied access unfairly under the terms of the settlement agreements. VICC has also worked with transfer students and their families, as well as suburban educators and students, to help ease the students' transition from the city to the county public schools.[79]

In the Boston-area METCO program, each participating school district has a METCO director paid for by the suburban districts, and all of these directors are people of color. Their main responsibility is to coordinate METCO-related activities, help place the minority students in the suburban districts, and serve as a liaison to the families—helping both parents and students bridge the gap between Boston and the unfamiliar suburban communities.[80]

In the Indianapolis plan, which is now being phased out, each of the six participating suburban school districts employed a Marion County Coordinator of Integrated Education (MCCIE) with specific responsibilities to supervise staff, students, and programs as the African-American students began enrolling in their predominantly white schools. In fact, these coordinators were responsible for collecting data and submitting an Annual Desegregation Statistical Overview to the Indiana Department of Education, which also helped the federal court oversee the transfer program and assure that it was providing access to those who were supposed to benefit from the remedy.[81]

In the Milwaukee metro area, an organization called Parents Concerned about Chapter 220 was formed in the early 1990s to represent the educational interests of MPS transfer students. At the same time, according to the Wisconsin Advisory Committee, a variety of steps had been taken by several suburban school districts to address problems that the transfer students and suburban students faced in the course of the cross-district transfer process.[82] For instance, one suburban school district called Franklin hired its own Chapter 220 program administrator and human relations coordinator. Another district adopted a multicultural curriculum, and another created a new staff position to oversee the Chapter 220 program and provided counseling to the students and parents involved in some racial incidents at school. Some suburban school districts decided to employ a school-community liaison person to work with MPS transfer students and parents; others hired human relations specialists or liaison persons. And finally, other suburban districts in the Milwaukee metro area started a Host Family program, which provides a place for transfer students to stay overnight if necessary and a home base for these students when they are so far from home. At the same time, the Host Family program, which was also implemented in the St. Louis suburbs, provided an opportunity for greater interaction between city and suburban families.[83]

Yet perhaps the most impressive system of support and outreach for students and families crossing school-district boundaries—as well as racial, social-class, and cultural boundaries—is woven into the Minneapolis The Choice Is Yours program and supported by both federal and state funds. More specifically, the Minnesota State Department of Education and the Minneapolis Public Schools' outreach activities, coupled with a system of parent information centers in the local communities throughout the metro Minneapolis area, constitute a more comprehensive safety net for the transfer students and their families than is available through most of these other programs. Examples of the outreach efforts led by the Minnesota Department of Education include media campaigns in newspaper, television billboards, and radio advertisements; community outreach events; partnership programs with Head Start centers; and school choice videos in multiple languages. Meanwhile, the Minneapolis Public Schools hold annual school choice fairs, direct mailings, and parent information fairs, among other outreach activities. In addition, the state and federal funds support two parent information centers to distribute information, hold parent meetings, and house computer labs so that parents can research their school choices. The support from the federal grant appears to be a critical factor in enabling the state and district to offer such support to parents, thereby exemplifying the potential role that federal policy makers can play in assuring that the most disadvantaged families have real school choice.

Free Transportation. Another absolutely crucial component of these interdistrict desegregation programs that the states can and usually do provide is free transportation for students to and from school. In contrast to state open enrollment plans, most of which require students to pay for and often provide their own transportation, all eight of the interdistrict desegregation plans that we reviewed for this chapter offer state-supported free transportation for transfer students to and from their suburban or urban schools of choice. In most states this means that the state is the direct provider of transportation services; in others, such as the Tinsley plan in Palo Alto, the state of California reimburses the local districts for the cost of transporting students from East Palo Alto, using buses and drivers employed by a local high school district.

This free transportation is particularly important for students from low-income urban families that may or may not have cars or work schedules that would allow them to drive children to schools in suburban communities. We also know that parents on both sides of the urban-suburban dividing line lack exposure to and familiarity with neighborhoods inhabited by people of different racial/ethnic backgrounds.[84] Thus, free transportation is critical to assure meaningful choice for all students, and it is one of the key components of interdistrict integration plans that is too often missing from the free market–based choice programs, such as open enrollment plans.

Several of the reports that we read on these interdistrict plans emphasized the importance of the free transportation between urban and suburban neighborhoods in enabling the transferring of students to participate in these programs. For instance, in one report on the Milwaukee Chapter 220 program, the authors note that while the program provides transportation at no cost to the families for all participants, the interdistrict open enrollment program requires participating families to provide their own transportation and provides for low-income families to apply for reimbursement of their transportation costs.[85] The authors argue that while the transportation costs of the Chapter 220 program are quite high—in the $10–11 million range in recent years—it is a critical component in guaranteeing greater access to schools of choice for poor Milwaukee students in particular. In their survey of students participating in the Chapter 220 program, the authors found that the students' responses to questions about the transportation suggested that "the bus is very valuable to them" to enable them to attend the suburban schools in the first place and to participate in any extracurricular activities at their choice schools.

In stark contrast, students participating in the state's open enrollment plan need to have the means to transport themselves to and from schools. If they are from low-income families, they can be reimbursed for their out-of-pocket costs to participate in the program, assuming that they can put forth these resources and wait to be paid back at a later date. Due in part to the very limited population of low-income families that can afford to forego the transportation costs until a later date when they can get paid back, the number of actual reimbursements via this program are quite small—a total of $500,000 in 2000–2001 compared to the eleven million dollars needed to make the choices meaningful under the Chapter 220 program. The authors' interviews with local officials in school districts participating in the Chapter 220 program revealed that "district administrators frequently cited this significant difference between the programs as reason enough not to expect the Open Enrollment program to supplant Chapter 220."[86]

Similarly, the Aspen Associates report on the Minneapolis The Choice Is Yours program explains that the transportation of Minneapolis students to suburban schools under the CIY program was paid for by the state of Minnesota through its state desegregation transportation funding formula and provided by the Wide Area Transportation System (WATS).[87] As many of these interdistrict programs do, the CIY program assures that transfer students who participate in after-school activities in their suburban schools have activity buses available to them. And the Western Metro Education Program (WMEP) suburban districts provide transportation to ensure that parents of CIY students can attend school conferences and other family events.

In their surveys of parents of CIY participating students, the Aspen Associates authors found that only one-third of the parents whose children were attending suburban schools said that they would "definitely" choose the same school for their child regardless of whether free transportation was available.

Therefore, it is clear from our analysis of the most critical components of interdistrict desegregation programs that, while open enrollment programs are far cheaper for states to operate, they do not serve the same clientele. They are far less likely to enable meaningful school choices for those families and students who have the fewest choices of all. Making such choice meaningful and thus assuring that far fewer children are left behind in failing urban and high-poverty schools requires ongoing and meaningful state—and hopefully federal—support in the form of incentives for districts, outreach efforts, and free transportation. Providing such meaningful choice and access to the most disadvantaged students in the worst-performing public schools is not done on the cheap. It requires mandates, incentives, and guidelines for participating suburban and urban school districts, as well as critical support for parents and students in the form of outreach and transportation. Both the state and federal governments can play important roles in assuring all the necessary components are in place.

How Different Goals and Designs Lead to Different Outcomes: The Benefits of Equity-minded Interdistrict Desegregation Plans

In this section of the chapter, we review the limited research about the outcomes of these two very different interdistrict transfer policies and show how the fundamental differences in the goals and designs of the two programs have led to dramatic differences in outcomes for students and school systems. Our review of the research on the outcomes of these two types of interdistrict choice programs demonstrates that the laissez-faire open enrollment policies have led to greater racial and social stratification between districts.

Meanwhile, the interdistrict desegregation plans have led to greater diversity in the suburban districts and less racial isolation in urban schools. Furthermore, these programs have improved racial attitudes in the suburbs, increased academic achievement among transfer students over time, and had a long-term effect on the transfer students' careers and lives. As a result of their academic and social success, these programs are very popular with urban families who too often have failing neighborhood schools. Thus, the de facto relationship between the goals of NCLB and these regulated and carefully designed equity-minded school desegregation policies are powerful and offer a model for expanding choices using federal policy.

INTERDISTRICT OPEN ENROLLMENT AND UNEQUAL OUTCOMES: WHEN LAISSEZ-FAIRE POLICIES MEAN FEWER CHOICES FOR THOSE WHO NEED THEM THE MOST. Given the lack of support for participation of lower-income students, it comes as no surprise that virtually all evaluations of state interdistrict open enrollment choice programs show that low-income students and students of color are the *least* likely to participate in these programs.

For example, a 2006 evaluation of New Jersey's pilot interdistrict open enrollment choice program, which was a phased program that allowed one district per county to receive out-of-district students, found that "based on the fact that the percentages of blacks and Hispanics among choice students were lower than their percentages in the statewide public school population, it appears that the Program has not served those students as well as others."[88] This report stated that it was encouraging that more than 50 percent of the students participating in the choice program came from low-income districts, yet the authors were not able to obtain the data to determine whether the students transferring out of these low-income districts were low income themselves.

A 1998 evaluation of Georgia's interdistrict open enrollment choice plan also found that white students were overrepresented in choice participants and that African-American students were underrepresented in choice transfers. While whites made up only 63 percent of the students in "open" districts (districts allowing out transfers), they constituted 83 percent of choosers; African-Americans made up 34 percent of the students in open districts yet represented just 13 percent of transfers.[89]

In Massachusetts, which first passed choice legislation in 1991, a 1994 study found that the overwhelming number of students participating in the state's program—approximately 94 percent— were white, while just 2 percent were African-American, and 2 percent were Hispanic.[90] Students transferring out of high-minority districts were largely white as well.[91] Armor and Peiser's later study of interdistrict choice in Massachusetts also found that the students who transferred out of their home districts through interdistrict choice came from more affluent and educated households vis-à-vis students in their home districts.[92]

In Wisconsin, where the statewide interdistrict open enrollment transfer program began in 1998, a 2002 audit found that students of color were the least likely to participate in the transfer program, while white students were the most likely to participate—particularly if their home district was large.[93] And, as we noted above, the Dickman et al. report found huge racial differences in the enrollment of the Milwaukee Chapter 220 program versus the Wisconsin open enrollment plan.[94] They report, for instance, that although only 18 percent of the students enrolled in the Milwaukee Public Schools are white, the share of white students transferring out of the city schools through the open enrollment program is 63 percent.

And finally, Lewin reports that during the 1993–94 school year, white Omaha high school students made 96.1 percent of the transfer requests under the open enrollment policy, even though 27 percent of Omaha high school students were black. Furthermore, Lewin cites data from Iowa and Ohio that show that under these states' open enrollment laws, white students placed 97 percent of the interdistrict transfer applications from Des Moines and 98 percent of the applications to transfer out of Akron to the suburbs.[95]

Taken together, these data suggest that, absent explicit support and targeting of the most at-risk students, white and affluent students are disproportionately likely to take advantage of interdistrict choice, while African-Americans—and in two states, Latinos—are less likely to take advantage of choice options. Of course, these results are not really surprising for school choice policies designed to force greater competition for students between school districts in the context of high-stakes testing and accountability reforms. Under such laissez-faire and competitive policies, districts are probably more motivated to let in only more advantaged, high-scoring students than disadvantaged students with low scores.

These analyses, however, tell us little about the types of districts or schools that the relatively privileged open enrollment participants are choosing. In theory, if students were choosing more racially diverse schools, these participation rates might be less troubling; as the evidence presented in the next section will show, however, on balance students are transferring to districts that serve more affluent and whiter student populations compared to their home districts.

Unfettered Choices Advantage the Advantaged: How Current Interdistrict Open Enrollment Choice Policies Leave Poor Students of Color Behind. Existing evidence from state evaluations of interdistrict open enrollment choice policies shows not only that lower income students of color are less likely to participate, but also that those students who *do* participate tend to transfer to higher-income, less-diverse school districts. Together with the existing student transfer information presented above, it becomes clear that, as currently designed, open enrollment choice policies are allowing whiter and more affluent students to transfer to whiter and more affluent school districts.

Evidence from individual state studies of these interdistrict open enrollment plans have all found that, across states, higher-income districts are most likely to receive transfers and lower-income and high-minority districts are the most likely to "lose" students. Together with the evidence presented above about *who* is most likely to participate in school choice, it becomes clear that interdistrict open enrollment choice has likely become a vehicle for white and more affluent students to have access to more advantaged schools.

In Michigan, for example, the open enrollment choice law allows students to transfer from their home district to contiguous school districts. Districts must accept all students who apply as long as they have capacity, and oversubscribed districts must institute a random lottery for admission. No provisions are made for transportation or support. This deregulated open enrollment program has led to what Arsen et al. called "upward filtering" of students.[96] Their study found that students were much more likely to transfer out of central city school districts and into districts with higher parental income levels and home values. They also found that "on balance, students flow from districts with high concentrations of African-American students to districts with moderate enrollment of African-American students."[97]

Similar "upward filtering" trends were found in Massachusetts, which amended its law in 1993 to grant all students the right to transfer out of their home district while granting districts the right to vote to not receive students. A 2003 analysis of transfer trends by MassInc found that low-income districts were the least likely to receive transfers under open enrollment; students tended to transfer to districts more affluent than their home districts.[98]

Two additional analyses of interdistrict open enrollment transfer trends in Massachusetts also found that sender districts had higher minority enrollments and receiving districts had lower minority enrollments.[99] Armor and Peiser found that when choice students constituted a large portion of the receiving district's enrollment—more than 2 percent—there were large socioeconomic differences between sending and receiving districts, the latter of which tended to be significantly higher income.[100] Interestingly enough, both of these Massachusetts studies included the state's interdistrict desegregation program, METCO, in their analyses; thus, the actual racial and socioeconomic disparities are likely higher than reported here.

Meanwhile, Fossey's research on districts receiving twenty or more students from a single town found that these receiving districts tended to have higher parental income levels and education levels, and higher per-pupil expenditures.[101] In just one instance—in the cases of smaller districts—did interdistrict choice enhance racial diversity when virtually all-white districts received some students of color.[102]

Evaluations of Wisconsin's open enrollment choice program have found similar trends. Wisconsin's law, passed in 1997, grants students the right to transfer to any district in the state. A 2002 Legislative Audit Bureau report found that statewide, students were more likely to transfer to higher-income school districts, and that this was especially true for students leaving Milwaukee, the vast majority of whom are white.[103]

The Rutgers study of New Jersey's pilot interdistrict open enrollment choice program also found that higher-income districts were more likely to accept transfer students.[104] It also concluded that there was no significant impact on district racial enrollment in any district except one, but these data provide little insight into school-level trends.

These "upward filtering" trends could be seen as evidence that open enrollment plans increase disadvantaged students' access to suburban schools. Taken together with the data presented above on *who* is most likely to participate, however, the evidence suggests that current state interdistrict choice policies do not provide many disadvantaged students with access to better educational opportunities. Rather, these policies are more likely to provide an "escape route" that allows advantaged and affluent students within more diverse districts to transfer to districts with predominantly white and more advantaged student populations.

This was the finding of a recent study of interdistrict choice in the Denver metropolitan area that utilized a more recent data set that was able to link the demographic characteristics of student transfers and students' actual transfer patterns. The analysis showed that both higher-income students and white students were more likely to take advantage of interdistrict choice, and that those students transferred to school districts that had greater proportions of white and affluent students than their home districts. The analysis also found that lower-income students of color tended to use open enrollment to transfer into districts with greater portions of students from their own backgrounds. Thus, as a result of interdistrict choice, the predominately nonwhite urban and inner-ring districts in the Denver metro area gained lower-income students of color, while at the same time losing white and more-affluent students to the suburbs.[105] In this way, the study argues, interdistrict choice exacerbated existing regional between-district stratification by race and social class within the Denver metropolitan area.

These findings from interdistrict open enrollment research are consistent with research on other types of school choice policies, which has consistently shown that more advantaged families tend to take advantage of choice policies, and that deregulated school choice policies tend to further stratification between schools.[106] These findings suggest that any interdistrict open enrollment choice law designed to foster educational opportunity must contain, like the interdistrict school desegregation programs discussed below, strong provisions to prevent these stratifying trends.

Outcome Data and Interdistrict Open Enrollment Choice Programs: Few Meaningful Competitive Market Effects, No Achieve-ment Data. Evaluating the academic impact of interdistrict open enrollment is not yet possible as no evaluations have been conducted to date on the academic outcomes of these policies. While some evaluations indicated that parents seek to move to higher-performing districts as measured by overall scores, there is also evidence that parents move against average test score measures—as shown in the 2002 audit of Wisconsin's program by the state's Legislative Audit Bureau.[107] Yet researchers have yet to measure the effect of choice on the achievement of transfer students themselves, or upon the students in both the sending and receiving schools and districts that should be improving due to competitive market pressures.

The limited research on the "outcomes" of these open enrollment plans has been focused on understanding the responses of districts to the competitive market pressures that open enrollment plans are presumed to bring to bear on affected districts—the same pressures that are presumed to operate under NCLB as it currently stands. Yet the small body of existing research on the outcomes of these policies indicate limited competitive market effects on the districts left behind. For example, Armor and Peiser's 1997 study of interdistrict open enrollment in Massachusetts found that just three of the ten sending districts did make changes to recoup their losses: the most significant changes were not academic, but financial, as the districts almost universally noted that the student losses through open enrollment prompted the school boards in their districts to increase funding for programs to attract students back.[108] These changes therefore weren't about inefficient schools being prompted to utilize existing resources more effectively; these market forces consisted of a wake-up call about the need to adequately fund programs in the first place. Another group of changes described by a larger number of districts involved marketing in an effort to portray the school district and schools in a positive light—these changes were therefore not about recapturing market share by improving programs but by improving publicity.

A 1999 study of the response of school districts in Michigan to the state's interdistrict public school choice program showed that school districts weren't able to respond to the competition either because they were unclear about exactly why students were leaving, or because they believed that students were leaving for factors that were beyond their control—particularly the racial and ethnic composition of the school district.

> Most significantly, administrators reported instances where the movement of significant numbers of students across district lines appeared to be influenced by the racial composition of the student body in the districts that the students were leaving and the districts they were choosing . . . The most commonly reported determinant of interdistrict transfers, however, was the desire of parents to send their children to school in districts ranking a notch higher in the social status hierarchy. Administrators see little that they can do to counter these moves.[109]

Taken together, the evidence indicates that racial and class stratification trumps, or at least redefines, the so-called competitive market effects presumed to be generated under these laissez-faire choice plans. Indeed, when the evidence is assembled, the most consistent documented effect of these market-driven policies has been to provide advantaged students with an "escape route" out of more diverse districts into more advantaged ones. Yet as we show below, student outcomes from the equity-minded interdistrict school desegregation programs are significant and long-lasting for participating students as well as the suburban students and adults in the districts who receive them.

OUTCOME DATA AND VOLUNTARY INTERDISTRICT DESEGREGATION PLANS: HOW GREATER ACCESS TO HIGH-STATUS, HIGH-ACHIEVING SCHOOLS SHAPES HEARTS AND MINDS. It is important to note that, to our knowledge, no one has yet pulled together the research and knowledge on these unique interdistrict desegregation plans. This forced us to piece together the evidence on the outcomes of these programs from several different sources, including newspaper articles; historical and court documents, as well as journal articles, books, and unpublished research reports. The lack of compiled information on these programs tells us that their collective history has never been told. While we do not have the space in this chapter to tell this full tale, we do highlight here the lessons we have gleaned from our research that most directly speak to the potential of federal legislation to provide similar types of opportunities for children.

What outcome data from these urban-suburban desegregation plans we could find helped us understand why a more proactive, regulated antisegregation public policy is needed to help close the achievement gap along racial lines in this country. Indeed solid research findings and anecdotal information from these cross-district choice programs explain why simply fixing up segregated and poor urban schools will never solve these deep and structural inequalities across spaces and institutions in our society—physical divides that can be challenged only when disadvantaged students are allowed to cross the barriers that separate the rich from the poor, the black and/or Latino from the white, and so forth.

In fact, what we know from the social science research on school desegregation policies in general—that separate is not equal because of the effects of the broader inequality on public schools—is best illustrated by the small body of research we have on these interdistrict desegregation plans. This research explains what it means to students to leave the harms of segregation far behind them and enter a more privileged world where public schools provide access to a brighter future. And not only that, the evidence from these eight interdistrict plans helps us see why racial and social integration is important to the democratic development of children and adults who have lived in predominantly privileged spaces for so long. What cross-district desegregation plans can do—better and more efficiently than any other form of school choice policy—is allow people to cross racial and social-class boundaries that may well, if not addressed, be the beginning of the end for this increasingly diverse nation.

In this section of the chapter we briefly review what research and other published information exists on these eight interdistrict desegregation programs to illustrate these points. We have divided this review into four subsections—racial attitudes, academic achievement, long-term effects, and the popularity of these programs with parents of students in failing public schools.

Changing Racial Attitudes in the Suburbs. What is most striking about reviewing dozens of newspaper articles and research documents on these eight programs is a common theme that emerges across these very disparate metropolitan areas: that suburban residents, educators, school officials, and students grow to appreciate these programs more the longer that they continue. In many of these metropolitan areas, opposition to the interdistrict plans on the suburban side of the racial divide was fierce initially. As we noted above, often court orders and state laws were the only things that got these districts on board—that and the threat that they might lose their districts altogether through a metropolitan-wide school district consolidation program, such as the one in Wilmington, Delaware.

Yet, despite this initial opposition toward these programs in the 1960s, 1970s, or 1980s when most of them began, we see in more recent reports strong evidence of growing acceptance and even solid political support for these transfer plans in the suburbs. In some cases, such as one suburban school district in St. Louis, we see strong public opposition to efforts to end these once-dreaded programs. Indeed, in 2004 hundreds of students in affluent suburban Clayton High School walked out of class to protest any effort on the part of their local school board to end the voluntary interdistrict desegregation plan. According to one news report on this incident, the students organized the walkout to "show support for diversity in this top-ranked school district and for their friends . . . Organizers asked students to sign petitions to maintain the school's diverse student population."[110]

This youth activism in Clayton is symbolic of another theme that we see across these programs and sites, namely that the younger white suburban residents—both the current students and recent graduates of the desegregated schools—are some of the strongest supporters of desegregation. For instance, an opinion poll taken in the late 1980s, five years after the St. Louis interdistrict plan started, showed that suburban students were the most supportive of the plan among whites—more so than the suburban teachers and parents. In fact, 71 percent of the white high school students said that it was a good idea to mix black city kids with white county kids, while only 54 percent of white parents said this.[111] Ten years later, in 1998, after fifteen years of urban-suburban desegregation in the St. Louis metro area, an opinion poll found even less hostility toward the program among whites.[112]

Still, perhaps what is most significant about the most recent history of the St. Louis Voluntary Interdistrict program, as we described it briefly above, is that after years of being ordered by a federal court to enroll the urban transfer students, sixteen of the suburban school districts involved in the program voted unanimously to extend the program for five years, even after the federal judge in the case decided that they could no longer be ordered to participate. Furthermore, thirteen of these sixteen districts voted to continue accepting new African-American transfer students during this extension even though the state funding for each transfer student was reduced to a flat rate of $8,000.[113] Apparently, after twenty-four years of participating in the program, the suburban school officials had come to value this plan for social, educational, and economic reasons. At the meeting in which this historic vote was taken, the chairman of the group of participating school districts and the superintendent of the affluent Clayton School District hailed the program after the vote, noting, "You all know how I feel about this program . . . It's a very special thing."[114]

Similarly, we saw in Indianapolis and Rochester as well as Boston that in more recent years, when these interdistrict school desegregation programs are threatened either in the courts or the state legislatures, it is not unusual for suburban school district officials and/or residents to stand up for these programs and try to preserve them. Indeed, an article in *Education Week* noted that when Federal District Court Judge Dillin ordered the interdistrict transfer program in Indianapolis in 1981, the suburban townships slated to receive the black urban transfer students vigorously opposed it: "But their stance changed over time, and they have in recent years fought the city's efforts to reclaim the students."[115]

Another sign of growing suburban acceptance of urban-suburban voluntary desegregation plans is that in several of these eight sites, over the years, more districts have signed on to accept students from the cities. For instance, in 2005, a ninth suburban school district signed on to Minneapolis's The Choice Is Yours program and began accepting urban transfer students. And in 2008 in Rochester, another suburban school district that had not historically participated in the forty-three-year-old urban-suburban transfer program signed on to the plan and began accepting minority students from the city.

Meanwhile, in 1994 a survey released by the Indiana Youth Institute found that both students who graduated from desegregated schools and their parents backed the interdistrict school desegregation plan: "Integrated education got overwhelming support."[116] The study found that "large majorities of both races said students who attend interracial school gain a positive advantage. Blacks from integrated schools received little serious racial bias . . . And data from suburbs found a 'remarkable level of friendship' among blacks bused from segregated city neighborhoods and white students from mostly white suburbs."[117]

And in the Milwaukee metropolitan area, another place where suburban support for racial integration was not initially forthcoming, the students who lived through the Chapter 220 program—both white and black—were highly optimistic about the impact of the program on their lives. For instance, a survey of urban and suburban students in schools participating in the Chapter 220 program concluded that most middle school and high school students indicated that it was easy to make cross-race friends in their schools and that most have done so. The survey also uncovered that it was not unusual for transfer students from the city of Milwaukee to report that they had been invited to the home of a student in the host district to attend a social event. Furthermore, the high school students in Chapter 220 schools were highly likely to report that their schools were integrated—92 percent. For middle school students it was 62 percent. In addition, the high school students surveyed expressed a strong interest in learning more about different cultures.[118]

Indeed, the evidence is quite strong, in the research and reporting on these eight programs and other work on school desegregation, that these plans become more accepted—embraced even—by suburbanites and graduates of the transfer program over time, as racial and social-class barriers are broken down.

   Student Achievement Data: When Access to Higher-status Schools Matters. Surprisingly enough there is very little solid research on the impact of these interdistrict voluntary desegregation programs on student achievement, but what little evidence there is suggests that for the students who transfer out of poor urban schools and into more affluent suburban schools, the long bus rides are worth it.

   The best analysis of student achievement in an interdistrict desegregation program comes from the old Hartford Project Concern and now Project Choice plan. In the early days of the Project Concern plan, the transfer students from the city of Hartford to suburban schools were randomly selected from the pool of possible applicants. Lottery winners were then strongly encouraged to participate in the transfer plan. This selection process created a desegregation program with as close to a perfect experimental design in terms of a control and treatment group as one can get in educational research. In other words, differences in student achievement and academic outcomes between the lottery winners and lottery losers are more meaningful because they are less tainted by a self-selection bias in favor of students with parents who are more involved in education and thus more active in choosing schools for their children.

   Thus, a 1970 report on student achievement among Project Concern students found that in reading, the randomly selected African-American students who transferred out of the Hartford Public Schools and enrolled in suburban schools had significantly higher test scores than students from similar backgrounds who remained in the urban schools. Furthermore, the longer these students who remained in their suburban schools and the younger they were when they started, the better they did.[119]

   More recent evidence from the newer version of Project Concern, the Project Choice program, which does not choose students via a lottery, demonstrates that participating Hartford students perform better on standardized achievement tests than those who remain behind in urban schools. More than half of Project Choice students are performing at or above proficiency on state standardized tests in both math and reading. In fact, the Project Choice students' test scores and proficiency rates are higher than their Hartford Public Schools peers and black and Latino students statewide.[120]

   Another, yet-to-be-published analysis compared achievement scores of fifth- through eighth-grade students in Project Choice to those of students who applied for the program but did not participate and instead remained in the Hartford Public Schools. This study found that students moving to suburban schools initially scored lower, but that their scores improved significantly as they spent more time in suburban schools, after which their reading results were much higher than those of the comparison group.[121]

These findings from Hartford and their suggestion of a long-term academic payoff for urban students of color who transfer to suburban schools echoes in some of the most important research on student achievement to come out of the St. Louis Voluntary Interdistrict Transfer program. This research, cited in the Wells and Crain study of the St. Louis program, demonstrates that African-American students from the city of St. Louis who transfer to suburban schools do not show significant gains on academic tests in the elementary grades, but that in the long run, for those who remain in the program, their achievement improves to far surpass that of their peers in the city's magnet or neighborhood schools by the time they reach tenth grade.[122]

This research, conducted by Lissitz in the early 1990s, shows that during elementary school, the students in the city of St. Louis's twenty-five magnet schools performed better than the suburban transfer students. In fact, the pre-transfer test score data on African-American students who went to suburban, magnet, and "regular" neighborhood city schools mildly supported this assertion, although the differences are not great. African-American students who attended city magnet schools had the highest pre-transfer test scores. Transfer students who attended suburban schools generally had lower pre-transfer test scores than magnet students but higher test scores than those of African-American students in neighborhood city schools. Thus, the elementary test scores reflected these pre-transfer test score differences.[123]

Yet, over time, the black students who transferred to the suburbs and remained there showed tremendous academic growth by high school, while the black students who attended city magnet schools had leveled off and those who remained in regular city schools never caught up. In fact, by tenth grade, the magnet school students had lost all of their initial advantage, which was at least partly due to self-selection factors.[124] Perhaps the most interesting aspect of Lissitz's analysis is that the transfer students who went to the suburbs consistently outperformed African-American students in magnet and neighborhood city schools in the eighth- to tenth-grade growth in test scores—the very years when students become more focused on what they are doing after high school and how their achievement may affect those future plans.[125]

In another analysis of student achievement and the St. Louis urban-suburban desegregation program, Freivogel reported that testing data released in August 2001 supported the earlier findings of the higher achievement by the time they get to high school among African-American students who transfer to suburban schools.[126] He noted that while achievement differences are small or nonexistent in the elementary grades, by middle and high school, African-American students in suburban schools were scoring about 10 percent higher in reading and math than the African-American students in non-magnet city high schools and middle schools. The students who transferred to the suburbs or chose to attend an urban magnet school were better off over the long run.

Furthermore, Freivogel concluded that the more significant evidence of the higher academic achievement among transfer students and magnet school students is graduation rates. He cites a 1995 report by the city's business leaders, which concluded that African-American students in the suburban transfer program and city magnet schools were graduating at twice the rate of their peers, who remained behind in the regular, non-magnet city schools. He reported that the graduation rate for the magnet students was 52 percent; for the transfer students, 50 percent; for students in the all-black St. Louis city high schools, 24 percent. Students attending the handful of city high schools that were integrated had an abysmal graduation rate of 16 percent.

In yet another analysis of the academic effects of the St. Louis interdistrict desegregation plan on African-American students, Trent found that, although many of the transfer students in the desegregated suburban schools were poor, their graduation rates far exceeded those of the black students who remained behind in racially segregated urban schools.[127] Similarly, Wells and Crain reported that the black urban-suburban transfer students were nearly twice as likely as their peers in urban schools to complete high school.[128] Furthermore, those who graduated from suburban schools were more than twice as likely to go on to two-year or four-year colleges than St. Louis Public Schools graduates.[129]

In his effort to analyze all of these data, Freivogel acknowledged that the disparate outcomes most likely relate to the poverty levels of the students across the different types of schools. For instance, the percentage of students from families that did not qualify for free and reduced price lunch, meaning those from families with incomes higher than 185 percent of the federal poverty level, was 36 percent for magnet school students, 24 percent for suburban transfer students, 10 percent for integrated city high school students, and 6 percent for students in all-black city schools.[130]

But, Freivogel noted, the positive academic outcomes of black students who transferred through the desegregation plan to suburban schools must also relate to the institutional effects of attending high-status, more affluent schools in which rates of college attendance for graduating classes are as high as 95 percent. Furthermore, in an analysis of the college-prep curriculum in the urban (non-magnet) versus suburban schools in St. Louis, Freivogel found that the city schools teach fewer foreign languages, have fewer counselors, and offer fewer advanced courses in math and science. They also lack music programs and up-to-date science labs and libraries.[131] Based on interviews and observations in city versus suburban schools, Wells and Crain drew similar conclusions.[132]

Thus, we should not be surprised to find that the transfer students said that the teachers and the curricula were far more challenging in the suburban than the city schools. It was also true that most of the whiter and wealthier suburban schools had greater resources, including newer buildings, more computers per student, and an abundance of textbooks. The suburban districts, even those with a lower per-pupil expenditure than the St. Louis Public Schools, had more real income—adjusted for special education and maintenance costs—to expend on rigorous educational programs.

Related to these unequal opportunities in suburban versus urban schools, the Lissitz study showed that between eighth and tenth grades, the African-American students who transferred to the suburbs and remained there until graduation improved not only their test scores but also their attitudes and feelings about themselves and their futures. A possible explanation for these findings is located in the personal stories of the urban-suburban transfer students we studied. These students told us they had learned that they could make it in a "white world" where students' futures are highlighted by real job opportunities and college preparation. They no longer feared leaving the predominately black north side of St. Louis and competing with whites in educational institutions or the job market. They had learned that they could succeed in such settings. They were not afraid to integrate into a predominantly white society.[133] The black students who transferred out to suburban schools did so because they believed that, in one way or another, the suburban schools were better equipped to help them attain certain goals. We concluded, based on our review of other research and our own extensive data collection in the St. Louis metropolitan area, that while not all African-American students who transferred to the St. Louis suburbs thrived, the vast majority accomplished more in the suburbs than they would have in their racially and socioeconomically segregated urban schools.[134]

Data on test score gains coupled with analyses of the curriculum and resources in city versus suburban high schools led us to conclude that attending a suburban school positively affected African-American transfer students' aspirations and expectations, especially in those critical years between eighth and tenth grades.[135] In fact, through our qualitative data collection in urban and suburban schools in St. Louis we came to better understand the "institutional" explanations for these statistics. In ways that echoed the large body of research on the harms of racial segregation in education, the successful transfer students in the Wells and Crain study told us of new worlds that had opened up to them within their high-status suburban schools.[136] They talked about their knowledge of college entrance exams and test prep courses, scholarship programs, internships, and jobs they said they never would have heard of in their urban schools. They said that they were exposed to significantly more challenging curricula, learned how to get along in a "white world," and befriended white students and teachers who often connected them to social networks that in turn connected them to opportunities in education and employment. They also talked about dispelling stereotypes that whites have of blacks so that they and those who come behind them might be more easily accepted.[137]

Through our in-depth research we came to realize the complexity of the experiences of the students who transfer to white suburban schools and the types of trade-offs that they face. Yet, in the end, we realized that their stories better explained why separate poor and all-black schools in highly segregated inner cities could never be equal to predominantly white and wealthy suburban schools in a society defined by the inequality embedded in these distinct urban and suburban spaces.[138]

Of course, the Wells and Crain analysis of the St. Louis Interdistrict Transfer plan does not paint a completely rosy picture of what happened to the African-American students. Indeed, many of these transfer students had to endure the racial and cultural insensitivity of whites in the suburbs in order to succeed there. Furthermore, as in many other desegregated schools, students in the suburban St. Louis schools were too often resegregated across classrooms within the schools via a tracking system that led to predominantly black remedial classes and predominantly white honors and AP classes. Although the degree of racial insensitivity appeared to be diminishing over time, the prejudice found in the white suburbs was real and often painful.[139]

Still, the extent to which the whiter and wealthier suburban schools were objectively "better" than the segregated, high-poverty urban schools is truly immeasurable. Every variable used to assess school quality in this country—test scores, drop-out rates, attendance, college-going rates, and so forth—is intertwined with factors related to racial discrimination and segregation in America. School quality, therefore, is strongly related to the educational needs of the students and the meaning that educators make of those needs. Although opponents of the St. Louis plan claim that money spent busing black students to suburban schools would be better spent "fixing up" the all-black schools in the city, the students who ride the buses every day to the suburbs are fighting for access to institutions with the best reputations and most influence in a predominantly white society.[140]

Interestingly enough, beyond these comprehensive studies of Hartford and St. Louis, there are few other studies on the academic impact of these interdistrict desegregation programs. One such study, conducted in 1989 in Milwaukee, concluded that while the desegregation program within the Milwaukee Public Schools had failed to increase the academic achievement of black students, black students who attended suburban schools through the Chapter 220 program outperformed their counterparts in city schools.[141] In another analysis of state test score data from suburban school districts accepting transfer students of color from Boston through the METCO program, researchers found that while METCO-receiving districts tend to be higher scoring initially, METCO participation slightly lowers the overall average test scores within district schools. This is most likely due to the fact that METCO participants are more disadvantaged when they enter the suburban schools and thus have lower average test scores than their more privileged suburban counterparts. Still, this study also found that, in both school-level data for Massachusetts and micro-level data from one large school district that accepts METCO students, there is no impact of the METCO program on the test scores of white, non-METCO students. Furthermore, in the more in-depth analysis of this one large METCO-participating district, these researchers found that the METCO students benefited from time in the program, generally showing more test score improvement between the third and seventh grades than resident students in this district.[142]

Meanwhile, annual evaluation reports of the Minneapolis The Choice Is Yours program have shown uneven results in the few years for which data are available. For instance, in 2004–5, the first year for which student achievement data were available, test results suggest that the low-income students who transferred from urban to suburban schools appeared to benefit academically. In contrast, the 2005–6 student achievement data reveal that the students who transferred to the suburbs were outperformed by a comparison group of students who were eligible for the suburban transfers due to their low-income status but chose to remain in city schools.[143] Given that this program began in 2000–2001 and given the unevenness of the first two years of test score data, we conclude that it is too early to assess the academic impact of this interdistrict transfer plan. Indeed, if the research on the St. Louis transfer plan is any indication, it make take several years before the full benefit of this program will be understood.

Long-term Outcomes for Mobility and Opportunity. The need for a longer-term assessment of the student achievement data from these interdistrict desegregation plans speaks to the potential long-term effects of these programs on the lives and opportunities of students of color—as they matriculate through the suburban schools and well beyond. Once again, some of the most important research on these longer-term effects comes from Project Concern, the original Hartford urban-suburban transfer program.

In the 1980s and early 1990s, Robert L. Crain and colleagues conducted a study of seven hundred African-American parents and/or former students. The sample was divided between graduates of the Project Concern program and a control group of young adults who had been chosen to participate in the program via the lottery but who decided not to transfer to the suburbs. In their report, the authors concluded that black students who attended suburban schools through Project Concern were more likely to graduate from high school and complete more years of college than members of the control group who remained in the Hartford Public Schools. The finding on dropping out of high school was particularly strong for male Project Concern participants, whose dropout rate was 0 percent while 36 percent of male control group students in the city dropped out.[144]

In addition, the authors found that the black Project Concern graduates had a greater sense of interracial comfort in predominantly white settings. The male Project Concern graduates were also less likely to have sensed discrimination during and after college and to have had far fewer encounters with the police. Male and female graduates, on the other hand, were more likely to have closer contact with whites, such as living in integrated neighborhoods or interacting with more white friends in college.

A second study of Project Concern adult graduates found that black graduates of suburban, predominantly white schools are far more likely to work in professions that had traditionally employed fewer blacks.[145] For instance, these black suburban school graduates were more likely to end up employed in white-collar jobs, mostly in the private sector, while those in the control group were more likely to have government or blue-collar jobs. Furthermore, Project Concern graduates were more likely to have "consistent" career plans based on their occupational aspirations, work history, and post-graduation activities.[146]

Similarly, in her study of African-American graduates of the Boston METCO program, Eaton asked if these alumni would do it all over again if they had the chance.[147] She found that the vast majority said that they would do it again. Furthermore, she found that these METCO graduates said they felt more comfortable around whites and that they had greater access to more prestigious educational and job opportunities.

This limited body of research on the long-term effects of these interdistrict desegregation programs echoes a larger body of research on the long-term effects of school desegregation policies in general. Research on employers, for instance, demonstrates that African-American graduates of a white suburban high school are more likely to be hired by a white-owned business than similar graduates of all-black, inner-city schools: "Knowledge that a job candidate graduated from a suburban school with a good reputation rather than an inner-city school is likely to signal to employers that the quality of education is better in the suburban school."[148] Similarly, Zweigenhaft and Domhoff found that most African-American students from low-income neighborhoods who attended prestigious private prep schools through a program called A Better Chance (ABC) used their prep school credentials to gain access to higher-status universities and successful careers.[149]

Clearly, this body of research on the long-term effect of cross-district desegregation speaks to the "institutional effects" of desegregation discussed above and thus helps underscore the reasons why proactive policies such as these are needed to both overcome the harms of racial and socioeconomic segregation and to tear down the spatial and physical barriers between the haves and the have-nots in our society. As we explain in the following section, these are exactly the characteristics that are lacking in the free market–founded open enrollment policies and programs.

High Demand: When Program Popularity Is Not about Markets but Inequality. Not all of these programs keep waiting lists of students who have applied for a seat in a suburban school but did not get one due to a lack of capacity. In some cases, once placements are made and the school year begins, the slate is wiped clean and parents whose children were not enrolled in a suburban school need to fill out a new application if they want to be considered for the following year. But despite the lack of systematic data across sites, we do know that in each of these programs, every year there are more applicants than spaces available.

For instance, in St. Louis, where the Voluntary Interdistrict Transfer plan has been losing state funding and thus capacity to serve the number of students that it did in the 1990s, for the 2007–8 year 3,662 black students from the city applied for only 1,163 available spaces in suburban schools. In other words, only

31 percent of the urban-to-suburban transfer applicants were placed in suburban schools.

We see more evidence of the popularity of these programs with urban families in the application figures from other programs. According to the coordinator for the Chapter 220 application process in the Milwaukee Public Schools, for the 2006–7 school year, approximately 2,000 students from the city applied to transfer to the suburbs, but there were only 370 total new seats available in suburban school districts. In Rochester, officials who work with the Urban-Suburban Transfer Program there said that each year between 400 and 500 students apply for between 70 and 100 spots in suburban schools. Similarly, the Tinsley Transfer program in California, which is fairly small in scale and places only about 166 new students each year in kindergarten through third grade, usually gets more than 200 applicants a year.

In 2006–7, there were 200 minority students from Hartford on the waiting list for Project Choice, mostly students in grades higher than second grade. Furthermore, Frankenberg argues that it is important to note that of all urban applicants for transfers to suburban schools, more ended up on the waitlist than actually were placed in a suburban school for that school year.[150] But the largest and most notorious waiting list is attached to Boston's METCO program, where estimates place the number of minority students from the city on the list to attend a suburban school at between 12,000 and 13,000. Furthermore, as of 1996 about 25 percent of the parents who signed up for METCO did so before their children were one year old.[151]

Clearly, there is demand for interdistrict desegregation programs that are grounded not in free market rhetoric but in meaningful choices for the students who have been most disadvantaged by the status quo in public education in the United States. More research is needed on how suburban schools are measuring capacity and what role funding levels play in their ability to accept additional transfer students. In addition, we need sound public policy that expands these meaningful choices for the most disadvantaged students by providing more incentives for suburban school districts to accept urban transfer students and funding for the infrastructure, which might include capital funding to build new structures in suburban districts, and support services needed to make these choices matter for poor families of color. Thus, in the final section of this chapter, we turn our attention to more specific policy recommendations.

RECOMMENDATIONS: USING FEDERAL ACCOUNTABILITY MANDATES TO EXPAND CHOICES FOR STUDENTS IN HIGH-POVERTY SCHOOLS

Born of court orders and political compromises, interdistrict school desegregation policies are not perfect in design. But ironically, their shortcomings tend to result not from their lack of free market orientation but rather from a lack of regulation—especially in their lack of strong requirements that suburban school districts enroll a certain number of transfer students or a more sophisticated lottery and recruitment system to curtail self-selection among students who choose to leave versus those who stay.

Despite these shortcomings, interdistrict desegregation plans are a marked improvement over interdistrict open enrollment choice policies when it comes to providing real choices to students most likely enrolled in failing schools. These desegregation plans are all designed—first and foremost—to assure that poor students of color who live in low-income and racially isolated communities are able to transfer to schools in more affluent and predominantly white communities. The most successful of these programs have also succeeded in getting suburban school districts to participate in meaningful numbers. Historically, this has been most often accomplished through court ordered agreements; in the cases of Boston and Rochester, however, moral persuasion and the benefits of diverse school environments for preparing children for the twenty-first century seem to have done the trick for a substantial number of suburban districts and schools. And as the stories of St. Louis, Milwaukee, and Indianapolis attest, even suburban districts initially forced to participate in interdistrict desegregation programs can come to support them.

And while none of these programs has yet met the full demand from eligible families in their cities, they do teach us about the possibilities of public policies to expand educational opportunities. Meanwhile, open enrollment interdistrict school choice plans teach us both about the limits of the free market metaphor for school choice policy, and the ways in which school choice options can do more harm than good by exacerbating existing inequalities in the name of competition.

Absent a slew of new court orders to desegregate public schools, which seems highly unlikely, we have to consider alternative policy mechanisms to spur urban-suburban district transfer programs modeled after the interdistrict desegregation plans and not open enrollment plans. Indeed, more than one commentator has noted the connection between what NCLB has espoused and the design of these interdistrict desegregation plans. For instance, Freivogel wrote as NCLB was still being debated in Congress that the St. Louis interdistrict plan contains many of the key elements of President George W. Bush's educational reform proposal—what was soon to become NCLB:

> It permits parents of children in failing schools to send their children to more successful public schools. And it reconstitutes failing schools with new principals and educational programs—elements of the education reform program supported by President George W. Bush and Sen. Edward M. Kennedy, D-Mass . . . As a notable example of the last century's great educational experiment of desegregation and as an example of this century's educational reform model, St. Louis has lessons to offer the rest of the nation. The single most telling lesson is that neither school desegregation not accountability has created an equal education for African-American children.[152]

Taken together, research on interdistrict open enrollment choice policies and interdistrict desegregation plans illustrates that the design of these policies matters a great deal. Thus, we argue that the federal government, which, until NCLB, had never used its powers to mandate school choice, has the unique ability to create equity-minded choice programs that break through existing school district boundary limits. The way in which these policies are crafted, however, will matter a great deal in terms of student outcomes. These are issues that members of Congress should consider in reauthorizing NCLB, if their goal is indeed to provide meaningful school choice that leaves no child behind.

We base the following recommendations on the cautions gleaned from our examination of interdistrict open enrollment policies and the possibilities embedded in the interdistrict desegregation plans. Most important, any new federal policies to foster interdistrict public school choice must have the following characteristics to support a noncompetitive but equity-minded framework for school choice policies:

1. target and support meaningful school choices for the most disadvantaged students,

2. foster and support significant participation of suburban districts, and

3. further the goals of diversity and equity in public education.

    Given the research findings that we discuss above, we suggest the following policy components under each of these characteristics.

1. TARGET AND SUPPORT MEANINGFUL SCHOOL CHOICES FOR THE MOST DISADVANTAGED STUDENTS

    This characteristic would embody the following legislative components to help the new legislation achieve the goal of greater equity.

TARGET STUDENTS WHO HAVE HAD THE LEAST CHOICES IN EDUCATION AND RESTRICT STATE-SUBSIDIZED CHOICES FOR OTHERS. Lessons from open enrollment and interdistrict desegregation clearly illustrate that for interdistrict school choice under NCLB to expand opportunities for students who are the least advantaged, choice opportunities need to be targeted toward certain students and regulated to prevent increased stratification. The federally supported interdistrict transfer process, therefore, should be targeted toward students who have had the fewest opportunities in public education and who are most likely to be enrolled in failing schools. Given the Supreme Court's recent ruling on the Louisville and Seattle cases, it is unlikely that these policies can target students directly according to their racial identification. Still, in order to avoid the kind of racial segregation and stratification that open enrollment plans have exacerbated, these new policies must reach the most disadvantaged students via targets based on the following "opportunity of place" student criteria:

◆   enrollment in a failing school,

◆   family poverty, and

♦   residency in a racially isolated community with highly concen-
    trated poverty.

Students who meet all three of these criteria should have top
priority for suburban transfers. Once communities, schools, and students who are most disadvantaged in terms of access to high-quality
education are identified based on these criteria, several steps need to
be taken to assure the participation in the transfer program.

Furthermore, careful controls must be instituted to ensure that
students are allowed to choose only among schools in which they do
not negatively affect the socioeconomic balance. Another clear need
is to ensure that all students are provided information and support in
making choices so that the least advantaged students are not the ones
that are "left behind."

PROVIDE SUPPORT FOR CHOOSING FAMILIES VIA COORDINATION OF
SERVICES AND INFORMATION. To foster participation of the most
disadvantaged students, funding should be allocated within the reauthorization of NCLB to pay for the types of metropolitan public
school choice coordination centers shown to be highly effective with
interdistrict desegregation plans. These centers, such as the VICC office in suburban St. Louis, should conduct outreach and information
campaigns about interdistrict school choice plans through mailings,
local meetings, and community networks. These centers should also
administer the application process and coordinate the transportation
and transfers with families and school districts. These coordinating centers could also create and staff parent information centers in
targeted communities, modeled after those in the Minneapolis The
Choice Is Yours program. Successful interdistrict desegregation programs have demonstrated the need for providing ongoing support to
parents and students who transfer through centers such as these.

PROVIDE FREE AND ACCESSIBLE TRANSPORTATION. Lessons from
open enrollment versus interdistrict desegregation plans illustrate
that transportation is critical to the participation of disadvantaged students. Under current NCLB legislation, school districts
must spend between 5 percent to 15 percent of Title I, Section
A, funding allocations to "provide or pay for transportation for
public school choice" as long as the student's home school is still
in school improvement status.[153] These funds should be made

available to bus students who fit the above criteria to high-achieving schools across district lines. Additional funding will be required to pay for interdistrict school choice bus routes, which will be longer and thus more expensive. Busing routes need to be established and worked out centrally via the public school choice coordinating centers to assure both full transportation support for disadvantaged students and the most efficient transportation system possible. To foster the participation of the students least likely to choose, these funds should be provided not as a reimbursement plan (as is currently in place for many open enrollment laws) but should be utilized to pay for bus passes or additional buses that would transport students either to suburban schools or to places on routes that would allow students to access suburban school district bus lines.

2. FOSTER AND SUPPORT SIGNIFICANT PARTICIPATION OF SUBURBAN DISTRICTS

Federally supported interdistrict choice policies should appeal to the sensibilities of suburban educators, parents, and students regarding the importance of racial and ethnic diversity in education, but they should also assure that suburban districts will accept urban transfer students up to an agreed-on number or percentage of their total student bodies. The following legislative components could help the suburbs reach these goals.

LEGISLATION THAT INSPIRES SUBURBAN SCHOOL DISTRICTS TO DO THE RIGHT THING. As we have noted throughout this chapter, the goals and framework of a school choice policy matter. Suburban school districts in the eight areas we looked at have been more likely to resist accepting interdistrict transfer students from the most disadvantaged communities and schools when the policy is framed around competition between schools for students, funding, and high test scores. They are much more willing to accept lower-socioeconomic-status children from a poor school district under voluntary interdistrict desegregation plans than they have been through their state open enrollment laws, even when, as in the Boston METCO case, the per-pupil funding for these transfers is higher under open enrollment.

Furthermore, in Minneapolis where the interdistrict socioeconomic urban-to-suburban integration plan and the statewide open enrollment plan are intertwined, we see that the mechanisms of open enrollment choice can be shaped toward creating more equity, not less. Although we believe the Minneapolis The Choice Is Yours plan needs more tweaking to assure that it is not disproportionately transferring low-income white students out of city schools (which could be achieved through the targeted student criteria listed above), it is a model of how to take the two interdistrict school choice policies analyzed in this chapter and merge them into a more equity-minded model. In short, we argue based on the history of the interdistrict desegregation programs that when policies are framed by the goals of educational equality as well as the creation of more diversity in otherwise extremely racially homogeneous schools, the districts do, over time, become highly committed to them as long as they are given some incentive to do so.

Financial Incentives to Help the Suburbs Cover the Cost of Educating Transfer Students. Suburban school districts do need financial incentives or "carrots" to help cover the costs of educating students who transfer into their schools. Such incentives should match their average annual per-pupil expenditure when possible, or else be slightly below that amount but include federal and state compensatory education funding to address students' more specific needs. Furthermore, states, with financial support from the federal government, should provide capital funding to suburban school districts that can prove a lack of capacity. These one-time capital grants would help suburban educators make the case to their constituents about the benefits of participating in interdistrict choice programs.

Safe Havens for Participating Suburban Districts under AYP. Under increasing pressure from NCLB, suburban districts may be unlikely to accept new urban transfer students who may (at least initially) lower their test scores and cause them to not make AYP in at least one student racial/ethnic category in the disaggregated data. Such transfer programs after all will require many suburban districts to become accountable for an increasing number of racial/ethnic subgroups. Without a temporary "safe haven" provision, suburban districts would be less likely to accept urban transfer students, particularly those who are low achieving. While the progress of these new transfer students should be monitored and districts should be held accountable for adding value and helping them achieve to a high standard, initially their state test scores should not be used to keep suburban districts from making AYP.

The recent proposal of Senator Joe Lieberman on revamping NCLB school choice provisions suggested providing a safe harbor for one year from AYP calculations for the new out-of-district student transfers. Yet we argue that a separate, non-AYP related monitoring system be set up to evaluate the progress of these students over a five-year period in their new schools. After five years, the transfer students should be merged into the overall student population in terms of test score accountability.

Support and Training for Educators in Suburban Schools. Successful school desegregation plans have shown that to enable suburban districts to adequately serve transfer students who have different racial/ethnic, socioeconomic, and cultural backgrounds than the majority of educators and students in suburban schools, support and training will be required for teachers and administrators in the receiving districts. Such training and support should help educators address and explore their inherent biases and preconceived notions of urban students, to ensure that transfer students receive equal opportunities within their new schooling environments. Also, suburban educators, to the extent that they can in the current era of high-stakes state tests, should rethink their school curriculum to reflect the diversity of perspectives and voices, in particular in history and English literature courses. A more multicultural, multi-perspective approach to education should also be supported via in-service and training funds.

3. Further the Goals of Diversity and Equity in Urban and Suburban Public Education

Given that some portion of students in failing urban schools are going to need to remain in those or other urban schools, federal policy needs to also consider what to do with the schools left behind. In addition, while we have not explained the urban school reform dimension of five of these interdistrict school desegregation plans—Milwaukee, St. Louis, Hartford, Minneapolis, and Tinsley—in any detail in this chapter due to a lack of space, it is important to note that these non-competitive policies did also try to help the students left behind when more students transferred out of urban schools in cities. Most of these resources were targeted toward school improvement efforts and urban magnet schools.

The most challenging dilemma facing any form of school choice policy is the question of how to address the needs of students and schools that do not choose. There are several possibilities for doing this that would support the non-competitive framework we are suggesting for the federal interdistrict school choice policy under NCLB.

EXTRA RESOURCES FOR SCHOOLS LEFT BEHIND. One component of several of the court ordered interdistrict school desegregation programs has been to allow urban school districts to keep a portion of the state funding for the students who transfer out. This increases the per-pupil funding for students who remain in failing schools, which can be used to shrink class sizes and institute a host of other school improvement reforms.

REGIONAL MAGNET SCHOOLS. Another possibility, which has been used in four of the eight desegregation plans—Hartford (and other Connecticut cities), St. Louis, Milwaukee, and Minneapolis—discussed here is creating new popular magnet schools that draw white students from the suburbs and thus have a regional attendance zone. These regional magnet centers, as they are also being instituted in Omaha, Nebraska, to create interdistrict choice options, must be carefully designed to ensure that they maintain a stable socioeconomic and regional balance. Also to make these schools attractive to diverse students from all over the metro areas, they must offer specialized programs that are popular, such as technology or science. We know from the four interdistrict desegregation plans noted here that these magnet schools can serve as beacons of excellence in otherwise low-performing school districts and that suburban students will choose to transfer to them if they are attractive enough. The real challenge is then to filter some of the curriculum and best practices that can be developed in these regional magnet schools into neighborhood urban schools.

FOSTER CROSS-DISTRICT COLLABORATION AND GROWTH. When school district officials, educators, parents, and students across a metropolitan area can think beyond their own school boundaries and work with schools and communities clear across town, they can come to know the "other" not as a competitor but as a collaborator in educating and nurturing the next generation of citizens. Schools and districts can form partnerships that cross significant boundary lines and develop shared educational experiences and projects. Two middle schools across the urban-suburban divide, for example, could hold a joint science fair with students collaborating on projects using the Internet and face-to-face meetings facilitated through science teachers. School plays and other performances could be jointly produced with students and educators from two or more schools working collaboratively. The possibility for cross-school and cross-district collaboration are endless; such projects could not only bring students together across geographic and cultural divides, but they could also spur school improvement programs by spreading learning opportunities across separate and unequal schools.

CONCLUSION

The central argument of this chapter is that educational policies—from those passed by the U.S. Congress all the way to those adopted by local school boards and educators within schools and classrooms—need to be framed by an understanding of education as a nurturing and caring profession that is best supported not by policies that force schools to compete, but by policies that foster collaboration and the expansion of educational opportunities. When we think of school choice programs that would allow students to escape failing schools and gain access to high-quality schools, we must think beyond school district boundaries and a paradigm of schools competing for rank, resources, and high-achieving students. Such a paradigm will never serve the most disadvantaged students well. And, in the long run, this framework will ultimately fail our increasingly diverse society as a whole.

Furthermore, we would like to add that in a small way, the federal government has been supporting one of the two key components we are calling for—interdistrict transfers—through the Voluntary Public School Choice Programs. This federal grant program has, in recent years, given priority to grant applicants proposing interdistrict choice plans. In fact, Minneapolis's The Choice Is Yours program is a recipient of one of those grants (see Table 4.1, p. 208). This is one step toward the kind of federal support that is needed to solve the problems of children left behind in poor, failing schools. But this program is relatively small—only $25 million spread across fourteen grantees—and it lacks the kind of guidelines and requirements that assure that these funded programs are providing the first and most choices to those students who have historically had so few options in the educational system, the second key component of our framework. Still one step down the path toward more meaningful and equity-minded school choice policies should be celebrated—and then built on for the future.

Table 4.1 begins on page 208 and runs through page 215.

Table 4.1
Overview of Eight Largest Interdistrict
School Desegregation Plans

	Year Started and Impetus/ Current Legal Status	Peak/Current Enrollment	Race/Ethnicity of Transfer Students
St. Louis Voluntary Interdistrict Transfer Plan	1983 Federal court case followed by a court order and a series of settlement agreements After 2008, suburbs will participate voluntarily	13,000 urban-to-suburban transfers and 1,500 suburban-to-urban magnet school transfers 8,000 from city to the suburbs; very few suburban-to-urban transfers	Black students from city to sixteen participating suburbs White students from suburbs
Hartford Project Choice	1997 State court case followed by a court order and a series of settlement agreements	1,070 urban-to-suburban transfers	Black and Latino students from the city of Hartford to the twenty-seven participating suburbs White students from the suburbs can enroll in one of the city's magnet schools, but few do

Guidelines/Incentives for Suburban Districts	Waiting List/Capacity Information
Strong guidelines under the original court order required the suburban districts to increase their black enrollment to between 15 percent and 25 percent In the future, suburban districts will define capacity Under the court order, suburban districts and the St. Louis Public Schools received their per-pupil funding for each transfer student After 2008, suburban districts will receive a flat payment of $8,000 per transfer student per year	For the 2007–8 school year, about 3,662 African-American students from the city of St. Louis applied to transfer to suburban schools; there were only 1,163 seats available; this equals a 31 percent placement rate
Weak guidelines for suburban districts to take Harford students Suburban districts were receiving only $2,000 per pupil for each city student who transferred in; that amount rose to $2,500 in 2007	By 2007, of the twenty-seven participating suburban school districts, ten provide less than 1 percent of their seats to Hartford students; the state's school facility capacity data suggest there may be thousands more potential seats in existing suburban schools

(continued)

(continued)	Year Started and Impetus/ Current Legal Status	Peak/Current Enrollment	Race/Ethnicity of Transfer Students
Boston METCO	1966 State legislation	As of 2007, there were 3,300 urban-to-suburban transfer students	75 percent of the METCO transfer students are black, 16 percent Hispanic, and 4 percent Asian; these students transfer to thirty-seven suburban school districts
Milwaukee Chapter 220 Program	1976 Chapter 220 Program created by state legislation 1987 Federal court case and court order followed by a settlement agreement to mandate suburban participation in Chapter 220 1993 The settlement agreement expired and the program has operated under a yearly contract between the Milwaukee Public Schools and the suburban districts ever since	6,000 urban-to-suburban transfers in 1993 Now, 3,000 urban-to-suburban transfers; about 423 suburban-to-urban transfers	Chapter 220 urban-to-suburban transfers were 72 percent black; 9 percent Hispanic, and 13 percent Asian in the late 1990s These transfer students enroll in twenty-two suburban school districts White students transfer into the city magnet and charter schools from the suburbs

Guidelines/Incentives for Suburban Districts	Waiting List/Capacity Information
Suburban participation is voluntary with weak guidelines for how many students each district must take Suburban districts receive $3,700 per pupil for each student who transfers from Boston	The waiting list for METCO, which is carried over from year to year, is reported to be as high as 13,000
Total goal for program under the court order instead of individual goals for each district Suburbs receive per-pupil funding for each transfer student MPS also receives per-pupil funding for suburban-to-urban transfers	For the 2006–7 school year, 370 total seats were open in suburban school districts, and there were about 2,000 applicants for those seats from minority children in the city of Milwaukee

(continued)

(continued)	Year Started and Impetus/ Current Legal Status	Peak/Current Enrollment	Race/Ethnicity of Transfer Students
Rochester Urban– Suburban Transfer Program	1965 Begun voluntarily by suburban and city schools Supported by state legislation	About 500–600 urban-to-suburban transfers each year	Mostly black and Latino students A white student in Rochester sued to participate but failed
Indianapolis– Suburban Township Desegregation Plan	1981 Federal court case and court order 1998 A new settlement agreement was reached that declared Indianapolis Public Schools unitary and set 2005 as the last year of new urban-suburban transfers	In the early 1980s, about 7,000 urban-to-suburban transfers Now phasing out	Black students from the city to the suburbs only

Guidelines/Incentives for Suburban Districts	Waiting List/Capacity Information
No guidelines for districts; suburban districts decide their capacity The State of New York pays for the transfer program; suburban districts receive the Rochester Public Schools' per-pupil funding amount for each city student who transfers into one of their schools; this funding level is often close to or greater than the per-pupil spending in the suburban districts	Each year, about 70–100 city transfer students are placed in suburban schools and about 400–500 apply.
City students were assigned to suburban schools based on where they lived; suburbs had to accept those students who lived in their paired zone in the city Suburbs receive a payment from the state for each urban transfer student that they enroll; this payment is roughly equivalent to their per-pupil costs	There were no waiting lists for this program because students did not apply (continued)

(continued)	Year Started and Impetus/ Current Legal Status	Peak/Current Enrollment	Race/Ethnicity of Transfer Students
Tinsley Interdistrict Transfer Plan	1986 State court case and resulting court order and settlement agreement between East Palo Alto and eight more affluent and predominantly white nearby suburban school districts	206 per year for grades K–3 Students matriculate through 8th grade	Latino, black, and Asian (particularly Tongan) students
Minneapolis The Choice Is Yours Program	2001 State court case and resulting settlement agreement that used the state's existing open enrollment policy to target poor children in the city of Minneapolis for transfers to suburban schools via a new program called The Choice Is Yours	2,000 urban-to-suburban transfers	Based on SES and not race: only 53 percent black; 22 percent white; the rest is "other" (a mix of Latino and Hmong)

Guidelines/Incentives for Suburban Districts	Waiting List/Capacity Information
Strong guidelines for receiving school districts

Receiving districts get 70 percent of the revenue limit (per-pupil expenditure) of the Ravenswood Elementary School District in East Palo Alto | The program usually receives more than 200 applications each year for the 166 seats available for new K–3 students |
| Weak guidelines in terms of assuring that suburban districts will take students

Suburbs receive state per-pupil plus compensatory funds that the transfer student was eligible for in the Minneapolis Public Schools. | A lottery assigns students to schools based on the choices that they submit, and virtually all students receive either their first- or second-choice school |

NOTES

CHAPTER 1

1. Richard D. Kahlenberg, *Tough Liberal: Albert Shanker and the Battles over Schools, Unions, Race, and Democracy* (New York: Columbia University Press, 2007), 320.

2. Ibid., 6.

3. Jennifer O'Day and Marshall S. Smith, "Systemic Reform and Educational Opportunity," in *Designing Coherent Education Policy,* ed. Susan Furhman (San Francisco: Jossey-Bass, 1993), 250–312; Marshall S. Smith and Jennifer O'Day, "Systemic School Reform," in *The Politics of Curriculum and Testing,* ed. Susan Fuhrman and Betty Malen (Bristol, Penn.: Falmer Press, 1990), 233–67.

4. Kahlenberg, *Tough Liberal,* 326–27.

5. Ibid., 322.

6. Bruce Fuller, Joseph Wright, Kathryn Gesicki, and Erin Kang, "Gauging Growth: How to Judge No Child Left Behind?" *Educational Researcher* 36, no. 5 (2007): 268–78.

7. See Center on Education Policy, *Answering the Question That Matters Most: Has Student Achievement Increased since No Child Left Behind?* June 2007. Fuller et al., "Gauging Growth,' 268–78. See also Scott J. Cech, "12-state Study Finds Falloff in Testing Gains after NCLB," *Education Week,* August 1, 2007, 9.

8. Writing in the *American Prospect,* for example, Richard Rothstein declared: "NCLB is dead. It will not be reauthorized—not this year, not ever." Richard Rothstein, "Leaving 'No Child Left Behind' Behind," *American Prospect,* January–February 2008, 50.

9. National Education Association, *Funding Gap: No Child Left Behind,* 2008, http://www.nea.org/lac/funding/images/fundinggap. pdf. The NEA relies on appropriations funding information from the U.S. Department of Education. See U.S. Department of Education,

"Department of Education Budget Tables," http://www.ed.gov/about/
overview/budget/tables.html?src=rt. The authorization levels are from
the No Child Left Behind Act of 2001, 107th Congress, 1st session,
2001, H.R. 1, http://www.ed.gov/policy/elsec/leg/esea02/107-110.pdf.
According to the NEA, its NCLB totals differ slightly from those of the
department because the NEA includes programs such as Education for
Homeless Children and Youths since this program is amended by NCLB,
while the department does not. A handful of programs account for the
difference.

10. William Duncombe, Anna Lukemeyer, and John Yinger, "Dollars
Without Sense: The Mismatch Between the No Child Left Behind Act
Accountability System and Title I Funding" (see p. 30 in this volume).

11. Ibid., p. 20 and pp. 70–71, Table 2.13.

12. Lauren B. Resnick, Mary Kay Stein, and Sarah Coon, "Standards-
based Reform: A Powerful Idea Unmoored" (see p. 130 this volume),
and Paul Barton, *"Failing" or "Succeeding" Schools: How Can We Tell?*
American Federation of Teachers, 2006, 5.

13. Kahlenberg, *Tough Liberal*, 326.

14. John Cronin, Michael Dahlin, Deborah Adkins, and G. Gage
Kingsbury, *The Proficiency Illusion*, Thomas B. Fordham Institute, October
2007, http://vcww.edexcellence.net/doc/The_Proficiency_Illusion.pdf. See
also Chester E. Finn Jr., "Dumbing Education Down," *Wall Street Journal*,
October 5, 2007, A16.

15. Duncombe, Lukemeyer, and Yinger, "Dollars without Sense" (see
p. 74 this volume).

16. Kahlenberg, *Tough Liberal*, 328.

17. Paul Barton, *Staying the Course in Education Reform*, Educational
Testing Service, April 2002, 14. See also Paul Barton, *Unfinished Business:
More Measured Approaches in Standards-based Reform*, Educational
Testing Service, December 2004, 4.

18. Resnick, Stein, and Coon, "Standards-based Reform" (see p. 127
this volume).

19. Ibid. (see p. 129 this volume) See also Barton, *Unfinished Business*, 3.

20. Kahlenberg, *Tough Liberal*, 338–39.

21. The Bush administration, recognizing the problem, recently
announced a move to allow up to ten states to distinguish degrees of failure
in schools. See Sam Dillon, "U.S. Eases 'No Child' Law as Applied to Some
States," *New York Times*, March 19, 2008.

22. Resnick, Stein, and Coon, "Standards-based Reform" (see p. 129
this volume).

23. Lynn Olson, "A Better Measure of Student Growth?" *Education Week*, November 8, 2006, 17; and Barton, *"Failing" or "Succeeding" Schools*, 13.

24. See, for example, Cynthia G. Brown, *Choosing Better Schools: A Report on Student Transfers under the No Child Left Behind Act*, Citizens' Commission on Civil Rights, 2004, 3.

25. U.S. Department of Education, Office of Planning, Evaluation and Development, Policy and Program Studies Service, *State and Local Implementation of the No Child Left Behind Act: Volume I — Title I School Choice, Supplemental Educational Services, and Student Achievement*, Washington, D.C., 2007, xi. See also Government Accountability Office, *No Child Left Behind Act: Education Needs to Provide Additional Technical Assistance and Conduct Implementation Studies for School Choice Provision*, December 2004, 15; Brown, *Choosing Better Schools*, 6.

26. See, for example, Richard D. Kahlenberg, "A County's Failing Policy," *Washington Post*, June 24, 2002, A19, detailing the effort by Montgomery County, Maryland, to discourage families from transferring out of failing schools.

27. Jennifer Jellison Holme and Amy Stuart Wells, "School Choice beyond District Borders: Lessons for the Reauthorization of NCLB from Interdistrict Desegregation and Open Enrollment Plans" (see pp. 141 and 144 this volume).

28. Ibid. (see p. 146 this volume).

29. U.S. Department of Education, *State and Local Implementation* of the No Child Left Behind Act, xi.

30. Holme and Wells, "School Choice beyond District Borders," (see p. 144 this volume)

31. James E. Ryan, "The Perverse Incentives of the No Child Left Behind Act," *New York University Law Review* 79, no. 3 (June 2004): 962.

32. U.S. Department of Education, *The Condition of Education 2006* (Washington, D.C.: Government Printing Office, 2006), 47.

33. *PISA 2006: Science Competencies for Tomorrow's World*, vol. 1 (Paris: Organisation for Economic Co-operation and Development, 2007), 194.

34. See Richard D. Kahlenberg, *All Together Now: Creating Middle-class Schools Through Public School Choice* (Washington, D.C.: Brookings Institution Press, 2001), 47–76; and Richard D. Kahlenberg, *Rescuing* Brown v. Board of Education: *Profiles of Twelve School Districts Pursuing Socioeconomic School Integration*, The Century Foundation, 2007, 7.

35. Kahlenberg, *Rescuing* Brown v. Board of Education (citing forty districts). Since publication of the report, additional districts have decided

to employ socioeconomic status as a factor. See Megan Hawkins, "D.M. Schools to Judge Diversity by Income," *Des Moines Register*, February 20, 2008; Molly Walsh, "Burlington School Board Moves Forward on Magnets," *Burlington Free Press*, February 1, 2008; Emily Guevara, "BISD Replaces Race-based Transfers with Policy Based on Students' Economic Status," *Beaumont Enterprise*, February 3, 2008; Antoinette Konz and Chris Kenning, "Jefferson Co. Schools Unveil Desegregation Plan," *Louisville Courier-Journal*, January 28, 2008; and Amanda Bedgood, "Schools of Choice Get New Entrance Criteria: Economic Status, not Race, Now Part of Consideration," *Lafayette Daily Advertiser*, February 21, 2008.

36. Kahlenberg, *Rescuing* Brown v. Board of Education, 13.

37. Holme and Wells, "School Choice beyond District Borders" (see pp. 157 and 183–195 this volume).

38. Ibid. (see p. 188–92 this volume).

39. Ibid. (p. 195 this volume).

40. Ibid. (pp. 208–15 this volume).

41. Ibid. (pp. 165–76 this volume).

42. Ibid. (pp. 172–74 this volume).

43. Ibid. (pp. 174–76 this volume).

44. Ibid. (pp. 167–69 this volume).

45. Ibid. (p. 187 this volume).

46. Ibid. (p.184–87, this volume).

47. See John Edwards, "Building One America by Creating Opportunity," http://www.johnedwards.com/issues/poverty/creating-opportunity/index.html; Mike Allen, "Edwards Has Plan to Diversify Schools," *Politico*, July 17, 2007; and "Integrating Schools: John Edwards Has Interesting Ideas about How to Do It," Editorial, *Washington Post*, July 23, 2007, A16.

48. Richard D. Kahlenberg, "The New Brown: Integration by Class, Not Race, Can Fix Schools in Poor Cities," *Legal Affairs*, May–June 2003, 30–35.

49. Richard Lee Colvin, "Public School Choice: An Overview," in *Leaving No Child Behind? Options for Kids in Failing Schools*, Frederick M. Hess and Chester E. Finn Jr., ed. (New York: Palgrave MacMillan, 2004), 13, 25.

50. Holme and Wells, "School Choice beyond District Borders," (see p. 202 this volume).

51. Ibid. (see pp. 202–3 this volume).

52. See, for example, Chester E. Finn Jr., "Com 'Pell'ing Proposal: An Opportunity for Low-income Students to Find Better Schools," *National Review* Online, January 30, 2008.

53. For the myriad problems posed by privatization, see the essays found in *Public School Choice Versus Private School Vouchers*, ed. Richard D. Kahlenberg (New York: Century Foundation Press, 2003).

54. Lauren Resnick and Chris Zurawsky, "Getting Back on Course: Fixing Standards-Based Reform and Accountability," *American Educator,* Spring 2005.

CHAPTER 2

1. H. F. Ladd, "School-based Educational Accountability Systems: The Promise and Pitfalls," *National Tax Journal* 54, no. 2 (2001): 385–400; L. Meyer, G. Orlofsky, R. Skinner, and S. Spicer, "The State of the States," *Quality Counts 2001,* January 10, 2002.

2. W. Erpenbach, E. Forte-Fast, and A. Potts, *Statewide Educational Accountability under NCLB,* Council of Chief State School Officers, Washington, D.C., 2003.

3. Education cost functions have been estimated for New York (W. Duncombe and J. Yinger, "Financing Higher Student Performance Standards: The Case of New York State," *Economics of Education Review* 19 [October 2000]: 363–86; W. Duncombe and J. Yinger, "How Much More Does a Disadvantaged Student Cost?" *Economics of Education Review* 24, no. 5 [2005]: 513–32; W. Duncombe, A. Lukemeyer, and J. Yinger, "Financing an Adequate Education: A Case Study of New York," in *Developments in School Finance: 2001–2002,* ed. W. J. Fowler Jr. [Washington, D.C.: National Center for Education Statistics, 2003], 127–54), Arizona (T. Downes and T. Pogue, "Adjusting School Aid Formulas for the Higher Cost of Educating Disadvantaged Students," *National Tax Journal* 67 [March 1994]: 89–110), Illinois (J. Imazeki, "Grade-dependent Costs of Education: Evidence from Illinois" [draft paper, San Diego State University, 2001]), Texas (J. Imazeki and A. Reschovsky, "Estimating the Costs of Meeting the Texas Educational Accountability Standards" [unpublished manuscript, 2004]; J. Imazeki and A. Reschovsky, "Is *No Child Left Behind* an Un [or Under] Funded Federal Mandate? Evidence from Texas," *National Tax Journal* 57 [September 2004]: 571–88; T. Gronberg, W. Jansen, L. Taylor, and K. Booker, *School Outcomes and School Costs: The Cost Function Approach.* Texas Joint Select Committee on Public School Finance, Austin, Tex., 2004) and Wisconsin (A. Reschovsky and J. Imazeki,

"Achieving Educational Adequacy Through School Finance Reform," *Journal of Education Finance* 26 [Spring 2001]: 373–96).

4. Duncombe and Yinger, "How Much More?"; W. Duncombe and J. Yinger, "Measurement of Cost Differentials," in *Handbook of Research in Education Finance and Policy*, ed. H. Ladd and T. Fiske (New York: Routledge, 2007), 238–56.

5. E. Hanushek and M. Raymond, "The Confusing World of Educational Accountability," *National Tax Journal* 54, no. 2 (2001): 365–84; H. F. Ladd and R. Walsh, "Implementing Value-added Measures of School Effectiveness: Getting the Incentives Right," *Economics of Education Review* 21 (February 2002): 1–17; D. N. Figlio, "Funding and Accountability: Some Conceptual and Technical Issues in State Aid Reform," in *Helping Children Left Behind: State Aid and the Pursuit of Educational Equity*, ed. J. Yinger (Cambridge, Mass.: MIT Press, 2004), 87–110; W. Sanders, "Value-added Assessment from Student Achievement Data: Opportunities and Hurdles," *Journal of Personnel Evaluation in Education* 14, no. 4 (2000): 329–39; T. Kane and D. Staiger, "The Promise and Pitfalls of Using Imprecise School Accountability Measures," *Journal of Economic Perspectives* 16, no. 4 (2002): 91–114.

6. Hanushek and Raymond, "The Confusing World"; Ladd and Walsh, "Implementing Value-added Measures"; Figlio, "Funding and Accountability"; Sanders, "Value-added Assessment"; Kane and Staiger, "The Promise and Pitfalls."

7. Meyer et al., "The State of the States."

8. B. Jacob and S. Levitt, "Rotten Apples: An Investigation of the Prevalence and Predictors of Teacher Cheating," *Quarterly Journal of Economics* 118, no. 3 (2003): 843–77; D. N. Figlio and C. E. Rouse, "Do Accountability and Voucher Threats Improve Low-performing Schools?" *Journal of Public Economics* 90, no. 1–2 (2006): 239–55.

9. States have also been moving slowly toward more accurate accounting for cost factors in their education aid formulas. See Y. Huang, "Appendix B: A Guide to State Operating Aid Programs for Elementary and Secondary Education," in *Helping Children Left Behind: State Aid and the Pursuit of Educational Equity*, ed. J. Yinger (Cambridge, Mass.: MIT Press, 2004), 331–51; and Duncombe and Yinger, "Measurement of Cost Differentials." At this point, however, no state fully accounts for all cost factors in its aid formulas.

10. C. Clotfelter and H. F. Ladd, "Recognizing and Rewarding Success in Public Schools," in *Holding Schools Accountable: Performance-based Reform in Education*, ed. H. Ladd (Washington, D.C.: Brookings Institution, 1996), 23–64.

11. Ladd and Walsh, "Implementing Value-added Measures."

12. Ibid.

13. Duncombe and Yinger, "Measurement of Cost Differentials."

14. J. Yinger, "State Aid and the Pursuit of Educational Equity: An Overview," in *Helping Children Left Behind: State Aid and the Pursuit of Educational Equity*, ed. J. Yinger (Cambridge, Mass.: MIT Press, 2004), 3–58.

15. Kane and Staiger, "The Promise and Pitfalls."

16. U.S. Department of Education, *No Child Left Behind: A Road Map for State Implementation*, Washington, D.C., 2005, http://www.ed.gov/admins/lead/account/roadmap/index.html; Center on Education Policy, *From the Capital to the Classroom*, Washington, D.C., September 2006; Erpenbach, Forte-Fast, and Potts, *Statewide Educational Accountability*.

17. U.S. Department of Education, *Growth Models: Ensuring Grade-level Proficiency for All Students by 2014*, Washington, D.C., November 2005, http://www.ed.gov/news/pressreleases/2005/11/11182005.html.

18. C. Hoxby, "Inadequate Yearly Progress: Unlocking the Secrets of NCLB," *Education Next* (Summer 2005): 46–51.

19. Center on Education Policy, *From the Capital to the Classroom*. In a review of state accountability plans in 2006, the Center on Education Policy found that "the U.S. Department of Education continued in 2006 to approve changes to state accountability plans that in effect make it easier for schools and districts to demonstrate AYP." Center on Education Policy, *No Child Left Behind at Five: A Review of Changes to State Accountability Provisions*, Washington, D.C., January 2007, 1–2.

20. U.S. Department of Education, *Growth Models*. States approved to use growth models include Tennessee, North Carolina, Delaware, Arkansas, Iowa, Florida, Alaska, and Arizona. The use of growth models does not relieve the state of the requirement of 100 percent proficiency by 2014.

21. J. E. Ryan, "The Perverse Incentives of the No Child Left Behind Act," *New York University Law Review* 90 (June 2004): 942–43.

22. M. Davis, "Study: NCLB Leads to Cuts in Some Subjects," *Education Week*, April 5, 2006.

23. As Heinrich puts it, an accountability system should "make it difficult for managers to increase their measured performance in ways other than increasing their actual performance." C. J. Heinrich, "Outcome-based Performance Management in the Public Sector: Implications for Government Accountability and Effectiveness," *Public Administration Review* 62, no. 6 (November/December 2002): 712–25.

24. National Center for Education Statistics, *Mapping 2005 State Proficiency Standards onto the NAEP Scores*, NCES 2007-482, Washington, D.C., June 2007.

25. J. Kim and G. Sunderman, *Large Mandates and Limited Resources: State Response to the No Child Left Behind Act and Implications for Accountability* (Cambridge, Mass.: The Civil Rights Project, 2004); Ryan, "Perverse Incentives."

26. New York's measure of proficiency also gives weight to students close to proficiency (level 2). These students are recorded as 100, while students making proficiency are recorded as 200. The resulting performance index ranges from 0 to 200. We divide this index by 200 to calculate the proficiency rates on table 1.

27. The sources of information on proficiency targets are California Department of Education (CDE), *2006 Adequate Yearly Progress Report: Information Guide*, Sacramento, Calif., 2006; Kansas State Board of Education (KSBE), *Adequate Yearly Progress (AYP) Revised Guidance*, Topeka, Kan., September 2006; Missouri Department of Elementary and Secondary Education (MDESE), *Missouri Adequate Yearly Progress*, Jefferson City, Mo., 2007; and New York State Education Department (NYSED), *School and District Accountability Reports: Implementing No Child Left Behind (NCLB)*, Albany, N.Y., March 2004. The proficiency targets for New York appear to have been revised downward for fourth- and eighth-grade exams for 2007 (NYSED, *School and District Accountability Rules: Implementing No Child Left Behind [NCLB]*, Albany, N.Y., February 2007). Unfortunately the most recent report on accountability in New York (2007) does not provide targets for any other year. We used information from an earlier report (2004), which did include fourth- and eighth-grade targets from 2002 to 2014. These targets probably overstate what New York's targets will be, at least for some years.

28. Missouri Department of Elementary and Secondary Education (MDESE), *State Board of Education Revises Scoring Standards for MAP Exams*, January 13, 2006.

29. MDESE, *Missouri Public School Accountability Report: 2005–06 School Year*, Jefferson City, Mo., 2006.

30. National Center for Education Statistics, *Mapping 2005 State Proficiency Standards onto the NAEP Scores*.

31. The Commission on No Child Left Behind highlighted the significant variation in state exams and standards and the mismatch between state proficiency rates and those in NAEP in the report. One of the recommendations of the commission was for the development of "voluntary model

national content and performance standards and tests" (127). States should be given the choice of adopting these tests and standards, or building "their own assessment instruments based on the national model standards" (137). If states kept their existing standards and tests, they should be periodically compared to the "national model standards and tests using a common metric" (127). Commission on No Child Left Behind, *Beyond NCLB: Fulfilling the Promise to Our Nation's Children* (Washington, D.C.: The Aspen Institute, 2007).

32. B. K. Fuller, K. Gesicki, E. Kang, and J. Wright. "Is the No Child Left Behind Act Working? The Reliability of How States Track Achievement," Working Paper 06-1, Policy Analysis for California Education (PACE), University of California, Berkley, 2006. Some of the increase in state scores could also be due to increased cheating (Jacob and Levitt, "Rotten Apples").

33. Kim and Sunderman, *Large Mandates and Limited Resources.*

34. Ryan, "Perverse Incentives."

35. One might also say that the ultimate objective is fair treatment of students, not schools, and NCLB allows students in sanctioned schools to switch to a different public school in the same district. In fact, however, shifting disadvantaged students to different schools would do little to address the factors outside the control of school officials and would therefore simply shift the underfunded costs inevitably associated with concentrated student disadvantage.

36. T. Downes, "What Is Adequate? Operationalizing the Concept of Adequacy for New York" (paper for EFRC Symposium on School Finance and Organizational Structure in New York State, Albany, N.Y., 2004); B. Baker, "Evaluating the Reliability, Validity, and Usefulness of Education Cost Studies," *Journal of Education Finance* 32 (Fall 2006): 170–201; Duncombe and Yinger, "Measurement of Cost Differentials."

37. D. Hoff, "The Bottom Line," in *Quality Counts 2005*, ed. V. Edwards (Bethesda, Md.: Education Week, 2005), 29-30, 32, 35-36. Cost functions are criticized by Hanushek ("The Alchemy of 'Costing Out' an Adequate Education" [paper presented at the Adequate Lawsuits: Their Growing Impact on American Education conference, Harvard University, Cambridge, Mass., October 2005]; and E. Hanushek, "Science Violated: Spending Projections and the Costing Out of an Adequate Education," in *Courting Failure*, ed. E. Hanushek [Stanford, Calif.: Education Next, 2006], 257–312) and defended by Baker ("Evaluating the Reliability"), Downes ("What Is Adequate?"), and Duncombe ("Responding to the Charge of Alchemy: Strategies for Evaluating the Reliability and Validity

of Costing-out Research," *Journal of Education Finance* 32 [Fall 2006]: 137–69). Hanushek's claim that cost functions ignore efficiency is belied by the efficiency corrections in Duncombe and Yinger (W. Duncombe and J. Yinger, "School Finance Reform: Aid Formulas and Equity Objectives," *National Tax Journal* 51 [June 1998]: 239–62; "Financing Higher Student Performance Standards: The Case of New York State," *Economics of Education Review* 19 [October 2000]: 363–86; "Estimating the Cost of Meeting Student Performance Outcomes Adopted by the Kansas State Board of Education" (study prepared for the Kansas Division of Legislative Post Audit, Topeka, Kan., 2005); Duncombe, Lukemeyer, and Yinger ("Financing an Adequate Education: A Case Study of New York," in *Developments in School Finance: 2001–2002*, ed. W. J. Fowler, Jr. [Washington, D.C.: National Center for Education Statistics, 2003], 127–54), Imazeki and Reschovsky ("Estimating the Costs"; "Does No Child Left Behind Place a Fiscal Burden on States? Evidence from Texas," *Education Finance and Policy* 1 [Spring 2006]: 227–46), and Reschovsky and Imazeki ("Let No Child Be Left Behind: Determining the Cost of Improving Student Performance," *Public Finance Review* 31 [May 2003]: 263–90).

38. W. Driscoll and H. Fleeter, "Projected Cost of Implementing the Federal 'No Child Left Behind Act' in Ohio" (report prepared for the Ohio Department of Education, December 2003); J. Imazeki and A. Reschovsky, "Is *No Child Left Behind*?" and "Does No Child Left Behind Place?"; W. Duncombe, A. Lukemeyer, and J. Yinger, "The No Child Left Behind Act: Have Federal Funds Been Left Behind?" *Public Finance Review*, vol. 36 (July 2008): 381–407.

39. C. Hoxby, "The Cost of Accountability" (NBER working papers, no. 8855, Cambridge, Mass., September 2002); Governmental Accounting Office (GAO), *Characteristics of Tests Will Influence Expenses: Information Sharing May Help States Realize Efficiencies* (Washington, D.C.: Government Printing Office, 2003); Driscoll and Fleeter, "Projected Cost of Implementing."

40. Separate spending data for special education in New York school districts were not available for all years used in the cost model; thus, special education spending was not excluded for any years.

41. Significant differences exist across states in how they measure the graduation rate, and states are given significant discretion in setting the graduation rate targets. E. Klemick, "Implementing Graduation Accountability under NCLB," *Education Week*, June 7, 2007.

42. For California, individual teacher data with salary information were not available. We used instead the minimum salary on each district's

salary schedule. This data is available from the California Department of Education.

43. For an audit of school lunch information, see *Kansas Legislative Division of Post Audit, K-12 Education: Reviewing Free-lunch Student Counts Used as the Basis for At-risk Funding, Part 1*, Topeka, Ks., November 2006. The correlation between the share of free lunch or subsidized lunch and the census child poverty rate in 2000 is about 0.70 in these four states.

44. J. Cullen, "The Impact of Fiscal Incentives on Student Disability Rates," *Journal of Public Economics* 87 (August 2003): 1557–89.

45. Duncombe and Yinger, "Financing Higher Student Performance Standards."

46. M. Andrews, W. Duncombe, and J. Yinger, "Revisiting Economies of Size in Education: Are We Any Closer to a Consensus?" *Economics of Education Review* 21, no. 3 (2002): 245–62; Duncombe and Yinger, "Measurement of Cost Differentials."

47. Large cities in Kansas include Kansas City, Wichita, and Topeka; in Missouri, St. Louis, Kansas City, Center, and Hickman Mills; and in New York, New York City, Buffalo, Rochester, Syracuse, and Yonkers. For California large cities are limited to those districts classified by the census as large central cities with enrollments of at least thirty thousand pupils.

48. B. Baker and W. Duncombe, "Balancing District Needs and Student Needs: The Role of Economies of Scale Adjustments and Pupil Need Weights in School Finance Formulas," *Journal of Education Finance* 29 (2004): 195–21; K. Carey, *State Poverty Based Education Funding: A Survey of Current Programs and Options for Improvement*, Washington, D.C.: Center on Budget and Policy Priorities, 2002; Duncombe and Yinger, "How Much More?"

49. Duncombe and Yinger, "How Much More?"

50. L. Olson and C. Jerald, "Barriers to Success," *Education Week*, January 8, 1998. The higher poverty weights in New York than in California are probably due in part to the use of percentage of free lunch students in New York compared to the percentage of subsidized and free lunch students used in the model for California.

51. The proficiency rate for New York also includes students who are close to proficiency but haven't reached it yet. See note 6.

52. If the spending increase in a district is negative, we set it to zero. We expect these spending estimates to be conservative for a couple of reasons. By focusing only on student performance in math and reading, we have ignored other measures considered in determining AYP, including participation rates, graduation rates, and performance on other exams. We also do

not disaggregate student performance into subgroups, which implies that poor performance in one subgroup can be averaged with strong performance in another subgroup.

53. National Education Association (NEA), *No Child Left Behind: The Funding Gap in ESEA and Other Federal Education Programs*, Washington, D.C., 2004.

54. P. Peterson and M. West, "The Contentious 'No Child' Law II: Money Has Not Been Left Behind," *Education Week*, March 14, 2004; J. Peyser and R. Costrell, "Exploring the Costs of Accountability," *Education Next* (Spring 2004): 22–29.

55. Research by the Center on Education Policy indicates that there is significant volatility in Title I funding across years, due largely to volatility in the child poverty rate estimates. For example, between 2006–7 and 2007–8 four states received an increase of over 10 percent in Title I (Part A) funding, and two states had decreases of over 10 percent. They found that "this volatility appears to be mounting with the passage of time since the 2000 census base" (8). Center on Education Policy, *Title I Funds—Who's Gaining and Who's Losing: School Year 2007-08 Update*, Washington, D.C., August 2007.

56. Goodwin Liu, "Interstate Inequality in Educational Opportunity," *New York University Law Review* 81, no. 6 (2006): 2044–2128.

57. Child poverty rates for 2000 are used for 2001 Title I aid, and rates for 2004 are used for 2006 aid. Data for 2004 was the latest available at the time of preparing this chapter. The source of data for 2000 is the 2000 census, and for 2004 the U.S. Census Bureau, *Small Area Income and Poverty Estimates*, http://www.census.gov/hhes/www/saipe/index.html.

58. The geographic cost index that we use is a comparable wage index (CWI) developed for NCES. L. Taylor and W. Fowler. *A Comparative Wage Approach to Geographic Cost Adjustment* (Washington, D.C.: U.S. Department of Education, 2006). A CWI typically uses information on wages in comparable private sector occupations to estimate labor costs in labor market areas. A CWI is constructed as an index of comparable wages in a labor market compared to those in the average labor market, either nationally or within a particular state. See Duncombe and Yinger, "Measurement of Cost Differentials."

59. W. Riddle, *Education for the Disadvantaged: ESEA Title I Allocation Formula Provisions* (Washington, D.C.: Congressional Research Service, 2001); Goodwin Liu, "Understanding Title I: Funding Equity Across States, Districts, and Schools" (unpublished paper, 2007).

60. Riddle, *Education for the Disadvantaged*; D. Smole, *Education Finance Incentive Grants under ESEA Title I* (Washington, D.C.:

Congressional Research Service, 2002); and *Education for the Disadvantaged: Overview of ESEA Title I-A Amendments under the No Child Left Behind Act* (Washington, D.C.: Congressional Research Service, 2005); Liu, "Understanding Title I."

61. The enrollment measure is average daily attendance, and the expenditure factor is prorated based on funding levels. The expenditure factors can't fall below 80 percent or be above 120 percent of the national average (Riddle, *Education for the Disadvantaged*).

62. The weighting is based on either the child poverty rate or absolute number of poverty students in a school, with weights ranging from 1 to 4 (ibid.).

63. Tax effort is calculated by dividing state expenditures per pupil by state personal income per capita, relative to the national average of this ratio. The effort factor is kept within the narrow bounds of 0.95 and 1.05 (ibid.). The equity factor is based on the coefficient of variation (CV) for per-pupil expenditure (average variation in expenditure as percent of average expenditure). Higher weights are assigned to children in poverty, and small districts (below two hundred students) are removed from the calculation. The equity factor is calculated as 1.3 minus the CV.

64. Smole, *Education Finance Incentive Grants under ESEA Title I.*

65. Liu, "Interstate Inequality"; and "Understanding Title I"; Riddle, *Education for the Disadvantaged.*

66. Liu, "Understanding Title I."

67. Among cost variables, we included the child poverty rate and its square, enrollment (in thousands) and its square, and a geographic cost index from NCES (Taylor and Fowler, *A Comparative Wage Approach*). For the other variables, we tried to proxy the actual variables used in aid distribution, including average per-pupil expenditure in a state, total public school enrollment in the state, the ratio of average state per-pupil expenditure over per-capita personal income, and the coefficient of variation for district per-pupil spending for districts of two hundred or more students (poverty students were weighted 1.4 in calculating district spending).

68. When 2001 Title I aid is included in the model for 2006, the model explains 67 percent of the variation in aid distribution (not reported), which illustrates the importance of the hold-harmless provision.

69. Aid tends to increase with enrollment size for total aid in 2006 and for the Targeted Grant and EFIG; the opposite is the case, however, for the Concentration Grant and Basic Grant. Because only the latter two types of grants were funded in 2001, enrollment is negatively related to aid.

70. M. Roza and P. Hill, "How Within-district Spending Inequities Help Some Schools to Fail," in *Brookings Papers on Education Policy: 2004,*

ed. D. Ravitch (Washington, D.C.: Brookings Institution, 2004); M. Roza, L. Miller, and P. Hill, "Strengthening Title I to Help High Poverty Schools" (working paper, Center on Reinventing Public Education, Seattle, Wash., 2005).

71. Roza, Miller, and Hill, "Strengthening Title I."

72. Ibid.

73. Driscoll and Fleeter, "Projected Cost of Implementing"; Imazeki and Reschovsky, "Does No Child Left Behind?"; Duncombe, Lukemeyer, and Yinger, "The No Child Left Behind Act."

74. Office of Management and Budget (OMB), *Budget of the United States Government: Fiscal Year 2009* (Washington, D.C.: U.S. Government Printing Office, 2008); Center on Education Policy, *Title I Funds*. Spending estimates, which are in 2005 dollars (2004 in Kansas), are adjusted to be in 2006 dollars using the consumer price index for urban consumers to make them comparable to the Title I aid information.

75. N. Gordon, "Do Federal Grants Boost School Spending? Evidence from Title I." *Journal of Public Economics* 88 (August 2004): 1771–92.

76. Duncombe and Yinger, "Financing Higher Student Performance Standards."

77. Current spending, $E(S)$, equals cost to meet current performance, $C(S)$, divided by efficiency, e, which has a maximum of 1.0. Now let $C(S^*)$ be the cost required to meet a standard, S^*. Then at the current efficiency level, spending required to meet the standard is $C(S^*)/e = E(S^*)$, which we can forecast based on our cost model. Then we want to solve for a new efficiency level, e^*, at which $[C(S^*)]/e^* = [E(S)]$. Now $C(S^*)/e^* = [C(S^*)/e] [e/e^*] = E(S^*)[e/e^*]$. So $e^* = [E(S^*)e]/[E(S)]$. Table 13 reports $(e^*-e)/e$.

78. W. Duncombe and J. Yinger. "Understanding the Incentives in California's Education Finance System" (report prepared for the Getting Down to Facts Project, 2007); W. Duncombe and J. Johnston, "The Impacts of School Finance Reform in Kansas: Equity Is in the Eye of the Beholder," in *Helping Children Left Behind: State Aid and the Pursuit of Educational Equity*, ed. J. Yinger (Cambridge, Mass.: MIT Press, 2004), 147–93.

79. A decline of this type also might be an indication of a favorable trend in cost factors that we cannot observe.

80. The estimate for California is consistent with an 8.8 percent improvement in efficiency, but it is based on only two years of data.

81. D. N. Figlio and C. E. Rouse, "Do Accountability and Voucher Threats Improve Low-Performing Schools?" *Journal of Public Economics* 90, no. 1–2 (2006): 239–55; Brian A. Jacob, "Accountability, Incentives, and Behavior: The Impact of High-stakes Testing in the Chicago Public Schools," *Journal of Public Economics* 89, no. 5–6 (2005): 761–96.

82. Schools also might be able to meet standards through cheating. For example, Figlio finds that schools hand out longer suspensions to students who make trouble at times when standardized tests are being given. "Testing, Crime, and Punishment," *Journal of Public Economics* 90, no. 4–5 (May 2006): 837–51.

83. Liu, "Understanding Title I."

84. 20 U.S.C. sec. 7907(a).

85. "No Child Left Behind and the Political Safeguards of Federalism," *Harvard Law Review* 119 (2005): 885–906; A. Wingfield, "The No Child Left Behind Act: Legal Challenges as an Underfunded Mandate," *Loyola Journal of Public Interest Law* 6 (2005): 185–216.

86. Proof Opening Brief of Plaintiff-Appellants Pontiac School District et al., filed March 22, 2006, in *Pontiac School District v. Spellings*, No. 05-2708 (U.S. Court of Appeals for the Sixth Circuit).

87. "No Child Left Behind and the Political Safeguards of Federalism"; Wingfield, "The No Child Left Behind Act."

88. *Connecticut v. Spellings*, 453 F. Supp. 2d 459 (D. Conn. 2006), 474–75.

89. *South Dakota v. Dole*, 483 U.S. 203 (1987).

90. *South Dakota*, 483 U.S. at 207.

91. *Pontiac School District v. Spellings*, No. 05-CV-71535 (E.D. Mich. November 23, 2005).

92. *Pontiac School District v. Secretary*, 512 F.3d 252 vacated (6th Cir. May 1, 2008).

93. *Pontiac School District*, 512 F.3d at 271, n7.

94. Liu, "Understanding Title I"; Roza and P. Hill, "How Within-district Spending."

95. National Center for Education Statistics, *Mapping 2005 State Proficiency Standards onto the NAEP Scores*; Commission on No Child Left Behind, *Beyond NCLB*. Following a suggestion in Duncombe, Lukemeyer, and Yinger ("The No Child Left Behind Act"), this comparison could be used by the secretary of education to rank state standards, and states could be given an opportunity to appeal their ranking.

96. R. Weiner and E. Pristoop, "How States Shortchange the Districts that Need the Most Help," in *Funding Gaps, 2006* (Washington, D.C.:

Education Trust, 2007), 5–9, available online at http://www2.edtrust.org/EdTrust/Press+Room/Funding+Gap+2006.htm.

97. The measure of inflation is the CPI for urban wage earners, with a base year of 2000.

98. We used spending in the general fund and in several special revenue funds as defined in the Standard Accounting Code System (SACS). Specifically we used spending in the Charter School Special Revenue Fund, Child Development Special Revenue Fund, Cafeteria Special Revenue Fund, Deferred Maintenance Special Revenue Fund, Special Reserve Fund for Other than Capital Outlay Projects Fund, Foundation Special Revenue Fund, and Special Reserve Fund for Postemployment Benefits. See Details in W. Duncombe and J. Yinger, "Understanding the Incentives in California's Education Finance System" (study prepared for the Getting Down to Facts Project, 2007).

99. Spending on special education, transportation, vocational education, food service, and school facilities is excluded. Details are discussed in W. Duncombe and J. Yinger, "Estimating the Cost of Meeting Student Performance Outcomes Adopted by the Kansas State Board of Education."

100. See W. Duncombe, "Estimating the Cost of Meeting Student Performance Standards in the St. Louis Public Schools" (report prepared for the Board of Education for the City of St. Louis, January 2007).

101. New York does not break out special education separately, so it was not possible to exclude this spending from total spending.

102. More information on this measure, dcaadm, is available from the NYSED Web site, http://www.oms.nysed.gov/faru/Profiles/18th/revisedAppendix.html.

103. The correlation between the share of free lunch (Kansas) or subsidized lunch (Missouri) and the census child poverty rate in 2000 is about 0.70 for both states.

104. "English learner students are those students for whom there is a report of a primary language other than English on the state-approved Home Language Survey **and** who, on the basis of the state approved oral language (grades kindergarten through grade twelve) assessment procedures and literacy (grades three through twelve only), have been determined to lack the clearly defined English language skills of listening comprehension, speaking, reading, and writing necessary to succeed in the school's regular instructional programs." See CDE Web site, http://www.cde.ca.gov/ds/sd/cb/glossary.asp#el.

105. Cullen, "The Impact of Fiscal Incentives."

106. To impute missing observations for this variable, we used the predicted value when this variable is regressed on share of enrollment with more severe disabilities. The latter is defined as the share of disabled stu-

dents who are not classified as having a "speech or language impairment" or "specific learning disability." See Duncombe and Yinger, "Understanding the Incentives in California's Education Finance System."

107. The salary scale between senior and junior teachers can reflect the power of the union in negotiating favorable contracts for senior teachers, who are more apt to be union members. H. Lankford and J. Wyckoff, "The Changing Structure of Teacher Compensation, 1970–94," *Economics of Education Review* 16, no. 4 (1997): 371–84.

108. Specifically, the natural logarithm of a teacher's salary is regressed on the logarithm of his total experience and indicator variables (0–1) for whether she had a master's, doctorate, or law degree (Kansas) or had a graduate degree (Missouri). Teacher salaries are also adjusted for inflation.

109. Duncombe and Yinger, "Understanding the Incentives."

110. Duncombe and Yinger, "Estimating the Cost."

111. The underlying theory behind the use of fiscal capacity variables indicates that the appropriate measure of aid is actually per-pupil aid divided by per-pupil income (H. F. Ladd and J. Yinger, *America's Ailing Cities: Fiscal Health and the Design of Urban Policy* [Baltimore: Johns Hopkins University Press, 1991]), commonly called an aid ratio. For New York, we were not able to use the aid ratio, because of high collinearity with other variables in the cost model. Per-pupil state aid was used instead. The aid variable for California and Kansas also includes federal aid.

112. In communities with little commercial and industrial property, the typical homeowner bears a larger share of school taxes (higher tax share) than in communities with significant nonresidential property. See ibid.; and D. Rubinfeld, "The Economics of the Local Public Sector," in *Handbook of Public Economics*, ed. A. Auerbach and M. Feldstein (Amsterdam: North-Holland, 1985) for a discussion of the tax share measure used in median voter models of local public service demand.

113. Duncombe and Yinger, "Understanding the Incentives."

114. Ibid. Revenue limits measure general school district revenues, which are constrained by court decisions in California. Some districts experienced large drops in their revenue limit in the late 1970s.

115. Duncombe, Lukemeyer, and Yinger, "Financing an Adequate Education."

116. Duncombe and Yinger, "Measurement of Cost Differentials."

117. J. Bound, D. Jaeger, and R. Baker, "Problems with Instrumental Variables Estimation When the Correlation Between the Instruments and the Endogenous Explanatory Variables is Weak," *Journal of the American Statistical Association* 90 (June 1995): 443–50; J. Stock and M. Yogo,

"Testing for Weak Instruments in IV Regression," in *Identification and Inference for Econometric Models: Essays in Honor of Thomas Rothenberg*, ed. D. Andrews and J. Stock (Cambridge, U.K.: Cambridge University Press, 2005).

118. Ibid.

119. M. Murray ("Avoiding Invalid Instruments and Coping with Weak Instruments," *Journal of Economic Perspectives* 20 [Fall 2006]: 111–32) recommends using a modified limited information maximum likelihood estimator developed by Fuller when instruments are weak. W. A. Fuller, "Some Properties of a Modification of the Limited Information Maximum Likelihood Estimator," *Econometrica* 45 (1977): 939–54. When we re-estimated the cost function for all the states using the Fuller method, the coefficients on outcomes and salaries change relatively little and remain statistically significant in all states but Missouri where the coefficient on outcomes is significant at the 20 percent level. The results of the instrument tests are available from the authors upon request.

120. J. Woolridge, *Introductory Econometrics: A Modern Approach*, 2nd ed. (Mason, Ohio: South-Western, Thomson Learning, 2003).

121. R. W. Garnett, "The New Federalism, the Spending Power, and Federal Criminal Law," *Cornell Law Review* 89 (2003): 1–94; J. E. Ryan, "The Tenth Amendment and Other Paper Tigers: The Legal Boundaries of Education Governance," in *Who's in Charge Here? The Tangled Web of School Governance and Policy*, ed. Noel Epstein (Washington, D.C.: The Brookings Institution, 2004); J. Dinan and D. Krane, "The State of American Federalism 2005: Federalism Resurfaces in the Political Debate," *Publius: The Journal of Federalism* 36 (2006): 327–74.

122. A. McColl, "Tough Call: Is the No Child Left Behind Act Constitutional?" *Phi Delta Kappan* 20 (2005): 604–10.

123. *South Dakota v. Dole*, 483 U.S. 203 (1987).

124. *South Dakota v. Dole*, 483 U.S. at 207–8, 211 (internal citations omitted). The court listed and discussed the first four of these and then discussed the fifth later in the opinion at page 211, but commentators have generally interpreted the opinion as establishing five requirements. See, for instance, Ryan, "The Tenth Amendment and Other Paper Tigers: The Legal Boundaries of Education Governance."

125. 20 U.S.C. sec. 7907(a).

126. *Pontiac School District v. Spellings*, slip op. at 7.

127. *Pontiac School District v. Secretary*, 512 F.3d 252 vacated (6th Cir. May 1, 2008).

128. *Pontiac School District*, 512 F.3d, at 272, citations omitted.

129. *Connecticut v. Spellings*, 453 F.Supp. 2d at 493.

CHAPTER 3

1. National Commission on Excellence in Education, *A Nation at Risk: The Imperative for Educational Reform*, 1983, Washington D.C., 28.

2. The Reagan administration had decreased federal education funding by one-third, while at the same time encouraging business leaders to become partners with school districts to fill the funding gap. The partnerships did emerge. In 1983 17 percent of all school districts had business partnerships. By 1989 that number had grown to 40 percent of districts, but it is not clear what the overall effect on students of these partnerships has been.

3. Business Roundtable, *The Essential Components of a Successful Education*, 1989.

4. Regan Walker, "Ed Summit's 'When' and 'Where' Are Set, But 'Why' Remains Unsettled," *Education Week*, September 6, 1989. In addition to FDR's Depression-era talks, Theodore Roosevelt held a White House-governors summit on conservation measures in 1908.

5. Julie A. Miller and Robert Rothman, "Bush's Advisory Panel Offers Suggestions for National Goals," *Education Week*, January 17, 1990.

6. Learning Research and Development Center and the National Center on Education and the Economy, *The New Standards Project: An Overview*, University of Pittsburgh, 1991.

7. *Curriculum and Evaluation Standards for School Mathematics, Professional Standards for Teaching Mathematics,* and *Assessment Standards for School Mathematics,* available online at http://standards.nctm.org/.

8. National Council of Teachers of Mathematics and the National Research Council, *Improving Student Learning in Mathematics and Science: The Role of National Standards in State Policy* (Washington, D.C.: National Academy Press, 1997).

9. Kenneth Clark, "The Social Scientist as an Expert Witness in Civil Rights Legislation," *Social Problems* 1, no. 1 (June 1953): 5–10; Kenneth B. Clark and Mamie K. Clark, "The Development of Consciousness of Self and the Emergence of Racial Identification of Negro School Children," *Journal of Social Psychology* 10 (1939): 591–99.

10. James Samuel Coleman, *Coleman Report on Public and Private Schools: The Draft Summary and Eight Critiques* (Arlington, Va.: Educational Research Service, 1982).

11. In his 1971 congressional testimony in preparation for creating the National Institute of Education (NIE), Senator Daniel Patrick Moynihan presciently called for not just equality of opportunity but also "parity of educational outcomes."

12. *Debra P. v. Turlington*, 730 F.2d 1405 (11th Cir. 1984).

13. Patti Breckenridge, "Black Students Score Big Gains for Florida's Basic-skills Exit Test," *Education Week*, May 30, 1984.

14. Jeannie Oakes, *Multiplying Inequalities: The Effects of Race, Social Class, and Tracking on Opportunities to Learn Mathematics and Science* (Santa Monica, Calif.: RAND Corporation, 1990). See also, Jeannie Oakes, *Keeping Track* (New Haven, Conn.: Yale University Press, 1985).

15. Mathematical Sciences Education Board, *Everybody Counts: A Report to the Nation on the Future of Mathematics Education* (Washington, D.C.: National Academy Press, 1989).

16. *EQUITY 2000: A Systemic Education Reform Model*, College Board, Washington, D.C., 2001, available online at http://www.collegeboard.org.

17. E. A. Silver and M. K. Stein, "The QUASAR Project: The 'Revolution of the Possible' in Mathematics Instructional Reform in Urban Middle Schools," *Urban Education* 30 no. 4 (1996): 476–521.

18. Michael W. Kirst, "Articulation and Mathematical Literacy: Political and Policy Issues," in *Quantitative Literacy: Why Numeracy Matters for Schools and Colleges*, Bernard Madison and Lynn Steen, eds. (Princeton, N.J.: National Council on Education and the Disciplines, 2003).

19. "Resources on the Kentucky Education Reform Act of 1990," Western Kentucky University Libraries Web site, available online at http://www.wku.edu/library/kera/.

20. This view of the centrality of thinking, and the possibilities for teaching thinking and reasoning, has been extensively elaborated over the succeeding two decades. See, for example, L. B. Resnick, *Education and Learning to Think* (Washington, D.C.: National Academy Press, 1987); John Bransford and Ann Brown, *How People Learn: Brain, Mind, Experience, and School* (Washington, D.C.: National Academy Press, 2003). It is still the leading scholarly view of how assessment should proceed in the classroom; see L. Shepard et al., "Assessment," in *Preparing Teachers for a Changing World: What Teachers Should Learn and Be Able to Do*, L. Darling-Hammond and J. Bransford, eds. (San Francisco, Calif.: Jossey-Bass, 2005).

21. R. K. Blank and P. Engler, *Has Science and Mathematics Education Improved Since A Nation at Risk?: Trends in Course Enrollments, Qualified Teachers, and Student Achievement*, Council of Chief State School Officers, 1992.

22. Richard Kahlenberg, *Tough Liberal: Albert Shanker and the Battles over Schools, Unions, Race, and Democracy* (New York: Columbia University Press, 2007).

23. The Southern Regional Education Board had developed education goals in 1986.

24. Marshall Smith and Jennifer O'Day, "Systemic School Reform," in *The Politics of Curriculum and Testing: The 1990 Yearbook of the Politics of Education Association*, ed. S. H. Fuhrman and B. Malen (New York: Taylor & Francis, 1991), 233–67.

25. As the NGA's 1986 report *A Time for Results* details, the goals focused on outcomes. In that report, the governors called for the states to increase achievement while decreasing the regulatory burden on schools. See Diane Ravitch, *National Standards in American Education: A Citizen's Guide* (Washington, D.C.: Brookings Institution, 1995).

26. *Measuring Progress toward the National Education Goals: Potential Indicators and Measurement Strategies,* National Education Goals Panel, March 1991.

27. Although using NAEP to roughly monitor state testing systems is the best option we have, researchers are not convinced that scores can be statistically linked between tests that were not designed to test the same content. See Michael Feuer, *Uncommon Measures: Equivalence and Linkage Among Educational Tests* (Washington, D.C.: The National Academy Press, 1999).

28. The National Council on Evaluation of Standards and Testing was comprised of officials from the White House, the Department of Education, members of Congress and state legislatures, scholars, and other experts in the field. It was co-chaired by Governors Roy Romer and Carroll Campbell, a Democrat and Republican, respectively.

29. Christopher Cross, *Political Education: National Policy Come of Age* (New York: Teachers College Press, 2004), p. 108.

30. "Reality Check 2000," *Education Week*, February 16, 2000.

31. Gender and migrant status is required to be reported but is not factored into calculations that determine adequate yearly progress (AYP).

32. Robert Linn, in an influential 2002 presidential address to the American Education Research Association, demonstrated the statistical improbability of reaching this goal and called for a radical revision of policy.

33. Given both the time allowed for states to mount their standards, testing, and accountability reporting, and the choices they had in how to establish the path to full proficiency in 2014, the full NCLB accountability is only now coming into full operation.

34. Lynn Olson, "Quality Counts at 10: A Decade of Standards-Based Education," *Education Week*, January 5, 2006.

35. L. B. Resnick, R. Rothman, J. B. Slattery, and J. L. Vranek, "Benchmarking and Alignment of Standards and Testing," *Educational Assessment* 9, nos. 1–2 (2003): 1–27.

36. Andrew Porter, "Measuring the Content of Instruction: Uses in Research and Practice," *Educational Researcher* 31, no. 7 (2002): 3–14.

37. Norman Webb, *Alignment of Science and Mathematics Standards and Assessments in Four States*, research monograph no. 18, University of Wisconsin-Madison, National Institute for Science Education, 1999.

38. Lauren Resnick and Lindsay C. Matsumura, "Academic Proficiency: Bright Hopes, Blurry Vision," *Voices in Education* 14 (Winter 2007). Suzanne Lane, "Validity of High-stakes Assessment: Are Students Engaged in Complex Thinking?" *Educational Measurement, Issues, and Practice* 23, no. 3 (2003): 6–14.

39. L. B. Resnick and D. P. Resnick, "Assessing the Thinking Curriculum: New Tools for Educational Reform," in *Changing Assessments: Alternative Views of Aptitude, Achievement, and Instruction*, ed. B. R. Gifford and M. C. O'Connor (Boston: Kluwer, 1992), pp. 37–75.

40. NAEP's proficient cut score was set in the early 1990s by the National Assessment Governing Board (NAGB), an independent policy-making body, with contributions from a wide variety of educators, business and government leaders, and interested citizens so that students' performance could be described against a standard of "what students should know and be able to do" and "how good is good enough?" Proficient performance is meant to connote solid academic performance and competency on a range of challenging subject matter.

41. National Center for Education Statistics, *Mapping 2005 State Proficiency Standards onto the NAEP Scales: Research and Development Report*, U.S. Department of Education, June 2007.

42. Some states (for example, Texas) deliberately set low cut-score criteria early in the standards process so as to not totally discourage educators and the public. Their intent was to gradually raise expectations as competence grew. To our knowledge, there has as yet been no evaluation of the overall effectiveness of this strategy.

43. American Diploma Project, *Ready or Not: Creating a High School Diploma That Counts*, Washington, D.C., 2004.

44. California Postsecondary Education Commission, *California Higher Education Accountability: Goal–Student Success Measure: California Community College Students' Degrees and Certificates*

Awarded and Successful Transfers, March 2007, available online at http:// www.cpec.ca.gov/Publications/ReportSummary.ASP?Report=1199.

45. D. Anagnostopoulos, "Testing and Student Engagement with Literature in Urban Classrooms: A Multilayered Perspective," *Research in the Teaching of English* 38, no. 2 (2003): 177–212; D. Koretz and L. Hamilton, "Testing for Accountability in K–12," in *Educational Measurement*, 4th ed., ed. R. L. Brennen, (Westport, Conn.: American Council on Education/Praeger, 2006) 531–78.

46. Center on Education Policy, *Instructional Time in Elementary Schools: A Closer Look at Changes for Specific Subjects*, Washington D.C., February 2008.

47. L. Shepard, "The Hazards of High-Stakes Testing," *Issues in Science and Technology* (Winter 2002–03): 53–58.

48. Resnick and Resnick, "Assessing the Thinking Curriculum."

49. P. Cobb, E. Yackel, and T. Wood, "Curriculum and Teacher Development: Psychological and Anthropological Perspectives," in *Integrating Research on Teaching and Learning Mathematics,* ed. E. Fennema, T. P. Carpenter, and S. J. Lamon (Albany, N.Y.: State University of New York Press, 1991) ; see also the performance assessments created by the California Assessment Program, the QUASAR Project, and the New Standards Project.

50. L. McNeill, *Contradictions of School Reform: Educational Costs of Educational Testing* (New York: Routledge, 2002).

51. Hamilton Lankford, Susanna Loeb, and James Wyckoff, "Teacher Sorting and the Plight of Urban Schools: A Descriptive Analysis," *Educational Evaluation and Policy Analysis* 24, no. 1 (Spring 2002): 37–62; S. W. Raudenbush, R. P. Fotiu, and Y. F. Cheong, "Inequality of Access to Educational Resources: A National Report Card for Eighth-grade Math," *Educational Evaluation and Policy Analysis* 20, no. 4 (1998): 253–68.

52. Models for this already exist and a few states try to maintain the practice. When, for example, the New Standards Project developed its model standards in literacy, mathematics, and science, every standards statement was accompanied both by sample questions and tasks that could be used to assess proficiency and examples of student responses that met the standard. *The New Standards Performance Standards,* Volume 1, 2, 3, The National Center on Education and the Economy and the University of Pittsburgh, 1997.

53. R. Glaser, "Instructional Technology and the Measurement of Learning Outcomes," *American Psychologist* 18 (1963): 510–22.

CHAPTER 4

1. A. S. Wells, *Time to Choose: America at the Crossroads of School Choice Policy* (New York: Hill and Wang, 1993).

2. J. Chubb and T. Moe, *Politics, Markets, and America's Schools* (Washington, D.C.: Brookings Institution, 1990).

3. U.S. Department of Education, Office of Planning, Evaluation, and Policy Development, Policy and Program Studies Service, *Title I Accountability and School Improvement from 2001 to 2004*, Washington, D.C., 2006, http://www.ed.gov/rschstat/eval/disadv/tassie3/tassie3.pdf.

4. G. L. Sunderman, J. S. Kim, and G. Orfield, *NCLB Meets School Realities: Lessons from the Field* (Thousand Oaks, Calif.: Corwin, 2005); U.S. Department of Education, *Title I Accountability*.

5. *The No Child Left Behind Act of 2001*, Public Law 107-110, 107th Congress, 2nd Session, January 8, 2002.

6. Ibid.

7. Ibid., 1486–87.

8. See, for example, V. Honawar, "10,000 Students Eligible to Transfer," *Washington Times*, August 10, 2002, A8; M. MacDonald, "Transfer Law Has Schools Looking for Right Answer," *Atlanta Journal-Constitution*, August 8, 2002, 1JF.

9. U.S. Department of Education, *Title I Accountability*. See also Brian Gill et al., *State and Local Implementation of the No Child Left Behind Act Volume IV—School Choice and Supplemental Educational Services—Interim Report* (Washington, D.C.: U.S. Department of Education, 2008).

10. M. Casserly, "No Left Behind in America's Great City Schools: Five Years and Counting," Great City Schools, Washington, D.C., 2006, available online at http://www.cgcs.org/publications/achievement.aspx.

11. Dianne M. Piché and William L. Taylor, eds., *Choosing Better Schools: A Report on Student Transfers under the No Child Left Behind Act*, Citizens' Commission on Civil Rights, Washington, D.C., 2004.

12. Sunderman, Kim, and Orfield, *NCLB Meets School Realities*.

13. "Creating Strong District Choice Programs," Office of Innovation and School Improvement, U.S. Department of Education, May 2004, available online at http://www.ed.gov/admins/comm/choice/choiceprograms/index.html.

14. J. E. Ryan and M. Heise, "The Political Economy of School Choice," *Yale Law Journal* 111, no. 2043 (2002): 2045–136.

15. See R. A. Mickelson, M. A. Bottia, and S. Southworth, *School Choice and Resegregation by Race, Class and Achievement*, University of North Carolina at Charlotte, 2008, for a review.

16. See "Creating Strong District Choice Programs."

17. R. A. Mickelson and S. Southworth, "When Opting Out Is Not a Choice: Implications for NCLB's Transfer Options from Charlotte, North Carolina," *Equity and Excellence in Education* 38 (2005): 1–15.

18. C. T. Clotfelter, *After Brown: The Rise and Retreat of School Desegregation* (Princeton, N.J.: Princeton University Press, 2004).

19. Sunderman, Kim, and Orfield, *NCLB Meets School Realities*; U.S. Department of Education, *Title I Accountability*.

20. U.S. Government Accountability Office (GAO), *No Child Left Behind Act: Education Needs to Provide Additional Technical Assistance and Conduct Implementation Studies for School Choice Provision*, report to the secretary of education, Washington, D.C., December 2004, 25.

21. M. Casserly, "No Child Left Behind in America's Great City Schools"; Sunderman, Kim, and Orfield, *NCLB Meets School Realities*.

22. Piché et al., *Choosing Better Schools*, 63, italics in original.

23. Sunderman, Kim, and Orfield, *NCLB Meets School Realities*, 45.

24. D. N. Plank and C. Dunbar, Jr., *Over the First Hurdle: Michigan's Implementation of the "No Child Left Behind" Act*, East Lansing, Michigan State University Education Policy Center, November 2006, available online at http://www.epc.msu.edu/publications/bysource.htm.

25. G. Macris, "Providence Parents Call School Choice a 'Sham,'" *The Providence Journal*, September 28, 2004, A1.

26. E. Gootman, "Schools Seeking Alternatives to Granting More Transfers," *New York Times*, September 30, 2003, A1, B7; M. Winerip, "No Child Left Behind Law Leaves No Room for Some," *New York Times*, September 10, 2003, B7.

27. C. Moran, "County Schools Face Sanctions," *St. Louis Post Dispatch*, October 16, 2004.

28. S. Saulny, "Few Students Seek Free Tutoring or Transfers from Failing Schools," *New York Times*, April 6, 2006.

29. "Creating Strong District Choice Programs."

30. The Commission on No Child Left Behind, "Beyond NCLB: Fulfilling Our Promise to Our Nation's Children," The Aspen Institute, Washington, D.C., 2007.

31. Sunderman, Kim, and Orfield, *NCLB Meets School Realities*; U.S. Department of Education, *Title I Accountability*.

32. Piché et al., *Choosing Better Schools;* Sunderman, Kim, and Orfield, *NCLB Meets School Realities*; U.S. DOE, *Title I Accountability*.

33. U.S. GAO, *No Child Left Behind Act*, 16n15.

34. U.S. DOE, *Title I Accountability*, 21.

35. See L. M. Lobao, G. Hooks, and A. R. Tickamyer, "Introduction: Advancing the Sociology of Spatial Inequality," in *The Sociology of Spatial Inequality*, ed. Linda M. Lobao, Gregory Hooks, and Ann R. Tickamyer (Albany: State University of New York Press, 2007), 1–25.

36. Clotfelter, *After Brown*.

37. X. de Souza Briggs, ed., *The Geography of Opportunity: Race and Housing Choice in Metropolitan America* (Washington, D.C.: Brookings Institution Press, 2005); P. Drier, J. Mollenkopf, and T. Swanstrom, *Place Matters: Metropolitics for the Twenty-first Century*, 2nd ed., rev. (Lawrence: University of Kansas Press, 2004).

38. D. S. Massey and J. Fischer, "The Geography of Inequality in the United States, 1950-2000," Brookings–Wharton Papers on Urban Affairs, Brookings Institution, Washington D.C., 2003.

39. Ibid., 26.

40. S. Sassen, *Cities in a World Economy* (Thousand Oaks, Calif.: Pine Forge, 2006).

41. Drier, Mollenkopf, and Swanstrom, *Place Matters*.

42. G. T. Kingsley and K. L. S. Pettit, *Concentrated Poverty: A Change in Course*, The Urban Institute, Washington, D.C., May 2003, available online at http://www.urban.org/publications/310790.html.

43. R. Puentes and D. Warren, *One-fifth of America: A Guide to America's First Suburbs* (Washington, D.C.: Brookings Metropolitan Policy Program, 2005).

44. Ibid.

45. M. Orfield, *Metropolitis: The New Suburban Reality* (Washington, D.C.: Brookings Institution Press, 2002).

46. Clotfelter, *After Brown*; S. Reardon and J. Yun, "Suburban Racial Change and Suburban School Segregation 1987–1995," *Sociology of Education* 74 (April 2001): 79–101.

47. U.S. DOE, *Title I Accountability*, xiii.

48. N. Lewin, "The No Child Left Behind Act of 2001: The Triumph of School Choice over Racial Desegregation," *Georgia Journal of Poverty Law and Policy* (Spring 2005): 95.

49. Piché et al., *Choosing Better Schools*, 11.

50. Macris, "Providence Parents."

51. S. Baldrige, "Why County Schools Won't Take City Kids: The Much-ballyhooed Federal No Child Left Behind Program Was Supposed to Allow School Choice For Some Students, But It's Just Not Working Here," *Lancaster New Era* (Pennsylvania), October 20, 2003, A1.

52. See S. Gewirtz, S. J. Ball, and R. Bowe, *Markets, Choice, and Equity in Education* (Buckingham, U.K.: Open University Press, 1995); G. Whitty,

"Creating Quasi-Markets in Education: A Review of Recent Research on Parental Choice and School Autonomy in Three Countries," *Review of Research in Education* 22 (1997), 3-47.

53. See, for instance, K. K. Metcalf, N. A. Legan, K. M. Paul, and W. J. Boone, "Evaluation of the Cleveland Scholarship and Tutoring Program," Indiana University School of Education, Bloomington, Ind., 2004, http:// crlt.indiana.edu/index.html; Mickelson, Bottia, and Southworth, *School Choice*; L. A. Renzulli and L. Evans, "School Choice, Charter Schools, and White Flight," *Social Problems* 52, no. 3 (2005): 398–418.

54. See U.S. GAO, *No Child Left Behind Act*; H. F. Ladd, "School Vouchers: A Critical View," *The Journal of Economic Perspectives*, 16, no. 4 (2002): 3–24; H. M. Levin and C. R. Belfield, *Vouchers and Public Policy: Where Ideology Trumps Evidence*, National Center for the Study of Privatization in Education, New York, June 2004; Mickelson at al., *School Choice and Resegregation by Race, Class and Achievement*; Ryan and M. Heise, "The Political Economy"; J. F. Witte, T. D. Stern, and C. A. Thorn, *Fifth-year Report: Milwaukee Parental Choice Program*, University of Wisconsin, Madison, December 1995.

55. Gewirtz, Ball, and Bowe, *Markets, Choice*.

56. Casserly, "No Child Left Behind, in America's Great City Schools," 7.

57. Piché et al., *Choosing Better Schools;* Sunderman, Kim, and Orfield, *NCLB Meets School Realities;* Casserly, *No Child Left Behind*.

58. Chester Finn, "Preface," in D. J. Armor and B. Peiser, *Competition in Education: A Case Study of Interdistrict Choice* (Boston: Pioneer Institute, 1997).

59. Wisconsin Joint Legislative Audit Bureau, *Open Enrollment Program: An Evaluation*, Wisconsin Legislative Audit Bureau, Madison, Wisc., August 2002, 3.

60. National Center for Education Statistics (NCES), *Schools and Staffing Survey, 1999–2000: Overview of the Data for Public, Private, Public Charter, and Bureau of Indian Affairs Elementary and Secondary Schools*, U.S. Department of Education, Washington, D.C., 2002; "Open Enrollment: 50 State Report," Education Commission of the States, accessed June 25, 2008, available online at http://mb2.ecs.org/reports/Report.aspx?id=268.

61. NCES, *Schools and Staffing Survey*.

62. In this chapter we focus on desegregation programs that have enabled students to cross over existing school-district boundary lines and not on school desegregation remedies that resulted in the merging of school districts either in the midst of a school desegregation case or shortly

before these cases began. Such mergers occurred in Wilmington, Delaware; Louisville, Kentucky; and Charlotte and Raleigh, North Carolina, but the likelihood of them being replicated elsewhere is slim. We have also excluded school choice programs—usually magnet schools—run by county offices of education in, for instance, several places in California and Bergen County, New Jersey. While these county-wide magnet schools are often racially diverse and draw students from more segregated school districts, they are more limited in scope and capacity than the interdistrict plans that we examine here.

63. "Open Enrollment: 50 State Report."

64. Ibid.

65. D. Arsen, D. Plank, and G. Sykes, *School Choice Policies in Michigan: The Rules Matter*, School Choice and School Change, Michigan State University, East Lansing, 2000.

66. Ibid., 34.

67. Ibid.

68. Ohio Legislative Office of Education Oversight, *An Overview of Open Enrollment*, Columbus, Ohio, December 1998, 8.

69. A. M. Dickman, S. A. Kurhajetz, and E. V. Dunk, *Choosing Integration: Chapter 220 in the Shadow of Open Enrollment*, The Public Policy Forum, Milwaukee, Wisconsin, February, 2003.

70. D. R. Doering, *Interdistrict School Choice in Georgia: Issues of Equity*, Fiscal Research Program, Georgia State University, Atlanta, Georgia, 1998.

71. A. S. Wells and R. L. Crain, *Stepping over the Color Line: African American Students in White Suburban Schools* (New Haven, Conn.: Yale University Press, 1997).

72. G. G. Hankins, "Like a Bridge over Troubled Waters: New Directions and Innovative Voluntary Approaches to Interdistrict School Desegregation," *The Journal of Negro Education* 58, no. 3 (Summer 1989): 345–56.

73. C. Hendrie, "Judge Spurns Indianapolis Bid to Recover Bused Students," *Education Week,* March 12, 1997.

74. *Buckley v. The Board of School Commissioners of the City of Indianapolis, Indiana.* (August 1, 1975), United States District Court for the Southern District of Indiana, Indianapolis Division. 419 R. Supp. 180. Memorandum of Decision.

75. While many interdistrict desegregation plans also allow suburban students to transfer into urban school districts—usually into magnet schools—we mostly discuss the mechanisms that ensure that poor students

of color gain access to high-quality suburban schools, because such interdistrict transfers most directly relate to potential changes to NCLB that would provide students in failing schools more meaningful choice. One of the eight programs that we examine, however, is a suburban-to-suburban transfer plan that allows students in East Palo Alto, California, to transfer to several nearby and more affluent school districts.

76. MassInc, *Mapping School Choice in Massachusetts: Data and Findings 2003*, Center for Education Research and Policy, Boston, 2003; Ryan and M. Heise, "The Political Economy."

77. Aspen Associates, "Minnesota Voluntary Public School Choice: 2005–2006" (prepared for the Minnesota Department of Education, Minneapolis, Minn., January 30, 2007).

78. P. Dougherty, "New State Role Called to Urban-Suburban Integration." *Education Week,* November 12, 1982.

79. Wells and Crain, *Stepping over the Color Line*; Judge G. W. Haney and S. Uchitelle, *Unending Struggle: The Long Road to an Equal Education in St. Louis* (St. Louis: Reedy, 2003).

80. E. Frankenberg, *Project Choice Campaign: Improving and Expanding Hartford's Project Choice Program*, Poverty and Race Research Action Council, Washington, D.C., September 2007, 31.

81. Carol Snorten, "An Analysis of the Effects of the Indianapolis Public Schools Desegregation Court Order, 1981–1982 through 1991–1992," Indiana University, 2005, Order No. DA3209577.

82. Wisconsin Advisory Committee to the United States Commission on Civil Rights, *Impact of School Desegregation in Milwaukee Public Schools on Quality Education for Minorities—15 Years Later*, Milwaukee, Wisconsin, August, 1992.

83. Wisconsin Advisory Committee, *Impact of School Desegregation*, 27.

84. Wells and Crain, *Stepping over the Color Line.*

85. Dickman, Kurhajetz, and Dunk, *Choosing Integration.*

86. Dickman, Kurhajetz, and Dunk, *Choosing Integration*, 20.

87. Aspen Associates, "Minnesota Voluntary."

88. "New Jersey's Interdistrict Public School Choice Program: Program Evaluation and Policy Analysis," Rutgers Institute on Education Law and Policy, November 2006, available online at http://ielp.rutgers.edu/projects/schoolchoice.

89. Doering, *Interdistrict School Choice*, 8.

90. R. Fossey, "Open Enrollment in Massachusetts: Why Families Choose," *Educational Evaluation and Policy Analysis* 16, no. 3 (1994): 320–34.

91. Ibid.

92. D. J. Armor and B. Peiser, *Competition in Education: A Case Study of Interdistrict Choice*, Pioneer Institute, Boston, 1997.

93. Wisconsin Joint Legislative Audit Bureau, *Open Enrollment Program*.

94. Dickman, Kurhajetz, and Dunk, *Choosing Integration*.

95. Lewin, "The No Child Left Behind Act."

96. Arsen, Plank, and Sykes, *School Choice Policies*.

97. Ibid., 38.

98. MassInc, *Mapping School Choice*.

99. Armor and Peiser, *Competition in Education*; S. L. Aud, *Competition in Education: A 1999 Update of School Choice in Massachusetts*, Pioneer Institute, Boston, 1999.

100. Armor and Peiser, *Competition in Education*.

101. Fossey, "Open Enrollment."

102. Aud, *Competition in Education*.

103. Legislative Audit Bureau, *Open Enrollment Program: An Evaluation*, Department of Public Instruction, Madison, Wisc., 2002.

104. "New Jersey's Interdistrict Public School Choice Program."

105. J. Holme and M. Richards, "School Choice and Stratification in a Metropolitan Context: Inter-District Choice and Regional Inequality," paper presented at the Annual Meeting of the American Educational Research Association, New York, N.Y., March 24–29, 2008.

106. See, for instance, Mickelson, Bottia, and Southworth, *School Choice*; A. S. Wells and A. Roda, "Colorblindness and School Choice: The Central Paradox of the Supreme Court's Ruling in the *Parents Involved* Cases," paper presented at the American Educational Research Association Annual Meeting, New York, N.Y., March 24–29, 2008.

107. Wisconsin Joint Legislative Audit Bureau, *Open Enrollment Program*, 20.

108. Armor and Peiser, *Competition in Education*, 86–89.

109. Arsen, Plank, and Sykes, *School Choice Policies*, 61.

110. Associated Press, "Students Protest Expected Change in Voluntary Transfer Program," September 22, 2007.

111. W. Freivogel, "St. Louis: The Nation's Largest Voluntary School Choice Plan," in *Divided We Fail: Coming Together through Public School Choice*, ed. Richard Kahlenberg (New York: Century Foundation Press, 2002), 23.

112. Ibid., 24.

113 . P. Hampel, "Districts Vote to Extend Desegregation Program," *St. Louis Post-Dispatch*, June 23, 2007, A12.

114. Ibid., A12.

115. C. Hendrie, "In Indianapolis, Nashville, a New Era Dawns," *Education Week,* July 8, 1998.

116. J. Ritter, "Across USA, Steps Forward and Steps Back/Indianapolis: A System that Seems to Be Working," *USA Today*, May 12, 1994, 9A,

117. Ibid.

118. Harold M. Rose and Diane M. Pollard, *Perspectives on the Chapter 220 Interdistrict Student Transfer Program: What Have We Achieved? Phase One Report,* Compact for Educational Opportunity, Milwaukee, 1993.

119. Frankenberg, *Project Choice Campaign*, 25.

120. Ibid., 2.

121. Ibid.

122. Wells and Crain, *Stepping over the Color Line.*

123. Ibid.; A. S. Wells, "The 'Consequences' of School Desegregation: The Mismatch Between the Research and the Rationale," *Hastings Constitutional Law Quarterly* 28, no. 4 (2001): 771–97.

124. Freivogel, "St. Louis."

125. Wells and Crain, *Stepping over the Color Line.*

126. Freivogel, "St. Louis."

127. W. Taylor, "Introduction and Overview: The Role of Social Sciences in School Desegregation Efforts," *The Journal of Negro Education* 66, no. 3 (Summer 1997): 196–202.

128. Wells and Crain, *Stepping over the Color Line.*

129. Ibid.; Wells, "The 'Consequences.'"

130. Freivogel, "St. Louis," 18.

131. Ibid., 20.

132. Wells and Crain, *Stepping over the Color Line.*

133. Wells, "The 'Consequences,'" 12.

134. Ibid., 12; Wells and Crain, *Stepping over the Color Line.*

135. Wells, "The 'Consequences,'" 12.

136. Wells and Crain, *Stepping over the Color Line.*

137. Wells, "The 'Consequences,'" 11.

138. Ibid., 10.

139. Wells and Crain, *Stepping over the Color Line*; Wells, "The 'Consequences.'"

140. Wells, "The 'Consequences,'" 9.

141. Wisconsin Advisory Committee, *Impact of School Desegregation*, 15.

142. J. D. Angrist and K. Lang, "Does School Integration Generate Peer Effects? Evidence from Boston's Metco Program?" *The American Economic Review* (December 2004): 1613–34.

143. Aspen Associates, "Minnesota Voluntary."

144. R. L. Crain, R. L. Miller, J. A. Hawes, and J. R. Peichert, *Finding Niches: Desegregated Students Sixteen Years Later*, Institute for Urban and Minority Education, New York, June, 1992.

145. R. L. Crain and J. Strauss, *School Desegregation and Black Educational Attainment: Results from a Long-term Experiment*, Johns Hopkins University Center for the Social Organization of Schools, Baltimore, 1985.

146. Frankenberg, *Project Choice Campaign*.

147. S. E. Eaton, *The Other Boston Busing Story* (New Haven, Conn.: Yale University Press, 2001).

148. A. S. Wells and R. L. Crain, "Perpetuation Theory and the Long-term Effects of School Desegregation," *Review of Educational Research* 64, no. 4 (1994): 531–55; Wells, "The 'Consequences.'"

149. R. L. Zweigenhaft and G. W. Domhoff, *Blacks in the White Establishment: A Study of Race and Class in America* (New Haven, Conn.: Yale University Press, 1991).

150. Frankenberg, *Project Choice Campaign*.

151. Eaton, *The Other Boston Busing Story*.p

152. Freivogel, "St. Louis," 1–2.

153. D. Smole, *School Choice under the ESEA: Programs and Requirements*, Congressional Research Service (Order Code RL 33506), Washington, D.C., January 23, 2007.

INDEX

ABOUT THE CONTRIBUTORS

SARAH COON is a Broad Resident in Urban Education at Achievement First, a charter management organization in New York and Connecticut. While writing the chapter for this book, she was the executive director of the University of Pittsburgh's Learning Policy Center, an organization that influences education policy with high quality research on teacher and organizational learning. Previously, she was research coordinator for the Governor's Commission on Training America's Teachers and program director for Apangea Learning's Community Outreach Initiative. Her interest in education policy developed as a teacher in low-income communities and she pursued this interest as a Coro Fellow in Public Affairs. Her classroom experience includes teaching fifth grade during the founding year of the KIPP San Francisco Bay Academy and teaching first grade as a Teach For America corps member. She holds a Bachelor of Arts in human services from George Washington University and Masters in public management from the Heinz School of Public Policy at Carnegie Mellon University.

WILLIAM D. DUNCOMBE is professor of public administration and senior research associate in the Center for Policy Research, The Maxwell School, Syracuse University. He is also the associate director of the Education Finance and Accountability Program at Syracuse University. His research specialties include estimating the cost of educational adequacy, school aid design, educational costs and efficiency, evaluation of educational programs, financial condition assessment, and budgeting and financial management of school districts. His work has appeared in numerous journals in public administration, education policy and finance, and economics. He has worked on education finance projects in several states, including California, Kansas, Maryland, Missouri, Nebraska, and New York.

JENNIFER JELLISON HOLME is an assistant professor of educational policy in the Department of Educational Administration at the

University of Texas at Austin. Her research agenda is centered on the politics and implementation of educational policy. Her work has been published in the *Harvard Educational Review* (2002) and *Equity and Excellence in Education* (2005). She currently is studying how low-performing high schools respond to state high school exit examination requirements.

RICHARD D. KAHLENBERG is a Senior Fellow at The Century Foundation, where he writes about education, equal opportunity, and civil rights. He is the author of four books: *Tough Liberal: Albert Shanker and the Battles Over Schools, Unions, Race and Democracy* (Columbia University Press, 2007); *All Together Now: Creating Middle Class Schools through Public School Choice* (Brookings Institution Press, 2001); *The Remedy: Class, Race, and Affirmative Action* (Basic Books, 1996); and *Broken Contract: A Memoir of Harvard Law School* (Hill & Wang/Farrar, Straus & Giroux, 1992). In addition, he is the editor of three Century Foundation books: *America's Untapped Resource: Low-Income Students in Higher Education* (2004); *Public School Choice vs. Private School Vouchers* (2003); and *A Notion at Risk: Preserving Public Education as an Engine for Social Mobility* (2000). He also served as executive director of The Century Foundation Task Force on The Common School, Chaired by Lowell Weicker, which produced the report *Divided We Fail: Coming Together through Public School Choice* (2002). His articles have been published in the *New York Times*, the *Washington Post*, the *Wall Street Journal*, the *New Republic*, and elsewhere. Kahlenberg has appeared on ABC, CBS, CNN, FOX, C-SPAN, MSNBC, and NPR. Previously, He was a fellow at the Center for National Policy, a visiting associate professor of constitutional law at George Washington University, and a legislative assistant to Senator Charles S. Robb (D-VA).

ANNA LUKEMEYER is an associate professor and chair of the Department of Public Administration at University of Nevada Las Vegas. Her research reflects her interest in the interaction of education policy, finance, and law. She is the author of *Courts as Policymakers: School Finance Reform Litigation* (LFB Scholarly Publishing, 2003), as well as other scholarly works addressing school finance, policy, and law. She received her J.D. from Southern Methodist University and her Ph.D. from Syracuse University.

LAUREN B. RESNICK is University Professor of Psychology and Cognitive Science at the University of Pittsburgh. Director of the prestigious Learning Research and Development Center from 1977 to 2008, she has researched and written widely on school reform, assessment, effort-based education, the nature and development of thinking abilities, and the role of talk and discourse in learning. She is founder and director of the Institute for Learning, a group that works with school districts to provide research-based solutions to improving the academic performance of students. She also co-founded and co-directed the New Standards Project, which developed performance-based standards and assessments that influenced state and school district practice. She has received multiple awards for her research, including the 2007 Award for Distinguished Contributions in Applications of Psychology to Education and Training and the 1998 E. L. Thorndike Award, both from the American Psychological Association, and the 1999 Oeuvre Award from the European Association on Research for Learning and Instruction (EARLI).

MARY KAY STEIN holds a joint appointment at the University of Pittsburgh as professor of learning policy and senior scientist at the Learning Research and Development Center. Her research focuses on schools and districts as contexts for teacher learning and on the relationship between research and policy. She is the founding director of the Learning Policy Center at the University of Pittsburgh. Over the past several years, she has been a principal or co-principal investigator of a number of grants from both public (the National Science Foundation) and private (Spencer, MacArthur) foundations. She has served on several national panels, including the National Academy of Education's Panel on Strengthening the Capacity of Research to Impact Policy and Practice.

AMY STUART WELLS is a professor of sociology and education at Teachers College, Columbia University. Her research and writing has focused broadly on issues of race and education and more specifically on educational policies such as school desegregation, school choice, charter schools, and tracking and how they shape and constrain opportunities for students of color. She is co-author of a forthcoming book, *Both Sides Now: The Story of School Desegregation's Graduates* (University of California Press, 2008), with Jennifer Jellison Holme, Anita Tijerina Revilla, and Awo Korantemaa Atanda. She is also the author and editor of numerous other books and articles, including co-editor with Janice Petrovich of *Bringing Equity Back: Research for a New Era in Educational Policy Making* (Teachers College Press, 2005); editor of *Where Charter School Policy Fails: The Problems of Accountability and Equity* (Teachers College Press, 2002); co-author with Robert L. Crain of *Stepping over the Color Line: African American Students in White Suburban Schools* (Yale University Press, 1997); and co-editor with A. H. Halsey, Hugh Lauder, and Phillip Brown of *Education: Culture, Economy, and Society* (Oxford University Press, 1997). She is the recipient of several honors and awards, including a 2007–08 Fellowship at the Center for Advanced Study in the Behavioral Sciences; a 2001–02 Fellowship from the Carnegie Corporation's Scholars Program; the 2000 Julius & Rosa Sachs Lecturer, Teachers College-Columbia University; and the 2000 AERA Early Career Award for Programmatic Research. In 1999–2000, she was a Russell Sage Visiting Scholar, and in 1995–96, she was a National Academy of Education-Spencer Foundation Post-doctoral fellow.

JOHN YINGER is Trustee Professor of Public Administration and Economics at the Maxwell School, Syracuse University, and director of the Education Finance and Accountability Program in Maxwell's Center for Policy Research. He has taught at Harvard University, the University of Michigan, and the University of Wisconsin; served as a senior staff economist at the President's Council of Economic Advisers; and co-directed several state-level tax or aid studies. His recent scholarly publications on education address education cost and demand functions, the design of state aid formulas, school district consolidation, the federal No Child Left Behind Act, the determinants of teacher attrition, and the performance impacts of whole-school reform programs. He is the editor of *Helping Children Left Behind: State Aid and the Pursuit of Educational Equity* (The MIT Press, 2004).